THE LEADER'S CODE

The Leader's Code

Ken Chapman, Ph.D.

iUniverse, Inc.

New York Lincoln Shanghai

The Leader's Code

iUniverse, Inc.

For information address:
iUniverse, Inc.
2021 Pine Lake Road, Suite 100
Lincoln, NE 68512
www.iuniverse.com

ISBN: 0-595-29587-8 (pbk)
ISBN: 0-595-66025-8 (cloth)

Printed in the United States of America

For Jeremiah George Chapman

Contents

Author's Preface

The Leader's Code is about the principles which have guided the best leaders across the years. The best leaders have always led by example by first leading themselves. Having mastered the art of self-management, the best leaders turn their attention to those who would choose to follow them. But the first concern of the best leaders is to lead one's self and to lead one's self well.

The final days of the American Revolutionary War give us a compelling example. The officers of the Continental Army had not been paid for several months. Unlike many members of the Continental Congress, the officers were not men of wealth. They were small farmers and merchants who had creditors to satisfy and mortgages to meet. They were in urgent need of having their salaries paid. The Continental Congress, on the other hand, was flat broke. The Congress pleade with the officers: "Give us thirty days. The British know they beaten. They will sign the peace treaty any day now and the F Government will issue our young republic letters of credit and pay you in full. However, you must stay with your troops s British Army will know we are willing to continue the fig sary."

Having heard the plea of the Continental Congr refused to wait. The officers began making plans to m gress meeting in session in New York. Anxious to tion, the Congress sent an urgent dispatch to f The Congress asked Washington to interced through the night and arrived at Washingt before seven a.m. After reading the congre asked where the officers were meeting. Learning that they were assembled in a nearby barn, he rode immediately to speak with them. When he arrived, he requested the opportunity to address the officers. The request was quickly granted. Standing before the assembled officers, General Washington took the congressional dispatch from his breast pocket and began to read. He had read only a few words when a senior staff officer interrupted, "General, you don't have to read the rest of the letter. We will wait." General Washington's biographer tells us the officers waited because they all knew that throughout the course of the war, Washington had never been paid. Whenever money was available from the Continental Congress, Washington had always insisted that his soldiers and then his officers be paid. Even more, at the darkest moment of the war, Washington had mortgaged his beloved Mount Vernon in order to pay the salaries of his men. The Continental Congress would eventually settle accounts with Washington. He would be paid for his service, and he would recover the mortgage on Mount Vernon. However, that day in that barn, Washington had never been paid and the assembled officers knew it. "The officers waited," states Washington's biographer, "because not a single man could think of a verbal argument to match the witness of General Washington's behavior."

The leader's code which guided General Washington is expounded in the pages which follow. Leaders first lead themselves. Leaders then focus on leading others to lead themselves. The personal influence which makes these two principles effective is found in the time-tested principle of *leading by example*. Leading by example is what *The Leader's Code* is all about.

THE LEADER'S CODE

A leader has faith in the magic of the human heart.
A leader believes in what people are like at their best.

A leader is patient with people as they learn and grow.
Leaders treat others as they would like to be treated.

A leader is supportive.
A leader voluntarily seeks to be helpful to others.

A leader is trustworthy.
Leaders manage their own words and behavior.
A leader self-corrects.

A leader is loyal to the best interest of the common good.
A leader is guided by an abiding faith in right.

A leader empathizes with others.
A leader seeks to understand others.

A leader speaks less and listens more.
A leader listens to understand.
A leader speaks to clarify and build trust.

A leader is honest, rational and civil.
A leader values common sense.
A leader honors basic human dignity.

A leader leads others to lead themselves.

A leader is candid.
A leader tells the truth with compassion.

A leader is a peacemaker and a coalition builder.

A leader is a team player who can follow as well as lead.
A leader understands the task of team building.

1

Leaders Know People Matter

A leader has faith in the magic of the human heart.
A leader believes in what people are like at their best.

People have an intrinsic need to be valued. Businesses, on the other hand, need to make a profit. At first glance, it seems that these two unchanging realities are in opposition. Some would argue that people cannot find meaning in organizations driven by a bottom-line perspective. Others would insist that productivity, as often as not, demands that the touchy-feely stuff be kept in check. Human beings may need to be appreciated and challenged, but that's not what business is all about. In a free-market system a business' first priority is to provide a return on investment. The needs of the employees must, at best, come second to profitability.

The premise of this book is that bottom-line reasoning simply misses the mark. For most people, their work is not just work. It is something of great importance. It is the purpose of their lives. And, as such, it is their work which most often defines the degree to which they will ever realize their intrinsic need to *matter*—to be valued, appreciated, challenged, and praised.

Organizational issues alone do not drive this need to *matter*. It is an egocentric leader who imagines that this dynamic is nothing more than an employee's desire to be *THE WINNER* of various political games which run amok in many organizations.

For most employees the need to *matter* is driven by forces which go unspoken but rarely unfelt. People work for what their efforts will bring to the people they love and care about. Their work sustains their families; buys their homes; puts food on the table; sends their kids to school; makes possible the happiness and rich memories of vacations, summer camps, ball games and holidays; and finally, allows them the dignity of a secure old age and burial.

These provide self-respect—they enable a person to affirm his or her intrinsic worth. These allow a man or a woman to experience the satisfaction of having "provided for my family." Their work is not just work. Their work is that which consumes the precious minutes and hours of their lives. That time, once spent, is gone forever. On one level or another, everyone knows this. People want the time they spend and the lives they live to matter.

The organization that can tap the energy, resourcefulness, and creativity of this *need to matter* will have empowered employees.

Empowered employees:

- are interdependent, not dependent.

- stay with a company because they want to, not because they have to.

- are loyal to mutually beneficial results, not to a legal entity.

- are focused on meeting the needs of others (customers, peers, employees, the organization) rather than worried about saving themselves.

- will openly and candidly share their ideas.

- are motivated to consistently perform at their best.

- find genuine ethical and philosophical (even spiritual) meaning in giving their best to a team which values their contribution.

This is what it means to *touch the magic of the human heart.* Not-for-profit organizations have understood this for decades. Have you ever noticed that some of the most poorly managed institutions (from a business, bottom-line perspective) go right on surviving, even thriving, year after year? Schools, churches, synagogues, universities, and various charities frequently go merrily on, even though their business practice would doom a for-profit organization. Have you ever wondered how this could be? These organizations survive because the people who are a part of them want them to survive. This is the magical power of the human heart. It is sweat and effort and energy, to be sure. More than that, it is the dogged determination a person brings to people and places where they know they matter.

Can you imagine the competitive advantage of an organization that successfully taps the magic of the human heart? Further, imagine such *heart* teamed with a sound business plan. Competitive advantage takes on a whole new meaning.

So where do leaders go to find the magic? Leaders go where people in all national, ethnic, or corporate cultures go to touch the magic. We go to fables and fairy tales.

Admittedly, this is an unsettling place for most business school trained, Hard-Knock U, bottom-line types to begin. Fables and fairy tales are about risk. Business is about minimizing risk and getting a good return on investment. Why, when you're orchestrating the music of a well-oiled machine (business), run the risk of letting some fool with a foghorn into the violin section? Why set up the delicate balance of people, production, and capital and then let a butcher with heavy thumbs mind the store?

Is it not more prudent (business-like) to be serious, rigid, controlling, respectable? No freedom, no empowered employees, no risk, no creativity; just a smooth, obedient machine presided over by an all-knowing and sober bank president with a gold watch. It just seems like good business.

That is, it seems like good business until you think about it and realize that risk, conflict, creativity, motivation, chaos, competitiveness, and profit are all cut from the same cloth: the magic of the human heart. These dynamics add up to good business. Messy as they are, they are part and parcel of human beings going about the business of business.

In order to get the best possible return on investment, an organization must get the best possible effort from its people. One without the other yields a declining return on investment and frustrated, demotivated employees.

Effective competitiveness means that an organization's people are candidly, assertively, and creatively interacting with one another. From a pool of well-advocated ideas, the single best idea will emerge. The trip, however, may look uncontrolled and chaotic. The risk can loom larger than the potential benefit. The whole thing can look like something that couldn't possibly have a good ending. The fact is, engaging the human heart feels a lot like the telling and hearing of fables and fairy tales.

It may be that Walt Disney was the first motivational theorist to recognize this strategy. At the very least, his creation of the job and title of "imagineer" is one of the best ever efforts to tap the resourcefulness of the human heart.

Disney understood that a business must turn a profit. He also understood the competitive spirit of an organization whose employees want to see it thrive. A business should not be just a place where a paycheck is issued, but a place where a person matters. Disney tapped the magic which comes from meeting an essential and perhaps the greatest human need: the need to be valued.

From the time we are small children, our fascination with fables and fairy tales is fueled by the need to matter. Fables and fairy tales are all about people and places where the honest efforts of a good person always prevail. We like these stories from our mother's lap onward because we know, no matter what others may say or insinuate, we are good persons with good intentions.

The phrase, *Once upon a time,* is more than the classic way to begin the spinning of a good yarn. It is a place where we go to remember what we are like at our best. A magical place is where people matter. If this magical place seems alien to business, it is business which has everything to gain by changing.

In the poorest work environment, employees punch clocks, meet schedules, and get the job done with *Once upon a time* waiting deep in their hearts. "One day the boss will ask my opinion…Someday I'll share this idea I've got…Surely the day will come when the company will notice me." *Once upon a time* is that time somewhere out there in a magical future, when the organization realizes; "I've got a heart I'd gladly give to a place where I matter."

A leader understands the magical "once upon a time" which resides in every human heart. A leader understands the magic of the human heart. A leader believes in what people are like at their best.

If you have reservations about the practical value of fables and fairy tales, try writing a fairy tale on the safe-and-sane view of business.

2

Leaders Honor Honest Mistakes

A leader is patient with people as they learn and grow.
Leaders treat others as they would like to be treated.

Once upon a time there was a princess who was under a curse. She was asleep and no one could wake her. The only way to break the curse was with an apple from the tree that grew in the middle of the garden at the western end of the world. What does the king do? Well, on the theory that a well-run, no risk operation makes the best of all possible worlds, he gets out his maps, briefs his generals, and sends a couple of well-supplied divisions to the garden to fetch the apple.

The whole thing is just a matter of getting an odd prescription from an inconveniently located drugstore that doesn't deliver. He uses his power, and the job is done. The apple is brought to the palace and applied to the princess. She wakes up; eats breakfast, lunch, and dinner forever after; and dies in bed at the respectable age of ninety-two.

Everyone knows, of course, that this is not the way to tell a good fairy tale. The story is too predictable. There's no magic. To begin with, the garden isn't on any of the maps. Only one man in the kingdom, the hundred-year-old Grand Geezer, knows where it is. When he is summoned, however, he asks to be excused. It seems that he is scheduled to die later that evening and therefore cannot make the trip. He happens to have a map, but there is a complication (isn't there always—if it's not one thing, it's another). The map has been drawn with magical ink and will be visible only to the right man for the job. The king, of course, inquires how this man is to be found. "Very simply," responds the Grand Geezer. "He will be recognizable by his ability to pat his head and rub his tummy at the same time, while whistling 'Puff the Magic Dragon.'"

The king calls in his nobles, all of whom are excellent musicians. They whistle, sing and chant (Gregorian) at the paper, but nothing appears. They do their darndest but have no luck. At last the king, in frustration, tells them to knock off for lunch and come back at two o'clock. Much too preoccupied to eat, the king strolls out onto the balcony and, lo and behold, what does he hear? Someone is walking down the road whistling 'Puff the Magic Dragon' while patting the top of his head and rubbing his tummy all at the same time.

It is, of course, the miller's son, a local high school dropout and village rowdy. The king, however, is not one to balk at ideologies when he needs help. He hauls the boy in, gives him the map, and packs him off with a bag of bagels (sourdough) and a bottle of Thunderbird. (Why waste good wine on an unsophisticated palate?)

That night the boy reads the map. It seems pretty straightforward, except for a warning at the bottom in block capitals: **AFTER ENTERING THE GARDEN GO STRAIGHT TO THE TREE, PICK THE APPLE AND GET OUT. DO NOT, UNDER ANY CIRCUMSTANCES, SPEAK TO THE THIRD PEACOCK ON THE RIGHT.**

Any child worth his Nintendo can write the rest of the story. The boy goes into the garden and gets as far as the third peacock on the right. The third peacock on the right startles him by asking, "Wouldn't you like a Butterfinger candy bar and a nice frosty mug of root beer?" Exhausted and parched from his long journey, the boy gobbles the candy bar and guzzles down the root beer. Before he knows it, he has fallen fast asleep. When he wakes up, he is in a pitch-black cave; a light flickers, a voice calls—and from there on all hell breaks loose. The boy follows an invisible guide with a cocked hat down rivers of fire in an aluminum dinghy. He is imprisoned by the Crown Prince of the Sala-manders. Finally he is rescued by a confused eagle (that looks a lot like John Candy) who deposits him at the eastern end of the world.

The boy works his way back to the western end in the dead of win-ter, gets the apple (having learned through trial and error not to speak to the third peacock on the right), brings it home, touches it to the princess' lips, awakens her, reveals himself to be the long-lost son of the Eagle King, and marries the princess. Then, and only then, do they live happily ever after.

It is the improbability and risk that make the story. There isn't a child on earth who doesn't know the crucial moment—whose heart, no matter how well he knows the story, doesn't skip a beat every time the boy comes to the third peacock on the right. There is no one still in possession of his humanity who doesn't recognize that moment as an opportunity for the boy to prove that he matters despite his past mis-takes. This is the second chance he's been hoping for, the chance to prove he can get it right.

The safe universe may be a nice place to visit, but when a man or a woman (i.e., employee) is looking for a chance to matter, he or she instinctively knows not to go to the overstuffed bank presidents with model worlds. Rather, they head straight to the same old disreputable crowd their family has always done business with—the yarn spinners, the chance givers, the risk takers—the leader who understands that human nature is a bit chaotic. When you believe you matter the chaos can quickly become superior performance. But first, employees must believe they matter. This is the magic of the human heart. It is the magic a person brings to people and places where that person knows an individual's best efforts are valued.

The best leaders honor honest mistakes by allowing employees the opportunity to recover from their mistakes. The best leaders are patient with people as they learn and grow provided the employee demon-strates the capacity to learn from a mistake.

The best leaders treat others as they would like to be treated—the leader grants the employee a second chance.

3

Leaders Listen

A leader is supportive.
A leader voluntarily seeks to be helpful to others.

Once upon a time a young girl named Susan lived in a small town. It was the same town and the same street where Susan's mother, grandmother, and great-grandmother had all spent their girlhoods. As Susan grew from birth to young adulthood, her mother and grandmother gave her much advice about how to live and grow and do the right thing.

In particular, Susan's grandmother, whom Susan called Nannah, tried to guide her toward socially acceptable behavior. Nannah felt her guidance was particularly important since Susan seemed, at least to Nannah, a bit too interested in doing her own thing. Susan was not one to be guided by conventional ways of thinking and acting.

For example, although encouraged to play with dolls, Susan preferred mud pies and sand castles of her own special design. When scheduled for piano lessons, Susan never managed to arrive at her teacher's house on time; the neighborhood baseball game proved too much of a distraction. As other girls her age went through predictable phases and fascinations, Susan continued to march to her own drummer.

Finally, when Susan showed up for her seventeenth birthday party wearing cut-off jeans and a white T-shirt rather than the pretty cotton dress Nannah had bought for the occasion, it proved too much for Nannah. That afternoon Nannah reached the end of her patience. Nannah took Susan aside right then and there and scolded, *"Susan, why can't you be more like other girls your age? I swear, some day when you get to heaven, The Lord himself won't know what to do with you...but mark my word, He'll want to know why you weren't more like other girls."*

As it turned out, Nannah was not the only person who had reached the end of her patience that afternoon. Susan's response was quick and clear. In a voice easily as exasperated as Nannah's, Susan replied, *"Nannah, I think He'd be more alarmed if He had to ask, 'Why weren't you more like Susan?'"*

Susan is a test for her Nannah's patience. Susan is also her own person. Susan has the courage to assert her own value, even if it means disagreeing with her grandmother. Or, as the psychologist would say, Susan has a healthy sense of herself. Susan is self-confident.

If you're reaching for a dictionary let me save you the trip. Healthy self-confidence means that Susan (whether she would use these particular words or not) feels efficacious—adequate to meet life's challenges.

Or, stated another way, self-confidence is the reputation we get with ourselves. If that reputation is good, we feel good about ourselves. If it is not, we feel bad about ourselves. The consequences of that reputation carry over into our personal and professional relationships. For example, the degree to which we like ourselves is the degree to which we are free to like others. The degree to which we are comfortable with ourselves is the degree to which we are comfortable with others. The person in your workplace who has difficulty getting along with others is, most likely, having an even harder time getting along with himself. When I do not value me, it is difficult for me to value others. When I do not value me, I cannot value the organization.

So, does this mean that as long as Susan's self-confidence is high she and Nannah can have nothing but a frustrating relationship? No, that is not what it means. Susan and Nannah are like a two-person company with the same goal: They both want Susan to be happy, but they have competing ideas as to how to get there. Susan wants some say in her life. Nannah believes that, as the more experienced of the two, she knows best. All self-respecting employees want some say in their work. Bosses often believe their greater experience better qualifies them to structure an employee's work. Susan wants her thoughts and preferences considered. Nannah wants her grandmotherly instincts respected. Self-confident employees want their thoughts and preferences considered. Bosses tend to think that they know best because they are in charge.

Susan will be more open to her grandmother's hopes and dreams (goals) if she knows that her grandmother will consider her hopes and dreams (goals). Employees invariably bring higher motivation and commitment to the organization when they have been part of the goal-setting process. Emotionally healthy, self-confident employees want some say in both the goal and the path to the goal.

Interestingly enough, employees often set their goals higher than those goals that are set without the employees' input. People will stretch themselves but often resent being stretched by others. Susan, Nannah & Company, Inc. experience all the growing pains of any organization where people insist on being valued.

This is a good place to consider what Susan, Nannah & Company, Inc. can do to strengthen the self-confidence of every person in the organization. You may ask, "Why bother?" And the answer is that people who believe in themselves can be empowered. People who do not believe in themselves cannot be empowered. When I believe in me, and I know the organization believes in me, I think of work as my work. Here are seven suggestions for building employee self-confidence and setting the tone for empowerment.

1. **Be more concerned about making others feel good about themselves than in making them feel good about you or the organization.** Most people don't care what you think until they know you care. Until I know that my personal goals will be considered, the goals of the organization are just a means of getting a pay-

check and nothing more. It is a wise leader who realizes that one of the greatest unspoken fears we all have is that we will be accountable to someone who does not care about us. So the leader who does not treat employees with respect and consideration encourages employees to feel bad about themselves. This pushes employees toward a preoccupation with how to feel better about themselves. On the other hand, employees who are encouraged to feel good about themselves are free to focus on meeting the needs of others (i.e., customers, peers, and the needs of the organization).

2. **Encourage employees to view their work as a journey with many lessons to be learned.** Everyone is enrolled in a full-time, informal school called life. It does not have to be the school of hard-knocks. There is much to be learned (painlessly) by listening to lessons those who have been there can teach us. It is not in our best interest, or in the best interest of the organization, to spend precious time and energy reinventing the wheel.

   On the other hand, it is also helpful to remember that people learn most willingly from persons they trust. Therefore, candid, full disclosure forms the foundation for corporate learning. Giving an employee a good performance review because the boss wants to avoid conflict is nothing short of setting the employee up to fail. Telling the boss what he or she wants to hear should not be rewarded. Telling the truth with compassion is a vital part of what it means to be a team player.

3. **Set employees free to try, to fail, to learn, and to move on.** Personal and organizational development is a process of trial, error, and experimentation. The faulty ideas are as much a part of the formula for success as the ideas that ultimately work. In such a setting people are not rewarded for merely making sure nothing goes wrong. They are rewarded for making a contribution. This means more than just doing a job. It means making a positive difference.

Here the foundation is loyalty: personal and organizational loyalty to employees who are making an informed, honest effort to make a difference! "Informed" means the employee has carefully thought about and worked through the idea prior to trying it out, including soliciting opinions and insights from others. "Honest effort" means the employee is acting in the best interest of the organization—not playing politics or attempting to cover up a prior mistake.

4. **Create a learning culture within the organization.** Refuse to allow learning to be something done at the occasional continuing education workshop. Have organizational leaders talk with employees about any newly acquired learning or skills. Reward people for demonstrating the acquisition of new skills. Provide frequent opportunities for employees to learn something new. Do not limit the learning opportunity to company business. Provide learning experiences which enhance the quality of the employees' life. For example, provide classes on personal financial management, retirement, or parenting. Remember, every time an employee makes the effort to learn something, he or she is practicing a skill which can only benefit the organization.

5. **Recognize and reward employees who maintain a positive attitude.** Personal attitude is a choice. Every person is responsible for how the choice he or she has made impacts others. No one is responsible for me but me. If I am willing to accept responsibility for my own life-view (attitude), it is a revealing indication that I will accept responsibility for myself in other areas as well.

The myth is that someone other than me is choosing my attitude for me. When another person is choosing my attitude (and this is never the case), it is often because I lack either the maturity or the courage (or both) to assert my right to choose how I will live and act. Such a perspective also flies in the face of mental health. We know that a core characteristic of mental health is the capacity to choose behavior. Therefore, if I want you to believe that I cannot choose to behave differently, in essence, I want you to believe that I am mentally ill.

No matter how smart or gifted an employee is, if his or her attitude is not constructive, it will affect the entire team. In most settings it takes time to build a can-do culture. Employees who choose not to have a constructive attitude will find it stressful to see constructive attitudes rewarded. Some will resist development of such a culture. Interestingly enough, the team members who have chosen to maintain a positive attitude will often deal very effectively with this resistance without the intervention of the team leader. Others will simply move on. Either way, over time what gets rewarded will get done and will become the norm.

Expecting others to be responsible for themselves is one of the more important ways of showing **respect** for another person. We protect small children. It is a given that they are too immature and naive to be held responsible for their attitude or actions. We feel much the same about the elderly who are senile. However, we are paying others a compliment (demonstrating respect) when we assume they are willing to be responsible for themselves. Such respect enhances the self-worth of individuals and teams. And healthy self-confidence builds a can-do culture.

6. **Ask at least one employee for his or her opinion each day—then be quiet and listen.** It could be argued that *listening* is the most effective motivational strategy a leader can practice. It is also the most neglected. Listening is personal. It builds mutual trust. It solicits the insights of those closest to the work being done.

Few people are naturally good listeners. Effective listeners acquire this skill by working at it. Recognizing that I may not be a good listener is the place to begin. Leaders will have to candidly critique their listening skills. As long as my listening skills go unexamined, I can tell myself "I listen well enough." It may be that I don't listen well enough. However, if I work at acquiring effective listening skills, I can.

Begin by asking questions like these: When others are talking, do I concentrate on what they are saying, or am I thinking about what I want to say when they finish? Do I ask questions about what others have said? Do I summarize what I've heard and test for understanding? The point is this, nothing changes until it becomes what it is. Until I believe I need to improve, I will see no need to make the effort.

One of the pitfalls of leadership is a pattern of thinking that others should be listening to me. I, on the other hand, should not have to waste time listening to others. After all, I'm the one with the knowledge, experience, and authority.

The higher you go in an organization, the less willing others are to risk your displeasure by asserting their right to be heard. Thus, they tell you what you want to hear or nothing at all. This is a precarious position for a leader. Leaders frequently fail because they make decisions based on poor or inadequate information. Ironically, in such instances, employees are often sitting on the very information the leader needs. When asked why they did not provide the information, their response is, "Nobody asked me"—which translates: "Nobody was listening."

The further you go in an organization, the more you must depend on others for accurate information.

Leaders who do not listen carefully and intelligently aren't going to get the facts they need, and people will resent their decisions. If you want to motivate me, listen to me. If you want me to believe that I am a valued member of the team, listen to me. If you want accurate and timely information, listen.

7. **Honor the uniqueness of each team member.** Finally, not only does Susan have a healthy sense of self-confidence, but at seventeen she already knows something about herself which every person feels and longs to have others recognize. Susan knows she is unique. Susan believes there is something special about her. Every person in every setting has an intuitive desire to have this recognized. If human beings share anything in common, it is the belief within ourselves that we are somehow special. It is the belief that there has never been anyone quite like us before, and there will never be anyone quite like us again. We are not just one in a million, we are the only one—the only one of us, at least.

The individual's need to feel special is met through family life and through the formation of personal relationships. No organization can ethically single out an individual as more special than others. We may even refer to our co-workers as family. However, a business, by its very nature, cannot be expected to meet an individual's need to feel special in the same way a family would.

What, then, does the idea of *honoring the uniqueness of each individual* have to do with the workplace? While a business cannot (and should not) seek to replace a family, an organization can *tap the energy of the unique contribution.* Every employee wants to feel that he or she contributes something special to the team. This does not mean encouraging employees to believe they are irreplaceable (that would simply be untrue). It does mean that as an effective team member, the individual is contributing something essential to the success of the team. If a team member is not contributing something essential to the team's success, why is the person on the team? Honoring the uniqueness of each individual means recognizing the something essential each person is contributing.

Typically, the recognition has to be as individual as the employee. With some, an occasional compliment is sufficient. With others, an award such as a plaque, a day off, a company jacket presented in the company of their peers is needed. It may be best to offer the reward in private as an employee may be harassed by peers because he or she was singled out. For still others, nothing short of increased wages or a bonus will do. Whatever the recognition, it must express appreciation for the individual's *unique contribution.* Then it will tap the *energy* we all bring to the people and places where we are special.

4

Leaders Model Courage and Consideration

A leader is trustworthy.
Leaders manage their own words and behavior.
A leader voluntarily self-corrects.

Once upon a time there lived a man named Bill. Bill owned a construction company which specialized in home building. Bill took great pride in the quality of the homes his company built. Bill used only the best materials and the most reliable methods. Bill spared no effort and cut no corners.

Bill was particularly proud of his crews. "The Best People Building the Best Homes" was his company motto. And, as far as Bill was concerned, his crews were just that—the best.

Carpenters, masons, plumbers, roofers, and electricians all knew their trade and took pride in their workmanship. For his part, Bill paid top wages and never failed to give his people the credit they deserved.

After many satisfying years of building homes, Bill began to think about retirement. As he thought about retiring, he thought about Pete. Pete was Bill's oldest and best foreman. When Bill retired, that's the day Pete had said he would hang it up, too.

Bill went to see Pete to tell him of his plans to retire. Bill told Pete he had one last job for him, "I'm headed out of town for about six months, Pete. While I'm gone I'd like you to take a crew out to that lot on Harvest Lane and build this house. Spare no reasonable expense. Make sure it is the kind of house in which a man would enjoy spending his retirement years." Bill then handed Pete a roll of plans and headed off on his trip.

Pete went to work. As he guided the crew through the initial phase of construction, he began to think about his future. "In all the years I've worked with Bill he's never been able to provide me with a retirement program. I've got social security and my savings. But will that be enough? Maybe it's time I started looking out for Pete."

In the following stages of construction Pete began to cut corners. Whenever he thought it would be difficult to detect, he used inferior materials. In other instances he replaced master craftsmen with inexperienced carpenters and masons, because they would accept lower wages. "Nobody'll know," Pete thought to himself. "I'll pocket the difference and be long gone by the time the shoddy construction is discovered."

In time, the house was completed. Bill returned from his trip. Seeing the house, Bill congratulated Pete on what Bill believed to be Pete's usual good work. Within a day or so, Bill asked Pete to meet him at the new house on Harvest Lane. At first, Pete was reluctant to go, "What if Bill has discovered the shoddy construction sooner rather than later?" Pete wondered to himself. Then Pete recalled how clever he had been in covering his tracks. "You'd have to live in that house for three or four years before it started falling apart," Pete reminded himself. "Bill couldn't possibly know this soon."

Pete headed on over to the new house on Harvest Lane, confident his deception would not be discovered. When Pete arrived, Bill was waiting on the large, airy front porch. Glancing at the house as he got out of the car, Pete thought to himself, "It is a beautiful house but not for long."

Bill greeted Pete with his usual warmth and immediately began telling him why he wanted Pete to meet him, "Pete, you've been a loyal friend and my best foreman for many years. I owe much of my success to you. I just couldn't retire without first letting you know how much I appreciate you. Here are the keys to the house. It is yours, lock, stock, and barrel. All I ask is that you live in it and enjoy it for the rest of your life."

As human beings we have an uncanny ability to act against our own best interest. Most of the time we recognize this inclination, and we control our impulses. Giving in to the urge to tell the boss where to go, or strangling the customer who used the blender we sold them to mix house paint and is now in our face demanding to know what they should do with it is not in our best interest. We can usually see temptations like these coming in time to put the brakes on what we'd really like to say.

At other times we are less perceptive. We commit selficide. Selficide occurs when I betray my best interest. It is acting against what is best for me. As a result, I usually end up destroying what I want most—to be seen as a person of integrity who can be trusted.

On one level, selficide is the failure to learn and grow from life's experiences. The failure to learn and grow means we make the same mistake more than once. It means that we teach others to think of us as persons who just can't quite get our act together. Or, worse, we unintentionally nurture the perception that we are not very smart. Such perceptions are not in our best interest. They constitute the committing of selficide.

On another level, selficide includes those momentary lapses when we forget that we have to live with the perceptions of others. We indulge ourselves, usually only for a moment (though it is often a moment long enough to get ourselves in trouble) in the fantasy of our self-sufficiency. We take a long, deep drag on our ego and imagine we can reach our goals without the support or cooperation of others. Our experience has taught us that no one succeeds for very long unless other people want us to succeed—and therefore invest in our success. Lost in the euphoria of our ego, we allow ourselves to forget. We forget that the cooperation of others is essential to our success. How others perceive us has a direct impact on our effectiveness.

The opposite of selficide is healthy self-interest. Pete's problem began when he confused self-interest with ego and committed selficide. Self-interest is not acting for self and against others. Healthy self-interest is good for us and for others. Self-interest is choosing long-term benefits over short-term gains.

We noted earlier that self-confidence is the reputation we get with ourselves. By contrast, integrity is the reputation we get with others. Bill's construction foreman, Pete, committed selficide the moment he decided he no longer needed Bill's trust. Personal integrity is a glass house each person builds and maintains over a lifetime. Our willingness to openly and reliably do the right thing by others determines how bulletproof the glass will be. Pete shot out his own windows. Or, to use another metaphor, Pete shot himself in the foot. In building a house he knew to be inferior, he was acting against his own best interest. As it turned out, it was a house he would have to live in. But, even if he did not live in it, he'd still have to live with the reputation of having built a sub-standard house.

The critical transition in Pete's thinking took place when he bought into the single greatest myth of the American workplace: I work for someone other than me.

The truth is, Pete never worked for Bill. All those years, Pete worked for Pete. Pete had always been self-employed. It just so happens that Bill was Pete's only customer. Everyone who works for a living is a company of one. Pete was never just Pete. He was always Pete, Inc.

As Pete, Inc., Pete has something important in common with all the other companies of one who are savvy enough to realize they are self-employed. Pete, Inc.; Lisa, Inc.; and Joe, Inc. all have destinies controlled by the same holding company, a holding company they may or may not know as Character Corp. Having their destinies controlled by Character Corp. means that their success is at the mercy of something more perilous than market forces.

Pete, Inc. is at the mercy of Pete's character. As a company of one, Pete's destiny is equal to, but never greater than, his personal integrity. If others find that Pete can be trusted, they'll keep doing business with him. If they discover that Pete cannot be trusted, they'll take their business elsewhere. Either way, the destiny of Pete, Inc. (what Pete does for a living) is controlled by the degree to which others experience him as trustworthy.

The most reliable way to keep Character Corp.'s stock up is to think of one's self as self-employed. My product is the value and trustworthiness of my character.

Here are the five benchmark questions you can use to evaluate how quality control is going in your company of one.

1. Is my vision of what I want my life (company of one) to be clearly defined?

2. Am I keeping my priorities straight?

3. Am I asking myself the difficult questions?

4. Am I overly concerned with image building?

5. Am I investing in the success of others?

1. Is my vision of what I want my life (company of one) to be clearly defined?

Most people offer a predictable response when asked, "What's your mission in life?" They will say they'd like to:

- be loved by their family.

- be thought of as a good person.

- abide by the golden rule.

- be remembered for having done something special

When pressed, however, most people do not have a conscious strategy for realizing their vision of what they'd like their life to be.

By contrast, a person of vision has a plan. Persons of vision have an idea how to get where they're going. That is not to say that every person or company of one must have an extensive Strategic Business Plan as one might find at AT&T or Wal-Mart. It does mean that a person of vision has a set of core principles which guides the course of his or her life. It is this clearly defined system of values against which all of life is judged that is the source of personal integrity.

As the source of personal integrity, a vision statement is the beginning of personal and organizational leadership. The vision statement will clearly identify the core principles by which I choose to live. It will provide overall direction. It will clarify my purpose and meaning. By referring to it and internalizing its meaning, I am more likely to choose behavior that serves my vision and reject behavior which does not. I am less likely to commit selficide.

An effective vision statement will provide answers to three essential questions:

- Do I matter?

- Where am I going?

- Who will go with me?

These three questions form the Chapman Paradigm (Illustrated below).

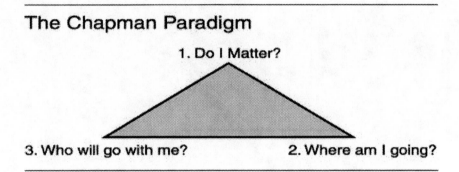

The Chapman Paradigm

1. Do I Matter?

3. Who will go with me?   2. Where am I going?

The first question is the esteem question: "Do I matter?" Self-esteem is the critical starting point for effective personal and public leadership. The degree to which I value "me" is the degree to which I am free to value others. The degree to which I value others is the degree to which I can build mutually beneficial relationships. This dynamic is illustrated by The Courage-Consideration Continuum shown on the following page.

The vertical axis of the continuum registers the degree to which I have the courage to advocate the value of my convictions. Through advocacy I affirm that I am a person of worth and value. As a person of worth, I have something of value to contribute to the human experience. By asserting the value of what I have to offer, I maintain my self-esteem.

The Courage-Consideration Continuum

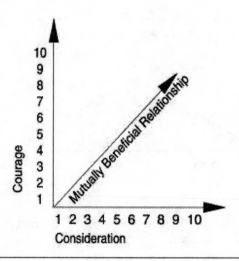

Assertiveness, however, is only the first step. I must demonstrate that I will be responsible for myself. This means honoring my commitments and accepting the consequences of my decisions—whether those consequences are good or bad. In this, I build and sustain a strong sense of self-worth and, therefore, feel efficacious, adequate to life and equal to the task of living as an adult among other adults.

Why do I feel hurt and confused when my courage fails me? Typically, this inadequacy happens when a person says or does something which leaves me feeling discounted, abused, mistreated, or wronged. If I fail to stop the abuse, fail to insist that the mistreatment be corrected, or fail to demand that the wrong be righted, my courage has failed me—and my sense of adequacy will suffer.

By failing to assert my value, I feel on the inside like I've affirmed the discounting. If I allow another to discount me long enough, the feelings of inadequacy will move from my inside to my outside. When on the outside, others will begin to experience me as having either an inferiority or a superiority complex. Feelings of both inferiority and superiority are driven by feelings of inadequacy. Inferiority is the "I'm less than human" response to being discounted. Superiority is the "I'm more than human—superman" response to being discounted.

By refusing to be discounted, I assert my self-worth. I answer "YES" to the question: "Do I matter?" In mustering the courage to assert my intrinsic value, I position myself to lead myself and others. Therefore, courage is the most essential virtue because it assures that all other virtues will be advocated.

The Courage-Consideration Continuum

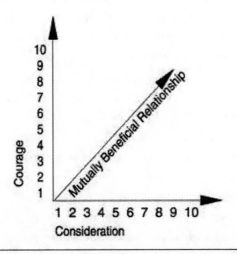

The horizontal axis of the continuum registers the degree to which I have consideration for the value of others. Consideration, in this context, is like the opposite side of the same coin. On one side is the courage to assert my values. On the other side is the consideration which allows others to assert their value. Consideration is willingly granting to others what we demand for ourselves—to be treated as persons of worth.

Consideration cannot be conditional. It must be granted whether the other person likes or dislikes me; treats me well or treats me poorly; affirms my value or discounts me. As long as I choose to interact with a person, I must grant him or her consideration. When and if the time comes when I feel I can no longer grant an individual consideration, we both then need to go our separate ways.

Consideration is a measure of my strength of character. It is driven by my value system, not by the value system of another. Otherwise, the consideration I extend to others will be nothing more than a tit-for-tat reaction to the behavior of others. My courageous self-confidence does not allow the inconsideration of another to regulate my consideration. I treat others with consideration because it is the core of who I am and what I am about. I am a person of courage and consideration. I will assert my value and I will respect the right of others to assert their value.

If either axis of the courage-consideration continuum is uneven, the relationship will eventually cease to be mutually beneficial. If the vertical (courage) is significantly weaker than the horizontal (consideration), I may well become little more than a doormat for others. If the horizontal (consideration) is weaker than the vertical (courage), I risk discounting others whether that is my intention or not.

The key is a proactive balance. In taking the initiative, I can work to keep each axis strong and balanced. I want strong vertical and horizontal axes because I want others to experience me as a person of both courage and consideration. Such a balance responsibly asserts my worth and respects the worth of others. Such a dynamic is mutually beneficial. A dynamic balance is an excellent place from which to lead.

The second question raised and answered by an effective vision statement is the question of goals and standards.

When I ask, "Where am I going?" I am establishing a direction and a benchmark. I am consciously choosing a path to a destination. In addition, I am establishing a standard for measuring progress toward a goal and the degree to which I maintain personal values in the process. I am not interested in merely traveling from point A to point B but in making the trip to my goals with my value system intact.

Let's say, for example, that after much thought and consideration I settle on a personal vision statement. I determine that vision to be as follows:

- I will tell the truth with compassion.

- I will live my own life.

- I will be loyal to my family, friends, and associates.

In addition, let's say that as a front-line leader I decide, after consultation with the leadership of my company, that I'd like to be a department manager someday. Becoming a department manager is my goal, a vital first half of the answer to the question "Where am I going?"

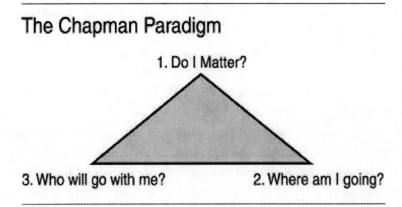

The Chapman Paradigm

1. Do I Matter?

3. Who will go with me?   2. Where am I going?

The other half of the answer is the benchmark. In this example, the benchmark is my commitment to truth telling, self-worth, and loyalty.

As I move toward the realization of my goal (becoming a department manager), I am concerned with more than the clever and the expedient. I want each action step to take me closer to my goal, and I want every action step to be consistent with my personal standards. Thus, when I evaluate my progress I ask not only the geographic question "How far have I come?" but also the standard question "Have I kept faith with my vision?" If I have been truthful and compassionate, the answer is yes. If I have refused to allow others to discount me, my answer is yes. And, if I have remained loyal to the best interest of family, friends and associates, my final answer is yes.

Maintaining a strong link between my goals and my standards assures the vitality of my personal integrity. Others will experience me as a person who can be trusted. My capacity to lead others will be enhanced. My stock will hold its value. My company of one will remain competitive. My character will continue to be a viable corporation.

The third and final question of a vision statement is the relational question, "Who will go with me?" Here my response builds on the answers for questions one and two. Asserting one's personal worth (Do I matter?) will have a direct impact on relationships. Being committed to a set of values (Where am I going?) will affect how others experience me.

The consequences will follow one of two paths. There will be those who will respect me for asserting my personal worth and being faithful to my values. They will be interested in associating with me if they find me to be a person of courage and consideration. They know I not only have the courage to be my own person, but I also have the consideration to allow another to be his or her own person as well.

On the other hand, a healthy sense of self-worth and integrity may make others uncomfortable. They may be so uncomfortable that they will be unable or unwilling to go with me. They may feel that my commitment to truth telling is naive. My self-confidence may seem threatening. They may consider my loyalty to family, friends, and associates an unnecessary nuisance. Any one, or all, of these commitments may make me someone they don't care to move through the years with.

The truly tough part of personal integrity is getting used to people moving in and out of our lives. We meet someone at a P.T.A. meeting or at the office and gradually become hopeful that the person will become a treasured friend and associate. Then, much to our disappointment, we discover that the individual finds our principles unsettling. They see nothing wrong with a little dishonesty, particularly if it gets them what they want. They don't mind being discounted, as long as it keeps them on the winning side of office politics. And, as for loyalty, it is for the naive and foolish. Gradually, they choose a course different from the one we are committed to. They exit our life. We, in turn, make the necessary but painful choice of principle over friendship.

Along with personal satisfaction, disappointment also comes with our vision. Occasionally, commitment to our principles will lead us to move through a period of time or a task alone. It is not that no one else on the planet shares our commitment to honesty, self-worth, or loyalty. The most principled person does not have a monopoly on ethical behavior. However, those who share our principles may not happen (by no design of their own) to be available. It is in keeping faith with our principles at such times that we are assured of being once again joined by others who share our principles.

If getting used to people moving in and out of our lives is the toughest part of integrity, then being unable to explain ourselves when appropriate is the most frustrating. Just as personal integrity can mean loneliness, it can also mean doing the right thing even when we cannot explain.

Sometimes the inability to explain has to do with the person to whom we are offering the explanation. It may be that the person has no context for understanding what we're talking about. The individual may be a person of integrity with a value system radically different from ours. Or, the person may simply be unprincipled, and the idea of doing the right thing may hold no interest. In such instances it is important to test our motives to make sure we are not being conde-scending or self-serving in our assessment of the other person.

At other times, doing the right thing may defy explanation. We can-not qualify why something is wrong for us, but in our heart, we know it is. While this has an emotional dynamic, it is also pragmatic. More often than not, we don't get to choose between the clearly wrong and the clearly right. We have to work in gray areas where a judgment call is required. Winning the respect of others when we choose what is clearly right will enable others to trust us when we have to work in the gray areas. Either way, choosing a principled course of action cannot be subject to our ability to explain. Doing the right thing even when we cannot explain just comes with the turf. Such instances not only mea-sure a person's commitment to his principles, they also prepare a per-son to lead.

Clearly defining my vision of my company of one allows me to focus on balancing my priorities, the second benchmark.

2. Am I keeping my priorities straight?

The second benchmark question for our company of one is the spe-cial relationship between balance and productivity. Deciding what is important and disciplining oneself to focus on what is important are essential to success.

Unfortunately, priorities have a tendency to get shuffled when we're not paying attention. The urgent pushes the important aside. With dozens of fires to put out, what really matters gets lost in the rush. The resulting scenario is predictable. A leader works hard, makes personal sacrifices, gets the job done, and becomes successful. And then, when it is too late, the leader discovers the enormous price of success: the mar-riage is in shambles, the children are strangers, and physical health is endangered. The resulting disappointment is not what the leader had in mind. Success was supposed to be much sweeter.

What happened? The leader, perhaps unintentionally, bought into the myth that success in one area of life assures happiness in all areas of life. Any life which has a single focus is unbalanced. The unbalanced life is a personal disaster waiting to happen. It may take twenty-five years for the harm to become evident. It may take only five years. This much we know: A leader who proactively seeks to live a balanced life is more productive over a longer period of time. By contrast the leader with a single focus, such as a workaholic, is three times as likely to experience burnout. The leader who focuses all of his or her energy on succeeding at the office may rise quickly but is also likely to fail sooner than the leader who seeks balance.

The key to long-term success is productivity driven by personal balance. Most of us want to succeed in every important area of our life. We want to experience professional success. But we also want to achieve personal, physical, mental, social, and ethical success.

The Life Wheel

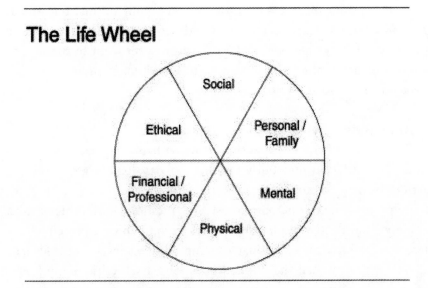

Here it may be helpful to think of success as a wheel. The wheel has six compartments, all connected and in one way or another dependent on each other. If each compartment is properly inflated and receives appropriate attention, the wheel will roll smoothly. If any compartment is over or under inflated, the ride will be bumpy.

By giving appropriate attention to each of the six areas, the leader is equipped with two potent advantages for long-term success: personal resilience and the capacity for self renewal.

Resilience is achieved by drawing one's emotional support from more than one source. If I'm experiencing success in all six areas of the wheel, then I can more easily bounce back from disappointment. If I have a bad day at work I can gain emotional renewal from going home or socializing with a good friend. But, if my work is my life, disappointment at work leaves me with no place to go for renewal. In time, my resilience—the capacity to recover from disappointment—is weakened. Thus, my ability to renew myself is depleted. Once my emotional resources are depleted, burnout is inevitable.

Does burnout mean it's over for me? No, many burned-out leaders recognize what's happened to them and begin the difficult process of properly inflating their wheel. Leaders do recover from burnout. The collapse of personal relationships and the loss of many productive years make burnout worth avoiding.

3. Am I asking myself the difficult questions?

The third benchmark question deals with my capacity to self-critique. It focuses on my ability to objectively evaluate my motives and actions. Quality control in my company of one requires that I self-critique prior to my critique of others. The questions I ask others I must ask myself. Effective leadership assures accountability. Principle-centered leadership makes sure that accountability begins with the leader.

When I ask myself the difficult questions, I self-critique my fitness to lead. If I fail to self-critique, my motives may appear to be self-serving. Once my motives become suspect, I risk losing the moral authority to ask others to do the right thing. Once I no longer have the right to ask others to do the right thing, my effectiveness as a leader is diminished, if not lost. By asking myself the difficult questions, I position myself to be effective.

I self-critique by thinking through my words and behavior:

- Have I said something I should not have said?

- Have I failed to say something I should have said?

- Have I done something I should not have done?

- Have I failed to do something I should have done?

I self-critique by thinking through my relationship to the organization:

- Why am I doing this?

- Who will be affected?

- How should it be done?

- When should it be done?

Why am I doing this? Am I doing this for the right reasons? Do I have the right motives? Is there an inappropriate personal agenda in my plans? Is it the right thing to do?

Who will be affected? Will anyone be harmed? Is the harm unavoidable? Have steps been taken to assure the harm is minimized? Have explanations been provided? Have questions been answered? Has open, candid communication been encouraged?

How should it be done? Have I carefully considered alternatives? Have I included others in the decision making process? What is the result I am looking for? Does the chosen course of action have the best chance of moving us toward the desired results?

When should it be done? Is this the right time? Is there a more appropriate time? Am I trading long-term results for a short-term advantage? Is the timetable realistic? Is the timetable mutually acceptable to the key players? Does the timetable allow for the unexpected?

4. Am I overly concerned with image building?

Benchmark question number four notes the difference between show business and substance. Integrity, by definition, is genuine. Character is not an image fabricated to manipulate others.

Madison Avenue has taught us that we must package ourselves in order to sell ourselves. Although attention should be paid to putting our best foot forward, character's focus is on relaying reality, not selling an act. Presenting myself as something other than what I am raises questions about my trustworthiness. Posturing may cause others to view my motives as bogus. Invariably, the value of my stock will go down.

Presenting a good professional image is an asset. Valid principle-centered leadership, however, does not depend on wearing designer fashions or knowing when to use the salad fork. The focus of integrity is on building a reputation, not merely projecting an image. Like principle-centered leadership, true professionalism includes a dogged commitment to the truth and seeing things for what they are.

Here are some questions which will assist a leader in gauging preoccupation with image building.

How good am I at telling myself the truth? Truth telling is an ethical concept which refers to the capacity to be loyal to the truth and the spirit of the truth. This raises the bar for honesty. It is not enough to merely refuse to lie. I must insist on never using the truth to suggest what is false either implicitly or explicitly. Implicitly, I can use the truth to suggest what is false by withholding information or by twisting the truth to create a false impression.

Explicitly, I can use the truth to suggest what is false by embellishing the truth. I can suggest something is more serious or less serious than it actually is by tone of voice or the words I choose. For example, for most of us the biggest personal barrier to telling ourselves the truth is cognitive dissonance. Cognitive dissonance is the capacity to lie to ourselves convincingly. We are all tempted by cognitive dissonance. Anytime someone tells us something unpleasant, it is tempting to rationalize or to engage in denial. We all want to be emotionally comfortable. Sometimes we want it badly enough to lie to ourselves.

Do I make decisions based on what is right or on what is most easily accepted? Do I have to take a poll before I can candidly relay information? Does opposition, even when it is self-serving, cause me to retreat? Do I shelve my convictions at the first sign of conflict? Am I committed to doing what I believe is best or is it more important to me to be liked?

Do I change my personality, speech, or actions according to the people I am with? Every healthy personality includes a desire to be liked. No one wants others to groan when we enter the room. We would like others to like us. But being a people-pleaser is an unacceptable price for being liked. Being liked does not have the same value as being trusted. Ideally, it is good to be both liked and trusted. But when a choice has to be made, it is personal integrity that secures the value of our stock. This does not mean that I am free to act like a bull in a china shop as long as I'm candid. The consideration axis of the courage-consideration continuum (page 27) requires me to treat others with courtesy. A lack of compassion in truth-telling is just another form of posturing.

Do I hog the credit when things go well and find someone to blame when things do not go well? Peers and employees usually find this kind of behavior unsettling. It de-motivates the team and strains relationships with the selection of each scapegoat. The most effective teams are bound together by mutual respect. Sharing the credit for success builds trust. Accepting responsibility for failure does even more to build trust. People instinctively know it takes less character to handle success than to overcome failure; the leader who will own his mistakes is a leader they want to see succeed. The leader who postures at the expense of others is a leader they would like to see fail.

5. Am I investing in the success of others?

The fifth and final benchmark question emphasizes the value of win-win relationships. In the story about the construction foreman, Pete attempts to construct a win-lose relationship. He assumes he can establish a long-term scenario in which he is the only winner. This is almost never the case. Long-term success is almost always the result of win-win partnerships built through years of cooperative effort.

Investing in the success of another speaks to the deepest needs and interests of the people around us. Everyone wants to experience some measure of success. Everyone believes individuals have a right to benefit from their efforts. Effective leadership takes these needs and interests into account. This sensitivity is not mushy or patronizing. It recognizes that it is unethical and self-defeating to treat others as a means to an end. People do what they do for their own reasons. Those reasons, more often than not, fit the vision a person has for his or her life. A principled leader respects that vision and works to build win-win relationships. Relationships which sustain long-term motivation and commitment are mutually beneficial.

Some of the more notable roadblocks to win-win relationships include pride, moodiness, perfectionism, oversensitivity, and negativism.

Win-win relationships rarely develop when others are treated as inferior. Most people find it difficult to accept a snobbish or know-it-all attitude. Few people view being discounted as an investment in their success.

Moodiness is an immature characteristic detrimental to personal relationships. Moody people tend to be fickle. Fickle individuals are perceived to be unreliable.

Perfectionism is an obsessive need to perform flawlessly. It stifles creativity and turns people away. Perfectionists can rarely affirm themselves; therefore, it's difficult for them to affirm others.

Oversensitive people are constantly licking their wounds. They look inward and are not aware of others. Naturally, it is hard to believe they care about the success of others.

Negativism poses the greatest threat to win-win relationships. It could even be said that negativism energizes all the other road blocks listed above. Negative people typically do not attract positive people. Positive persons know there is nothing mutually beneficial about naysayers.

On a practical level, here are some reliable suggestions for investing in the success of others.

Be patient.
As long as there is good reason to believe people are doing their best, cut them some slack. If a person is unable to do the job, tell him or her. As long as an individual is making acceptable progress, offer encouragement.

Be familiar with the problems of others.
Do your best to relate on a firsthand basis. Don't assume you know what there is to know because you came up through the ranks. Keep your knowledge and experience fresh. People must be able to trust you on the basis of today's facts, not on yesterday's experience alone.

Assure others of your confidence in them.
When an associate does a good job, tell him or her. When an employee improves performance, let him or her know. If team members express doubt about their ability to master a new process, bolster their confidence. Look for opportunities to let those who have earned your confidence know you believe in them.

Take care to give others credit for their efforts and their ideas.
Investing in others means allowing them to keep what is rightfully theirs. Most of us understand this as it applies to personal property. We certainly would not take anyone's car keys from their desk without permission and treat their car as if it were our own. Ethically speaking, a person's ideas and efforts fall under the same guideline. Every team member deserves to benefit from original ideas. Team members have a right to expect credit for their efforts. Leaders can stand on their own initiative. They do not steal the ideas or manipulate the behavior of others.

In our opening story, Pete committed the most fundamental mistake a leader can make—he failed to lead himself. The consequence of his failure to manage his own words and behavior was selficide. Principled leaders do not commit selficide. They are admired for the courage with which they self-correct and the consideration with which they relate to others. As a result, such a leader reaps the ever-increasing benefits of trust and respect.

5

Leaders Value Integrity

A leader is loyal to the best interest of the common good.
A leader is guided by an abiding faith in right.

Once upon a time there lived a man named Henry "Hank" Bedford Bannister, Jr. On February 19, 1996, Hank traveled to Yale to deliver the first of the Bannister Leadership Lectures that had been established in memory of his father. More than forty years earlier, Henry Bedford Bannister, Sr., had established Bannister Furniture Limited. Now president and CEO of Bannister Furniture Limited, Hank, as his father's successor, led a company widely respected as a good corporate citizen. It was a great place to work. It was a place where associates (employees) when asked, "Where do you work?" were proud to respond, "B.F.L."

That day in February Hank had endured a bad trip. The flight from Chattanooga to Hartford, with a connection through Nashville, had been delayed. Arriving in New Haven after midnight, Hank was exhausted from a long day and very little sleep the night before. He ordered dinner, ate, and then lay down to sleep without bothering to undress. About five o'clock the next morning Hank got up and began to shave. Hank still had not been able to formulate a plan for the lecture he was to present at 9:00. Procrastination had always been his number one developmental need, all the way back to the time he worked as an entry level clerk on the loading dock when his father had run the company. Somehow, he always came through in a pinch. Yet, he had come to New Haven without so much as a note card. He assumed it would all come to him somewhere between lift-off in Chattanooga and the podium in New Haven.

Just as he had his face lathered and was searching for his razor, the whole speech came to him out of nowhere. He dropped his razor and grabbed a pencil, dashing off the outline. As Hank distractedly returned to his razor, he cut himself badly. That cut was a hint of things to come.

Bannister Furniture Ltd. was more than a good corporate citizen and a great place to work. It was an ideal, a model for other corporations. It was a model led by honest, principled men and women with a vision. At the top of that model and at the center of that vision had always been the Bannister family. Henry, Sr., had gained national and international renown as the principled-centered leader of a new entrepreneurial age. After all, it was Henry's pristine business ethics which had brought Hank to New Haven. Yale was the alma mater of both Henry, Sr., and Hank. An endowment provided for The Henry Bedford Bannister, Sr., Chair in Principle-Centered Leadership. Business leaders and academics who admired the high ethical standards Henry, Sr., had brought to the competitive arena established the chair. Henry had demonstrated, once and for all, that an entrepreneur could turn a good profit while doing the right thing.

Now the leadership of B.F.L. and its prized reputation had fallen on Hank's shoulders. It was a role he had prepared for all his life. It was an honor and a challenge he gladly embraced some seven years earlier at his father's death. Like his father before him, Hank knew how to do the right thing. But somewhere between the knowing and the doing, the right thing had gotten lost in a price-fixing scheme. He had gotten sucked into a dubious competitive strategy and then had stayed long after he discovered it to be an illegal scam. The rumors about the scheme were no longer whispers but now were beginning to appear in print as incriminating internal memos were being leaked. Some people were taking sides; others were running for cover. The feds were formulating criminal anti-trust charges, and a public trial was not far in the future.

Hank's reputation and career were in danger, but much more was at stake. It was, in some measure, Bannister Furniture Ltd. It was everything Henry, Sr., believed in and stood for and what Hank had come to Yale to talk about.

So when Hank stood there looking into the hotel mirror with soap on his face and a razor in his hand, part of the reflection he saw was his own shame and disappointment. He could blame no one but himself for breaching his father's business ethic. A religious man, Hank saw in the mirror a judgment even more difficult to bear than God's: his own judgment of himself. When Hank had difficulty forgiving himself for disappointing his father, he remembered the words his father often spoke, "God is merciful, but none of us are very good at showing mercy for ourselves." That morning in New Haven, Hank felt no mercy, only shame.

Hank found himself casting his mind back across the years like the whip of a fly rod. Hanging in mid-air like a perfect trout lure just before it lands in the water was Henry's Code of Ethics. This document was in every lobby and office of Bannister Furniture Ltd. Principled, focused, and straightforward describe the perfect simplicity of the Bannister Ethic. Hank had known the code as long as he had known his ABC's.

The Code of Ethics was three direct questions:

Is it legal?

- Will I be violating either civil law or company policy?

Is it balanced?

- Is it fair to all concerned in the short term as well as the long term?

- Does it promote win-win relationships?

How will it make me feel about myself?

- Will it make me proud?

- Would I feel good if my family knew about it?

- Would I feel good if my decision was published in the newspaper?

For the first time since becoming company president and CEO, Hank realized his answers were now the wrong answers. Yes, he had broken the law and company policy. No, what he had done was not fair to anyone, and he felt neither pride nor pleasure at the prospect of his family and community finding out what he had done.

Standing there in the early morning twilight with his face lathered and bleeding, Hank asked himself the question men always ask when they discover a self-inflicted wound: *How could this have happened?*

The wound was self-inflicted, to be sure. It was also wrapped in self-pity. His reasoning had followed a predictable pattern. Hank winced when he thought how convincingly he had lied to himself. "To lie to one's self and believe the lie are the most cowardly things men do," would have been his father's assessment. Those who knew Hank's father and his homespun wisdom would have admiringly called this a "Henryism." Many "Henryisms" were beginning to return to Hank's memory as he pondered how it had all unfolded.

B.F.L. had always nestled in the mountain valley sixty miles northeast of Chattanooga. There, the Great Smoky Mountains gave B.F.L. a warm feeling factories usually lack. Bethlehem was the town's name. It had been founded around the turn of the century by a hearty band of Pennsylvania Amish. Unhappy with things up North, they had come South to this mountain valley. The "Andy Griffith Show" could have been filmed in Bethlehem with no need to add a single prop. Tree-lined streets; modest, neatly kept homes with wide front porches; steepled churches; a gazebo park at the center; and even the requisite town drunk graced the town of Bethlehem.

He was no Otis, but he made everyone feel better. His name was Morgan although most folks referred to him with a holier than thou air as "that drunk." Yet Henry, Sr., had been one of the few respectable people who would stop and pass the time of day with Morgan. When they happened to see Morgan, Henry liked to tell Hank, "People worth looking up to don't need anybody to look down on." And Hank had learned that lesson.

Even so, the Amish were still around and gave Bethlehem that final, sweet touch of quaintness with their horse-drawn buggies and black, Sunday-go-to-meetin' frock coats. Their handmade quilts drew tourists and tourists' dollars. The real money, however, was at B.F.L. Bethlehem held three thousand souls in her hands. Of these, four hundred ten won their daily bread at Bannister Furniture. Another dozen businesses gather B.F.L. table scraps, the kind small suppliers often glean from a larger customer's profits.

To say the least, B.F.L. was the economic soul of Bethlehem; B.F.L. and Bethlehem were interchangeable. B.F.L. was Bethlehem Furniture, and Bethlehem was Bannistertown.

Hank sat down on the bed in his hotel room. He thought to himself, "Suddenly, I feel tired. Maybe drained is a better word." Wearily Hank wiped the shaving cream from his face. Looking at the towel as it wiped away the mix of soap and blood, Hank's mind drifted back to when things had begun to go wrong...

Hank's dilemma is all too familiar. It raises the oldest ethical question: Why do good leaders make bad ethical decisions? Is it because these men and women who otherwise appear to be good people are in fact immoral? Such a question defies any common sense answer. The truth, I think, is less glamorous and less satisfying for those who like to use the actions of a few misbegotten souls to explain evil. Hank and his associates are ordinary men and women not very different from you or me. They found themselves in a dilemma, and they solved it in a way that seemed the least troublesome: *They decided not to disclose information which might hamper sales.* The consequences of their decision—both to the public and ultimately to B.F.L.—did not fully occur to them at the time.

The Bannister Furniture case illustrates the fine line between acceptable and unacceptable managerial behavior. Leaders are expected to strike a difficult balance—to pursue their companies' best interests, but not overstep the bounds of what outsiders will tolerate. Even the best leaders can find themselves in a bind and not know how far is too far. In retrospect, they can usually tell where they should have drawn the line, but no one manages in retrospect. We can only live and act today and hope that whoever looks back on what we did will judge that we struck the proper balance.

In a few years, many of us may be found delinquent for decisions we are making now about tobacco, clean air, and the use of some other seemingly benign substances. The leaders at Bannister Furniture may have believed that they were acting in the company's best interest, that what they were doing would never be found out, or even that it wasn't really wrong. These rationalizations endangered the company and contributed to its downfall.

Why do leaders do things that ultimately inflict great harm on their companies, themselves, and those whose patronage the organization depends? Although the particulars may vary, the motivating beliefs are much the same. Here we're examining them in the context of the corporation, but we know that these feelings are basic throughout society. We find them wherever we go because we take them with us.

When we look more closely at the Bannister Furniture case, we can delineate four commonly held rationalizations that can lead to misconduct. (1) A belief that the activity is within reasonable ethical and legal limits, that is, not really illegal or immoral. (2) A belief that the activity is in the individual's or the corporation's best interest, that the individual would somehow be expected to undertake the activity. (3) A belief that the activity is safe because it will never be found out or publicized, the classic crime and punishment issue of discovery. (4) And finally, a belief that because the activity helps the company, the company will condone it and even protect the person who engages in it.

Rationalization One:
The conduct is not really illegal or immoral.

The idea that an action is not really wrong is an old issue. How far is too far? Exactly where is the line between smart and too smart? Between sharp and shaded? Between profit maximization and illegal conduct? The issue can be complex. It involves an interplay between top management's goals and middle managers' effort to interpret those aims. Put enough people in an ambiguous, ill-defined situation and some will conclude that whatever hasn't been labeled specifically wrong must be okay, especially if there are rewards for certain acts. Top executives seldom ask their direct reports to do things that are against the law or are imprudent. But organizational leaders sometimes leave things unsaid or give the impression that there are things they don't want to know about. In other words, whether deliberately or otherwise, they seem to distance themselves from their reports' tactical decisions in order to keep their own hands clean if things go awry. Often they lure ambitious lower-level leaders by implying that rich rewards await those who can produce certain results and that the methods for achieving them will not be examined too closely.

How can leaders avoid crossing a line that is seldom precise? Unfortunately, most know that they have overstepped it only when they have gone too far. They have no reliable guidelines about what will be overlooked or tolerated and what will be condemned or attacked. When leaders must operate in murky borderlands, the most reliable guideline is an old principle—*when in doubt, don't*. That may seem like a timid way to run a business. One can argue that if this principle actually took hold among middle managers who run most companies, it might take the enterprise out of free enterprise. But there is a difference between taking a worth-while economic risk and risking an illegal or immoral act to make a few extra dollars. The difference between becoming a success and becoming a statistic lies in knowledge, including self-knowledge, not daring. Contrary to popular belief, leaders are not paid to take risks, they are paid to know which risks are worth taking. Also, maximizing profits is the company's second priority, not its first. The first is insuring its survival. Any leader can be tempted to take an inappropriate risk because of their companies' demands. But the same superiors who press you to do more and to do it better or faster or less expensively will turn on you should you cross the fuzzy line between right and wrong. They will blame you for exceeding instructions or for ignoring their warnings. The smartest managers already know that the best answer to the question, "How far is too far?" is "Don't try to find out."

Rationalization Two:
The activity is in the individual's or the corporation's best interest; the individual would somehow be expected to undertake the activity.

Believing that unethical conduct is in the person or corporation's best interest nearly always results from a parochial view of those interests. For example, Alpha Industries, a Massachusetts manufacturer of microwave equipment, paid $57,000 to a Rathion manager, ostensibly for a marketing report. The Air Force investigators charged that the report was a ruse to cover a bribe. Alpha wanted some contracts that the Rathion manager supervised. Those contracts ultimately cost Alpha a lot more than the amount paid for the report. After the company was indicted for bribery, its contract was suspended and its profits promptly vanished. Alpha isn't unique in this transgression. In 1984, the Pentagon suspended 453 companies for violating procurement regulations. Ambitious managers look for ways to attract favorable attention and to distinguish themselves from their peers. They do whatever will make them look good in the short run while ignoring the long-term implications. They skimp on maintenance or training or customer service, and they get away with it for a while. The sad truth is that many managers have been promoted on the basis of great results obtained in just those ways, leaving unfortunate successors to inherit the inevitable whirlwind. The problems they create are not always traced back to them. Organizations cannot afford to be hoodwinked in this way. They must be concerned with more than just results; they must look very hard at how results are obtained.

Rationalization Three:
The activity is safe because it will never be found out or publicized, the classic crime and punishment issue of discovery.

Believing that one can probably get away with irresponsible risk-taking is perhaps the most difficult rationalization to deal with because it's often true. A great deal of prescribed behavior escapes detection. We know that conscience alone does not deter everyone. For example, First National Bank of Boston pleaded guilty to laundering satchels of twenty dollar bills worth one-point-three billion dollars. Thousands of satchels must have passed through the bank's doors without incident before the scheme was detected. That kind of heavy, unnoticed traffic breeds complacency. How can we deter wrongdoing that is unlikely to be detected? We can make it more likely to be detected. Today's discovery process allows a plaintiff's attorneys to comb through a company's records for incriminating evidence. Had this process been in place when Johns-Manville concealed evidence on asbestosis, there probably would have been no cover-up. Mindful of the likelihood of detection, Johns-Manville might have chosen a different course and could very well be thriving today without the protection of the bankruptcy courts.

The most effective deterrent is not to increase the severity of punishment for those caught, but to heighten the perceived probability of being caught in the first place. For example, police have found that parking an empty patrol car at locations where motorists often exceed the speed limit reduces the frequency of speeding. Neighborhood crime watch signs decrease burglaries. Simply increasing the frequency of audits and spot checks is a deterrent, especially when combined with three other simple techniques—scheduling audits irregularly, making at least half of them unannounced, and setting up some checkups soon after others.

But frequent spot checks cost more than big sticks, raising the question of which is more cost effective. A common managerial error is to assume that because frequent audits uncover little behavior that is out of line, less frequent and, therefore, less costly auditing is sufficient. But this assumption overlooks the important deterrent effect of frequent checking. The point is to prevent misconduct, not to catch it.

Rationalization Four:
Because the activity helps the company, the company will condone it and even protect the person who engages in it.

The question to deal with here is "How do we keep company loyalty from going berserk?" At Johns-Manville, a small group of executives and a succession of corporate medical directors kept the facts about the lethal qualities of asbestos from becoming public knowledge for decades, and they managed to live with that knowledge. Johns-Manville, or really the company senior management, did condone their decision and protect those employees. Something similar seems to have happened at General Electric. When one of its missile projects ran a cost greater than the Air Force had agreed to pay, middle managers surreptitiously shifted those costs to projects that were still operating under budget. In this case, the loyalty that ran amok was primarily to the division. Managers want their unit results to look good, but GE, with one of the finest reputations in U. S. industry, was splattered with scandal and paid a fine of 1.4 million dollars. One of the most troubling aspects of the GE case is the company's admission that those involved were thoroughly familiar with the company's ethical standards before the incident took place. This suggests that the practice of declaring a code of ethics and teaching it to employees is not enough to deter unethical conduct. Additional safeguards are needed.

Top management has a responsibility to exert a moral force within the company. Senior executives are responsible for drawing the line between loyalty to the company and action against the laws and values of the society in which the company must operate. Further, because that line can be obscured in the heat of the moment, the line has to be drawn well short of where reasonable men and women could begin to suspect that their rights had been violated. The company has to react long before a prosecutor, for instance, would have a case strong enough to seek an indictment. Executives have a right to expect loyalty from their employees against competitors and detractors, but not loyalty against the law, against common morality, or against society itself. Leaders must warn employees that a disservice to customers, especially to innocent bystanders, cannot be a service to the organization.

Finally, and most important of all, leaders must stress that excuses of company loyalty will not be accepted for acts that place its good name in jeopardy. To put it bluntly, the corporation's leaders must make it clear that employees who harm other people, allegedly for the company's benefit, will be fired. In the end, it is up to top management to send a clear and pragmatic message to all employees that the highest ethical standards will be the foundation of their organization.

Suggested Guidelines for Ethical Decision Making

A fundamental safeguard for making ethical decisions is to ensure that all parties are fully aware of the issues (be sure there is plenty of light on the issue). Whenever in doubt, ask for help. The following process can guide you as you consider ethical decisions. It is important to begin at Step 1 and follow in sequence until you are confident you are making the best decision.

1. Know all the facts.

    • Make sure you have all the facts and information!

2. Is the action legal?

    • If the answer is "No," go no further.

3. Does it comply with company policy?

    • If the answer is "No," there is probably a good reason not to take the action. If you still feel the action is right, ask for advice.

4. Are you (or the other party) expecting something inappropriate or inconsistent with company policy, practice, etc. because of this action?

    • If you are taking this action for material gain, it is probably not ethical.

    • Make sure the action you are taking is to build a relationship with no strings attached and not for personal gain.

5. Who will be impacted by the decision?

    • Will people be positively or negatively impacted by your decision?

6. How will it look if the decision is made public?

    • If you would be ashamed to see a written account of this action in the newspaper, don't do it.

7. Could the action be interpreted as improper?

    • If this action could be perceived as unethical and you may have to explain your actions, either don't do it or ask for advice.

8. Ask.

    • If you get this far and still are concerned or unsure, ask for help.

    • If it's wrong, don't do it.

- If the action clearly breaks company policy and society's values, don't do it.

- If you don't know, ask.

- If you have an ethical issue, ask your manager or other leadership for advice until you get an answer.

Hank Bannister cared about right and wrong. He was proud of his father's business ethic and thought of himself as heir to that ethic. Even so, Hank became a statistic. Arguably, he was a good person who made a bad ethical decision. In the end, Hank asked the question we all ask when we discover the self-inflicted wound: "How could this have happened?"

Sadly, Hank knew all too well the rationalizations which led him to act against the best interest of Bannister Furniture, Bannister's employees, the community, and himself. Hank's failure was the failure to lead himself. Failing to lead himself, he could not lead B.F.L.

6

Leaders Are Empathetic

A leader empathizes with others.
A leader seeks to understand others.

Once upon a time there was a leader named Paul. Paul did not have a university degree. Paul had never been to business school. Paul's exposure to motivational theory was limited to the talks his high school coach used to give Paul and his teammates prior to the big game.

Paul was unorthodox. Even so, he was an effective leader. No one questioned that. People followed Paul instinctively. Given a choice, they chose to follow. Joining Paul's team was a prize employees strove to attain. Paul's motivational strategy brought out the best in people. Peers and associates felt valued and appreciated. Problems were considered normal. Paul viewed problems as nothing more or less than challenges for the team to meet and then to move on. Best of all, as far as the team was concerned, there were no human sacrifices offered up to the god of blame in Paul's department. Everyone shared the credit for success. Everyone was expected to contribute to the analysis and subsequent course correction associated with any failure. But there was no scapegoating.

When outsiders noted Paul's success, they assumed he was a summa cum laude graduate of a major management school. They were surprised to discover he was not. "How, then, could Paul's effectiveness be accounted for?" they frequently asked.

The answer is simple. People followed Paul because he knew first-hand where they were coming from. He knew their dreams, the source of their disappointments, and the hopes they held fragile within themselves. Paul empathized with others. And that was the key to his effectiveness.

Paul believed leadership was all about leading people to believe in themselves. As far as Paul was concerned, there was nothing a leader could not accomplish if who got the credit was not an issue. Paul liked to tell people, with a sparkle of humor in his eye, that he liked to go one step beyond MBWA (Management by Wandering Around). Paul found what he called MBBA (Management by Believing Around) far more effective. He encouraged his people. He took advantage of every opportunity to teach them to believe in themselves. Paul drove confidence, as well as competence, deep into his team. Believing that each person must believe in self before believing in anything else, Paul gave people a sense of confidence. Here's how Paul described his leadership philosophy:

> The longer I live the more I realize the importance of attitude. I suppose that's why I like to tell people, "I've got an attitude and I want you to have one too." Now, wait a minute, don't get me wrong. I'm talking about a **can-do attitude!** A can-do attitude is, to me, more important than the past, than education, than money, than circumstances, than failures, than successes, than what other people think or say. It is more important than appearances, cleverness, or skill. It will make or break a person or a company. The remarkable thing is that we all get to choose our attitude. And, just as remarkable, most of the folks we all work with would like to see each of us get an attitude—a can-do attitude, that is. Oh, I know that some people seem to have built-in filters that screen out boos and amplify hurrahs. But those are the people who never know when they're in trouble. They never let others help them. And people want all the help they can get in succeeding. People just want to know that when the tide comes in all the ships are gonna' be allowed to rise. People want to be able to trust the leader. They want to be able to believe that the leader knows where their vessel is

coming from and how far it has sailed—whether it is a big clipper ship or a small dinghy. They want their effort and their contribution, however small, appreciated. So that brings me back to attitude—in particular, the attitude of the leader. When the leader believes in the team, the team starts to believe in itself. For better or worse, most people live up or down to what is expected of them. The leader gives people a glimpse of what they can be at their best. We cannot change our past. We cannot change the fact that people will act in a certain way. What we can do is play the one hand we have, and that is our attitude. I am convinced that life is ten percent what happens to me and ninety percent how I respond to it. Therefore, a can-do attitude makes all the difference. You want a little pearl of wisdom from me? Well, here it is: Slip another person's shoes off their feet and walk around in their shoes for a while. Then, when you slip them back on the person's feet, make sure they fit better, feel better, and work better. Once you do, that person will follow you and they'll follow, not because they were told to, but because they want to.

Paul knows something profound about the qualities of an effective leader. He knows that the basis of life is people and how they relate to each other. Success, fulfillment, and happiness depend upon our ability to relate effectively. Paul has discovered that the best way to become a person others will follow is to develop the qualities we ourselves are attracted to in others.

If you are attracted to a sense of humor, courage, courtesy, candor, kindness, consideration, competence, good-will, and win-win relationships, then focus on developing these qualities in your own personality. The fact is the qualities we are attracted to in others are the very qualities which attract others to us. People are more alike than they are different. Everyone wants to find both humanity (a sense of compassion) and integrity in a leader.

The key to leading others is empathy. It is putting yourself in the other person's place and, once in the other person's place, demonstrating a sincere desire to know what life and work are like for that person.

How does a leader go about empathizing? Consider for a moment how you want others to treat you. Chances are, the qualities you value are not complicated at all. There's not a person reading this who doesn't like and respond to the following:

- Openness

- Encouragement

- Appreciation

- Forgiveness

- Understanding

First, you want others to be open with you.

You want the people around you to tell you the truth—even when it is unpleasant to hear. This includes not just the obvious that you don't want to be lied to, but also includes the desire that others be candid about what they think and feel. You want to live and work in an environment of openness where there are no hidden agendas. You want others to be open with you, and others want the same quality of openness from you.

Second, you want others to encourage you.

No one ever climbs out of bed in the morning grumbling to himself, "Boy, I hope the boss doesn't encourage me any more today. I don't know how much longer I can handle those 'attaboys.'" People complain, but never about being encouraged to take heart. Few people have more encouragement than they can stand. Think about it; most of your best friends are those who encourage you. You probably don't have many strong relationships with people who put you down. Typically, you avoid such people and seek out those who express belief in you. You want others to encourage you. And others want the same quality of encouragement from you.

Third, you want others to appreciate you.

Motivational theorists have made a convincing case for what they call the deepest principle in human nature—the craving to be appreciated. It is no coincidence that employee satisfaction surveys consistently rank the following as leading causes of employee dissatisfaction:

1. Failure to give credit for suggestions.

2. Failure to respond to grievances.

3. Criticizing employees in front of others.

4. Failure to ask employees their opinions.

5. Failure to provide information, in advance, when changes impact an employee directly.

6. Failure to offer feedback.

7. Failure to encourage.

Notice that every single item has to do with the failure to recognize the importance of the employee. Each item is an affront to the employees' self-esteem and says with clarity, "You don't matter." No one appreciates such treatment. You want others to appreciate you. Others want the same quality of appreciation from you.

Fourth, you want others to forgive you.

If you are like most people, your days include success and failure. The success you can probably handle. The failures, on the other hand, require recovery. Whether it is a failed project or a social gaffe, your course has to be corrected and apologies provided. You recover best when the people involved are willing to grant forgiveness and allow you to move on. You are drawn to people who harbor no grudges and plan no ambushes. You are drawn to people who will grant you another chance to get it right. You want others to forgive you. Others want the same quality of forgiveness from you.

Fifth, you want others to understand you.

How do you feel when you are misunderstood? What kinds of feelings well up inside of you—frustration, disappointment, resentment? These are common responses to being misunderstood.

Peter Drucker, often called the "Father of American Management," claims that sixty percent of all management problems are the result of faulty communications. A leading marriage counselor says that at least half of all divorces are the result of faulty communication between spouses. And, studies have shown that most repeat offenders have difficulty communicating with others. Communication is fundamental to understanding. When someone takes the time to listen to you, you feel they have made an effort to understand you. When someone is open, encouraging, appreciative, and forgiving, you find it easy to believe they are interested in where you are coming from. You want others to understand you. Others want the same quality of understanding from you.

Paul led like the idealized version of the Harvard Business School graduate. However, the secret to Paul's effectiveness lay in his understanding of human nature, not in his education. Paul knew that the basis of life is people and how they relate to each other. Paul gladly walked a mile or more in his employees' shoes. Paul was open with his people. He provided encouragement. He demonstrated appreciation. He forgave their honest mistakes. Paul's empathetic leadership built a high trust, high performance work team.

Leaders Communicate

A leader speaks less and listens more.
A leader listens to understand.
A leader speaks to clarify and build trust.

Once upon a time a handyman rang a doorbell in a wealthy neighborhood. Much to his surprise, the handyman was greeted warmly by the lady who came to the door. She stated that she was glad to see him because she had been hoping to find someone to do some painting. "Do you see that bucket of green paint there beside the doorstep?" she asked. "Yes," the man replied. "Well, I've been looking for someone to paint my porch. If you'll just go around back and put a coat of paint on it, I would appreciate it." The man replied, "Thank you," and went to work. A couple of hours later, he rang the doorbell again and informed the lady that the job was complete. She thanked him and said, "Well, let's go look it over." So they went around back and the lady discovered that the man had, in fact, put a nice coat of green paint on her Porsche. When questioned about it, the man explained, "Well, I thought you said to paint your Porsche, I didn't realize you meant porch."

This story illustrates one of the basic principles of communication. It is simply not accurate to assume that when we communicate with others, we transfer a precise piece of information from one mind to another. Words, gestures, and expressions do not, in themselves, have meaning. Instead, people attach meaning to them. Thus, when we attempt to communicate, we always run the risk of engaging in a failure to communicate.

Communication is the exchange of ideas between two people. Effective communication involves more than telling, it involves shared understanding. One-way communication rarely elicits the desired response. It must be understood as a two-way process. In the words of Peter Drucker, "Communications are practically impossible if they are based on a downward relationship." The basic reason for any type of communication is to prompt some form of behavioral response or action. But we often discover that what we say or do does not always elicit the kind of response that we want when we want it. A bank manager asks each of his tellers to ask every customer about opening a new savings account so that the branch can increase the number of new accounts. At the end of the week, there seems to be no increase and furthermore, very few tellers seem to be asking the question. What happened? The president of a software company requests that a proposal for a new client be on her desk the morning of an important meeting. That morning she discovers the proposal is not on her desk and the person responsible is out sick. What happened? These leaders probably did not recognize that successful communication is a two-way street. Although they may have given instructions, they did not really communicate effectively enough to get the desired results.

Before ideas can be accepted, they must be known and understood clearly by the listener. The most valuable contributions to society that we make during our lifetime are often the thoughts and ideas that we communicate. Expressing your creativity is a natural desire that offers a great deal of fulfillment. The more you realize the value of a new idea, the more enthusiastic you become about it. But unless you are able to stimulate the same kind of enthusiasm in others, your idea will begin to gather dust in the closet of your mind. The frustration of your attempt may even stifle future creativity and inhibit your personal growth.

No matter how well informed you may become, no matter how much knowledge you acquire in your chosen field, it is important to remember that very few have ever accomplished much or gone far in any human endeavor without the assistance and cooperation of other people. Friends, relatives, employers, business associates, customers; nearly everyone with whom you are in contact can speed or retard your journey toward your goals. It's easy to see, then, that effective communication and leadership are inseparable. I mentioned earlier that effective communication is a two-way process. However, we often view communication as a way of expressing our ideas to someone else. But we already know that human behavior is not a result of strictly logical and rational thought. Therefore, exchanging facts is only part of the process. The feelings and emotions that develop during the course of conversation strongly influence the behavior of those involved and ultimately the outcome of the conversation. Perhaps an employee enters your office and complains about not having enough time to complete a production report. It would seem that the status of production is being communicated when, in fact, the employee may be saying something very different. The employee may want to communicate the feeling of being overworked or the rationalization of a tendency to procrastinate. The employee may even want you to respond with anger to reinforce his or her own feelings of frustration.

Another example occurs when employees go over the head of their immediate leader in the chain of command. The intent may seem to be to get some action when in reality, perhaps even unknown to the person, the goal is to receive recognition or to undermine the immediate leader's position.

From your vantage point, there are two emotional factors that affect a conversation: 1) How you feel about the other person's ideas and 2) What you believe the other person feels about your ideas. In order for a salesperson to obtain an order, he or she must first discover the prospect's needs, then demonstrate or explain how their product will fill those needs, and finally ask for the order. If the prospect simply says,

"No," but doesn't explain why, the salesperson has no way of overcoming the prospect's objection. The salesperson doesn't know how the prospect really feels and whether or not the objection is actually warranted based on the information presented. Unless the salesperson can find out why the prospect feels the way he or she does, the communication process could come to an abrupt halt.

The same type of communication problem occurs in family relationships. A husband and wife may agree on the fact that they need a new automobile, but the husband discovers that the more he talks about it, the angrier his wife becomes. She certainly agrees outwardly they need a new car, but internally she is thinking about the fact that she will have to cancel the college courses she was planning to take to prepare for a promotion. Until she expresses her feelings, her husband will be unable to understand her actions. Any mention of the car will prompt a heated exchange and will probably affect communication in other areas of their family life.

Once you understand the role that emotions play in communication, you will begin to put yourself in the other person's shoes. As discussed in Chapter VI, this is called *empathy* and is a quality that can be cultivated by developing genuine interest in other people. Don't, however, confuse empathy with nodding your approval, sympathy, or simply agreeing with another person's point of view. Empathy is recognizing the fact that others are entitled to their beliefs just as you are, that they have certain needs to satisfy and goals to achieve just as you do. A doctor who confuses empathy with total agreement could do patients a great disservice. If the doctor agreed with their beliefs about their symptoms, knowing that clinically their appraisal was wrong, his faulty sense of empathy could be fatal. On the other hand, a physician with a good bedside manner is an individual with a strong inherent concern for the patients' needs, anxieties, and problems. The physician uses this emotional understanding to communicate to patients what must be done to affect a cure. As a result, both doctor and patient reach their objectives through mutual understanding. Such understanding may not have been possible without empathy in communication.

To be a truly effective leader, you must develop sensitivity to the needs and wants of your people. The secret is empathy, understanding, and caring. You must communicate through your words and your actions that you are interested in them as individuals. Your employees need to know that you appreciate their efforts and that their accomplishments are recognized. Rewards and recognition need not be expensive. A thank-you note, a pat on the back, or a round of applause can be even more important than monetary rewards.

Knowing your employees' needs, you can chart a course designed to give them what they want and, at the same time, achieve the company's goals. Your own goals may be reached by going around people, through people, or gaining the cooperation of people. It is not difficult to see that the easiest way to accomplish your objectives is with the help of those around you. If you feel that empathy is a characteristic which you need to develop more fully, set some specific goals in the area of personality development. The key to understanding others is to understand yourself. By examining your own experiences, anxieties, and fears, you will be able to relate more closely to the attitudes of others. Remember that your ideas are linked tightly with the results you want to obtain. By keeping your eye on your goals, you will become motivated by results and realize that those goals will only be met through communication that breeds acceptance, understanding, and trust. With this in mind, focus on the needs of others and you will develop empathy in communication.

We communicate every day with different types of people in different types of situations. In order to understand how to get your message across, it is important to examine three fundamental principles of successful, interpersonal communication.

1. The human mind functions in a very orderly fashion. It can only concentrate on one thought at a time. If you attempt to communicate a number of ideas rapidly and in an illogical sequence, the lis-

tener's mind will have great difficulty trying to follow and understand what you are saying. Before you present an idea, make a written plan, highlighting the objectives of your presentation and the main points. Make sure that the important facts are listed in a logical sequence. You may even want to share your presentation with a noninvolved third party to see if he or she clearly understands what is to be presented.

2. The human mind transposes words into pictures. Because words mean different things to different people, the responses that they produce may not be the same for everyone. The level of education, the region of the country that a person comes from, ethnic background—these and many other facts determine what mental pictures crystallize in a person's mind. As you begin to recognize the needs of others, you will use words that elicit an emotional response in harmony with those needs. Such empathy will enhance communications and ensure the accurate perception of your ideas.

3. Too many words clutter up communications. A good example of this was illustrated by an announcement made over a particular company's loud speaker system. It went like this, "Employees of Meniger, Inc. who are desirous of receiving additional copies of the new health benefit form should inform the receptionist of this office of the nature of their request in order to obtain, without delay, the extra copies they should like to have." Think how much simpler this would have been if the announcer had simply said, "If you want additional copies of the new health benefits form, ask the receptionist." When we fail to condense our communication, we leave the door wide open to time consuming misunderstanding and undesired responses. This is especially unfortunate if we need an immediate response to our communication. Become more conscious of your communication style and your ability to empathize with the feelings of others. As you develop a greater sensitivity to the needs and desires of family, friends, and associates, you will

gain their respect and open the door to even more effective communication.

For some reason, many people believe that the ability to speak articulately is an important prerequisite to achievement. Without diminishing the importance of good speech habits, it would serve us well to place greater emphasis on the quality of our listening habits. Benjamin Disraeli noted that nature has given us two ears, but only one mouth. This may be nature's way of telling us that listening is vital to our growth and development. Volumes have been written on the art of public speaking, how to deliver exciting speeches and even how to exercise your vocal chords in order to have a pleasant voice. But little has been written or presented on how to listen for understanding. If we agree that empathy and understanding are important traits, then we realize too that it is impossible to find out what someone else is thinking if we are doing all of the talking. Listening then, becomes our empathy skill.

In order to integrate good listening habits into your personal communication, you must know some of the "how to's" of listening and what to listen for. Here are ten suggestions for developing your listening skills:

1. **Take time to listen**.

   One of the biggest barriers to listening is that most of us have learned not to listen. It is a matter of survival in some sense. With so much racket in the world, we have to select what gets our attention. Tuning out has become such a natural and comfortable habit, we sometimes forget to tune in again, even when we need to. Listening is work, but it's worth the effort. So when you enter a situation where you know you need to listen, discipline yourself to enter a tuned-in mode. Bear down, suppress other thoughts, and focus. In time, the discipline of listening will become second nature, but only if it is practiced.

2. **Be attentive**.

Another natural inclination for listeners is to race ahead of the speaker—to jump to conclusions, prepare a response, or mentally criticize what the speaker is saying. The solution is to respond to the speaker every step of the way. Maintain eye contact. If you find your eyes drawn away, your mind won't be far behind. Also, demonstrate your interest by nodding, saying "uh-huh," and adopting an alert leaned-in posture. This will let the speaker know you care. He or she is far more likely to tell you what you need to know, and you are more likely to hear it. People talk about what is important to them. Whether you agree on the importance of the statement or issue, your lack of attention will be perceived as a lack of respect for their thoughts and opinions. Attentive listening, at its very best, means caring enough to take the time to pay attention. Easy to say—tough to do. Hearing involves focusing, being attentive to the individual and what is being said.

3. **Do not talk when you are listening**.

It is like talking with your mouth full—it's rude. It is easy for a conversation to degenerate into nothing more than alternating monologues. There is a difference in listening and waiting for your turn to talk. At the very least, constantly interrupting the speaker communicates insensitivity. At the worst, it is a subtle power play that leaves the other person feeling discounted and ignored.

4. **Listen with an open mind**.

Most of us have a natural tendency to hear what we want to hear. On the other hand, we also tend to filter out what we do not want to hear. For example, suppose a colleague tells you, "I'll have that project ready for you on Wednesday if all the materials come in." Because you want the project completed by Wednesday, you latch on to the first part of the statement. You make your plans with the expectation that Wednesday is the day. It is not until Wednesday and the project isn't done because the materials didn't come in, that you remember everything that was said. It's important to listen with an open mind. When you open your mind and approach a topic from the other person's point of view, you have a good chance to round out a complete picture of the facts surrounding the situation. Once you prove yourself capable of doing this, the other person is inclined to want to prove that he or she is just as capable of being fair and open minded as you are.

5. **Listen to more than the words.**

    Research indicates that at least sixty percent of a speaker's message is communicated nonverbally through tone of voice, facial expressions, and body language. Much of this information is received and processed unconsciously. Although you're unaware of it, your brain makes hundreds of calculations per second. When you're listening to someone, consider his or her posture, intonation, facial expressions, and gestures. Be careful not to give these non-verbals more weight than they deserve; however, trust your intuition. If a message sounds right, yet feels wrong, a red flag has been raised. Look and listen a little closer, and you will be glad you did. Listen for feelings. People tend to repeat those things that are important to them. Listen not only to what they say, but how they say it. Voices express emotion through pitch, intonation, hesitation, and speed of delivery. By listening to what people say and how they say it, you will discover the feelings behind the words.

6. **Ask questions politely.**

    One of the best techniques for attentive listening is asking questions. This can be particularly effective with people who ramble—it helps them focus, it lets them know you are serious about gaining needed information. If you are dealing with a rambler, feel free to interrupt occasionally, politely of course, with a question. It encourages them to come to the point. Questioning also works well with shy or inarticulate people. Letting them know exactly what you're looking for makes the conversation easier for them.

7. **Don't shoot the messenger**.

Sometimes people, particularly busy, task oriented people, fly off the handle when they hear bad news. Have you ever been guilty of this reaction? If you want people to cover up problems and keep the hard facts from coming to the surface, this approach works well. If, on the other hand, you want to be kept abreast of the information you need to do your job, stay calm. Welcome the arrival of bad news. In many instances, it is more valuable than good news. Let the people around you know that you want the facts whether the facts are good or bad.

8. **Take selective notes**.

It can be difficult to listen and write at the same time; however, it is essential in business to have an accurate recall of what was said. The pitfall is that you may be too busy writing to keep up with what is being said. The trick is to take selective notes, writing down key words, phrases, concepts and statistics. Try not to be too conspicuous. The speaker could be intimidated if you take down every word he or she says. And, in the event you are having a one-to-one conversation, you may want to say to the other person, "I need to keep a record of what we're saying. My memory is not great, so please don't be offended. I'm just trying to keep up with the important points we have agreed to."

9. **Get to "yes" or "no."**

Sometimes you need a quick answer without all the details. Under time constraints, consider saying, "I need a yes or no answer." Or, "Please briefly give me your best insight at this moment." "Give me a headline," can also work. People are accustomed to newspaper headlines delivering the essence of the story. Most of all, when you need a brief, to the point answer, ask for the person's help in getting the information as quickly as possible. This appeals to the better nature of most people. Not all, but most of us like to think of ourselves as helpful. However, rushing to the core of the issue must not be the pattern of your communication, it must be only an occasional event.

10. **Summarize**.

This is absolutely essential in those situations where you have to understand exactly what is said. When the speaker comes to a natural pause after finishing a point, paraphrase what he or she has said. Begin the summary with a phrase such as, "This is what I heard you say." Or, "My understanding of what you said is…" Then ask the speaker if what you heard or understood is correct. This provides the speaker with an opportunity to clarify or confirm what he or she said.

You can use these helpful hints regularly in your communication efforts. As others notice your attentiveness to their remarks, they will no doubt increase their respect for you and your concern for their feelings. People want you to believe in them just as you want them to believe in you. When you display empathy for another human being, you heighten self respect. The most loved, the most respected, and most successful leaders everywhere are invariably those who have the capacity to empathize with the feelings of others and who openly show it. Good listeners are good empathizers. In fact, the best way to express your interest and your empathy for another is to simply listen.

8

Leaders Are Mentors

A leader is honest, rational and civil.
A leader values common sense.
A leader honors basic human dignity.

Once upon a time there was a woman named June. June was the widow of a successful entrepreneur. Over a period of twenty-six years her late husband, Walter, had built a family-owned corner drugstore into a chain of 58 stores with annual sales in excess of one hundred, eighty-six million dollars.

June and Walter were the parents of one son, Michael. Michael was a high school sophomore when his father died. Therefore, his entry into the family business had to wait. As Michael grew toward adulthood and completed college, his mother assumed (though she never actually discussed it with him) that Michael would follow in his father's footsteps. Michael would someday run Double Discount Drugs. As president and CEO, Michael would fulfill his father's dream of one hundred stores with annual sales of over two hundred million. This, June believed, was the only course her son's life could take.

June was to be disappointed. When Michael completed undergraduate school, he announced he would not be entering the family business. Greatly distraught, June went to see an old family friend and confidante. In a matter of minutes she poured out her disappointment. The old friend, who happened to be a retired high school principal, listened patiently as June wandered through various stages of grief—denial, anger, depression and back to anger. June's pain was not new to the former principal. He had witnessed this frustration in other parents. He knew June's disappointment was genuine, so he agreed to have a talk with Michael.

Michael arrived for their appointment early. Rather than being reluctant to talk, Michael jumped right into the reasons for his decision. Michael explained, "I would have loved to take over the family business. But you need to understand the relationship I had with my father. He was a driven man who came up the hard way. His objective was to teach me self-reliance, but he made a mistake by trying to teach me that principle in a way that was demoralizing. He thought the best way to teach me self-reliance was to never encourage or praise me. He wanted me to be tough and independent."

"Two or three times every week we played catch in the yard. Sometimes we'd play catch with a baseball, at other times with a football. Either way the goal was always the same. I was to catch the ball ten times straight. I would catch that ball eight or nine times, but always on the tenth throw, he would do anything to make me miss. He would throw it on the ground or over my head, but always so I had no chance of catching it."

Michael paused for a long moment and then finished, "He never let me catch the tenth ball—never! No matter how hard I tried, he always set me up to fail. And I guess that's why I have to get away from my father's business; I want to catch the tenth ball."

Michael's father believed character and leadership are developed through the arbitrary exercise of authority. Nothing could be further from the truth. Both character and leadership are developed through the power of personal influence. Walter believed he was preparing Michael to be president of Double Discount Drugs. He failed to recognize the top three responsibilities of a mentor: to nurture, to encourage, and to set the person up to succeed.

Leadership is an art. Therefore, it cannot be taught as a science (i.e., catch a set number of balls and you qualify). Leadership is not the hammering out of an authoritarian skilled in the arbitrary exercise of power. Leadership is the weaving of a relationship. That relationship, woven well, results in mutual trust and influence. At its core, effective leadership is the capacity to influence the behavior of another due to the quality of the relationship.

Personal influence is, more than anything else, an ethical dynamic. The myth is that leaders transmit the values of the organization. The truth is that leaders are the values of the organization. Leaders do not merely relay a message to employees; leaders are the message. This is why the best evidence of effective leadership is found primarily in the followers. Thus, leaders have a moral obligation to be honest, rational, and civil in relating to followers and all other persons. Leaders have a moral obligation to set people up to succeed.

For example, have you ever observed two managers of equal position, rank, and authority within an organization? One leader's objectives seem to be successfully accomplished with a degree of ease. The other leader seems to always be under the gun, resolving one crisis after another by throwing around authority. If you have witnessed this dynamic, then you know firsthand that persons of equal authority do not necessarily possess the same degree of power. What is the difference between authority and personal power? The concepts have been used interchangeably over the years. However, they are not the same.

Personal power is the capacity to act in ways which influence the behavior of others. It is a personal attribute, and like all personal attributes, it can be developed. It is a skill leaders develop in their everyday relationships with reports, peers, superiors, and friends. Personal power is granted to the leader by those who trust and believe in the character of the leader. The leader *earns* personal power. It is not a part of the authority the organization bestows along with a title. It is won in the trenches of the workday. It is won through honest, rational, and civil treatment of others.

Authority, on the other hand, may be defined as a contractual right granted by an organization in keeping with a position. It is a right granted by the organization to organize work, settle disputes, control operations, make and implement decisions, administer, and manage. It is, in a nutshell, the right to be the boss.

A leader who abuses authority diminishes his or her personal power and, ultimately, the ability to influence others. People subjected to constant use or abuse of authority will develop subtle and effective ways of subverting it in order to protect themselves. Excessive use of authority often produces behavior in others which resembles the reaction of a child responding to restrictions imposed by a parent. The child rebels, not necessarily because the parent's expectations are unreasonable, rather because they are imposed through the exercise of authority—"Do it because I said so. I'm the parent and you're not." Typically, authority diminishes rather than enhances an adult-to-adult relationship in the work environment.

Authority does fill a necessary and important function in the life of an organization and can be an efficient tool of management when used judiciously. An effective leader will not shun the use of authority when the situation demands it but will avoid creating situations in which authority is the only recourse.

Authority has no chance of assuming its appropriate place in an organization (much less a relationship) if it is exercised arbitrarily or as a means of manipulating others. In that context, Michael is not the exception. Michael is the rule. People will simply not accept being set up to fail again and again; they instinctively know such an arrangement is unfair. The relationship between a leader and a follower has ethical implications. Among those implications are the follower's right to be treated fairly and the leader's obligation to qualify for the right to lead by being open, honest, and fair.

More than likely, Michael's father was well-intentioned. He very much wanted to nurture in his son those qualities essential to effective leadership. Unfortunately, he forgot that relationships count more than structure. There was something Michael needed prior to the ability to run Double Discount Drugs. Michael needed to believe his father wanted a relationship with him. He needed to believe his father would invest in his success. Michael wanted from his father what every follower wants from every leader—a reason to believe the relationship matters. This means relating to others in a fundamentally responsible manner. It means going far beyond the expediency of treating others as little more than a means to an end. It means asking the ethical question: What is the right thing to do?

The right thing to do may depend, to some extent, on the situation and context. However, whatever the situation or context, certain ethical mandates always apply. The leader has a moral obligation to be honest, rational, and civil in relating to others. This is not slightly less true as it applies to a subordinate. If anything, it is all the more essential in relationships with subordinates. The measure of a leader's character is not how he or she relates to a peer or superior. The measure of a leader's character is the degree to which he or she is honest, rational, and civil in relating to a follower (subordinate). This is why principled leaders are the last boy and girl scouts in a society increasingly in need of honest, rational, and civil leadership. And, not by coincidence, this often determines how successful a leader will be in developing personal power. Honest, rational, and civil behavior are foundational to building personal power.

First, honesty is the cornerstone of ethical leadership. It means truth-telling to be sure. It includes a commitment to being candid. However, in this context, it can best be described by the word quality. Typically, we use the word quality to describe products, services, or both. It is also a good word to use in talking about the quality of our relationships, and the quality of our communications, and the quality of our promises to each other. Also, it is reasonable to think about quality in terms of truth and integrity.

If you look up integrity in the dictionary, you will discover that, among other definitions, integrity is: A) *The quality of a relationship;* and B) A cross-reference to the word honor. There you will discover that honor means a *fine sense of one's obligations.* Clearly quality, integrity, and honor are the supporting pillars of honesty. The result is what Abraham Lincoln called "the honorable obligations of honesty."

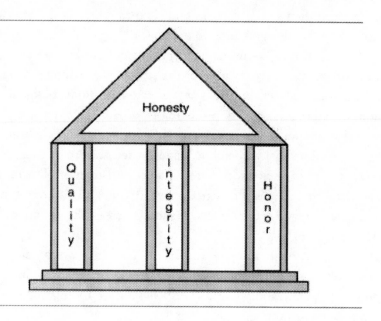

The question follows: What are the honorable obligations of honesty? The answer can be best understood in the context of rights, obligations, and responsibilities. Followers have certain rights. Leaders have certain obligations. Leaders and followers are bound by mutual responsibilities. These mutual responsibilities include the following rights and obligations:

The right to understand. Everyone has a right to understand his or her environment. This includes the right to be provided with information about decisions, events, or issues which impact us directly. Leaders have an obligation to create opportunities for understanding, whether through meetings, newsletters, or one-to-one conversations. Leaders and followers are bound by a mutual commitment to use all information (whether it is information concerning persons or the organization) responsibly.

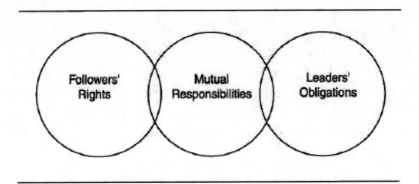

The right to contribute. Everyone has a right to be needed by the organization. This is the right to contribute to organizational success and to share the reward and satisfaction of achievement. Leaders have an obligation to ensure employees have clearly defined and measurable goals and to recognize employees for their contributions. Leaders and followers are mutually responsible for setting each other up to make a valued contribution.

The right to ownership. Everyone has a right to be involved in the decision-making process at some level. This provides a sense of ownership—the sense that my life and work is, to some degree, within my control. A sense of ownership also bolsters self-esteem. Leaders have an obligation to solicit input from team members and assure that the way work gets done does not demean the people involved. Leaders and followers are equally responsible for following through on their ownership commitments.

The right to be accountable. Everyone has a right to know how they are doing. Without feedback on performance it may be difficult, even impossible, for a person to grow, develop, and meet personal and organizational needs. Every team member has a right to know when his or her performance is unacceptable. Leaders have an obligation to provide team members with candid, constructive feedback. To withhold feedback is to deny the team member the opportunity to improve. Followers have a responsibility to consider constructive feedback in a context of goodwill.

The right to appeal. Everyone has a right to appeal or challenge the decision of a leader without the threat of retribution. This ensures that authority will not be used arbitrarily. Typically, the knowledge that I can appeal is as important as the appeal itself. Leaders have an obligation to provide open, non-threatening access to the appeal process. Leaders and followers are mutually responsible for:

- talking to each other, not about each other.

- owning what I say: I must be willing to say in your presence anything I would say in your absence.

- ensuring each person's freedom to talk with any person in the organization, regardless of department or title.

- closing the loop. I may go over my boss' head, but he or she must be brought into the loop prior to final resolution.

Second, the ethical leader has an obligation to be rational. Rational leadership is defined primarily by a leader's decision (and it is a decision) to be guided by reasonable expectations. The **rational** leader is a **reasonable** person.

The reasonable leader is a leader who brings a good measure of common sense to all issues. This means, among other things, that a rational leader will not require team members to be super-human—working long hours for an indefinite period of time, isolated from family, friends, and normal, healthy, life-enriching opportunities. Such common sense understands the reasonable constraints of doing business.

The leader has an obligation to assure the success of the organization. However, such effort must be tempered by a bottom-line ethical reality. Every legitimate organization has a right to survive, but it does not have the right to survive at any cost. Resisting the temptation to survive at any cost includes obeying the law, providing a safe work environment, and ensuring equitable pay. Just as essential as responsible leadership is the obligation to relate to team members in an ethically rational manner. Rational leadership includes the following obligations:

1. **Assuring informed consent.**

   People should be provided enough information to enable them to make an informed decision. Looking for a reason not to withhold information should be the norm. Withholding information should be the exception. Requiring a person to make a decision with inadequate information, particularly if the information is being deliberately withheld, is unreasonable and unethical.

2. **Eliminating bogus time constraints.**

   Manipulating a person through bogus time constraints holds the potential of setting the person up to fail. Sometimes decisions have to be made and actions have to be taken in very tight time frames; however, this is not always the case. Rational leadership carries the responsibility of the long view. Not just the long view in strategic terms, but in people terms. Looking ahead and anticipating what decisions will need to be made is an essential element of effective leadership. This includes providing team members with as much time as possible to think and decide.

3. **Respecting the conscience of others.**

   No two persons experience reality exactly the same way. It is rare for two people to have in common an identical set of life experiences. Such diversity is normal, but can result in disagreements on the basis of conscience. The rational leader wants people to succeed or fail on the basis of performance, not on the basis of religion, political affiliation, or life-style choice. The only way to avoid conflicts of conscience is to respect the conscience of others.

Third, civility is vital to the success of any organization. Though often underrated and neglected, civility oils the machinery of human interaction. Successful organizations are built on cooperation. Effective leaders know the critical role civility plays in sustaining cooperation. Respect for others and consideration for their feelings are the attributes of a courteous person. Everyone, without exception, appreciates being treated with courtesy. It is the most up-front means we have of knowing that we are valued. Disrespect expressed through attitude, action, or conversation sends a clear message: *You are of lesser value than I.* Such an idea is unacceptable. Simple courtesy is the minimum civility due employees. When our mothers' taught us to use the magic words, *please* and *thank you,* they were right on target. Courtesy costs nothing. It may, however, generate an unlimited return.

A great deal of money is spent each year educating employees on the importance of courtesy when dealing with customers and business associates. But an organization does not become imbued with courtesy just by talking it up. One cannot buy courtesy, nor does it come as a result of an official request. All efforts to develop good manners among employees are a waste of time unless the leadership is as courteous toward employees as it would have them be toward peers and customers.

The practice of courtesy within an organization must begin with the leadership. It must extend from the top to the bottom. It must include everyone, particularly those who have no authority or position which might be thought of as commanding respect. Simply stated, it means that the same simple, human courtesy granted to the president of the organization must be granted to the secretary, the frontline supervisor, or the custodian.

The good manners of the leadership have a profound effect on the cooperation and effort put forward throughout the organization. A leader who is courteous to reports inspires civility, and the cumulative result is a department where there is teamwork and minimum friction.

The myth is that civility is indicative of weakness. Nothing could be further from the truth. Courtesy is not a sign of weakness; it denotes the self-confidence and inner strength so necessary to self-discipline. People respect the leader who treats others with courtesy, attracting the best people and the best *from* people. People who possess dignity and self-respect want to work with a leader whose attitude toward them is friendly and courteous, the minimum requirement for a successful relationship.

Here are some behaviors to keep in mind as you lead your team to greater civility.

- Treat everyone with the same courtesy you would extend to the president of the company.

- Use (but don't overuse) the magic words *please* and *thank you.*

- Avoid petty or mean-spirited comments about others.

- Make sure your humor is not at the expense of another.

- Be open to being *wrong.*

- When proven wrong, be quick to acknowledge that you were wrong.

- When appropriate, be quick to offer an apology.

- Speak to people.

- Call people by name.

- When people come to your office, treat them as guests in your home—offer them something to drink.

- When you visit the office of a report, act as if you were a guest in another person's home.

- Don't second guess the motives of others.

- Don't patronize.

- Tell the truth with compassion.

A quick survey of human behavior will demonstrate that few things are as uncommon as common sense. Arguably, this observation falls in the same category as "the obvious is not always obvious." For example, to one on the outside looking in, it would seem obvious common sense that Michael would want to catch the tenth ball. That bit of common sense was lost of his father, Walter.

It may be obvious that leaders must be honest, rational, and civil, but every employee can relate at least one story that proves common sense does not come with a job title. Leaders who would be mentors must first lead themselves through honest, rational, and civil behavior—then and only then, can a leader nurture (mentor) those qualities in others.

9

Leaders Motivate

A leader leads others to lead themselves.

Once upon a time a wealthy entrepreneur bought a huge ranch in Wyoming. As soon as he was settled, he invited some of his closest associates to see it. After touring some of the 3,500 acres of mountains and rivers and grasslands, he ushered everybody into the house. The house was as spectacular as the scenery, and out back was the largest swimming pool anyone had ever seen. However, it was not a pool in which anyone would want to swim. The pool was filled with alligators and poisonous snakes of every description.

The eccentric owner explained, "I value courageous risk-taking above everything else. As far as I'm concerned, the courage to take a risk is what made me a billionaire. In fact, I think that courage is such a powerful virtue I'll make each of you the same offer. The first person who is courageous enough to dive in that pool and swim the length of it can have his choice of my house, my land, or my money." Of course everybody had a good laugh at the rancher's robust, but absurd, challenge and proceeded to follow the owner into the house for lunch.

Suddenly, the clamor of footsteps and laughter was interrupted by a splash! Turning around, they saw one of their number swimming for his life across the pool, thrashing at the water as the snakes and alligators swarmed after him. After several death-defying seconds, the man climbed out of the pool, unharmed, on the other side.

The host was absolutely amazed, but stuck to his promise. He said, "You are indeed a man of courage, and I will stand by my word. What do you want? You can have your choice—my house, my land, my money—just name it and it's yours." The young man looked at him with anger and revenge in his eyes and said, "Mr., all I want is the name of the guy who pushed me into the pool."

There are many misconceptions about motivation. One of the most common is the belief that motivation is nothing more than a sophisticated form of manipulation. The effective practitioner, this theory holds, would not have to push anyone in the pool or call out the snakes and alligators. The effective manipulator simply offers the appropriate carrot. The carrot, presented with the right measure of enthusiasm, will do the job. Men and women will jump in the pool in droves. This is the most common motivational myth.

Persuading a person to do something for your reasons and not for their reasons is not motivation. It is manipulation. Nor is motivation pushing someone to take what they otherwise believe is the wrong course of action. That is intimidation. Both manipulation and intimidation will often move a person to action. They will not, however, motivate a person.

That brings us to the second most common misconception about motivation: Once you have persuaded a person to move, you have effectively motivated him. Leaders frequently ask and seek to answer the question which follows this assumption: What is the simplest, surest, and most direct way of getting someone to do something? The answer, of course, is to ask. And, if the person does not want to do it? Demand that it be done! This is the last and first resort of the dictatorial leader who may add, without blushing, "Punish those who disobey." This type of leader will get results. The surest way of getting someone to do something with the greatest economy of words is to make sure there is a heavy price for not doing what is asked. But this is not motivation. It is just another form of manipulation called intimidation.

Manipulation masquerading as motivation comes in many forms. Here are just a few:

Physical Intimidation/Threat

This is a literal application of the concept and was frequently used in the past. It has, however, four major drawbacks: 1) It diminishes any sense of good will the employee might have toward the organization; 2) It is inconsistent with the image of benevolence most organizations cherish; 3) Since it is a physical attack, the employee may feel compelled to kick back; 4) Physical intimidation/threat does not work.

Negative Psychological Intimidation

Negative psychological intimidation seeks to motivate by manipulating a person's emotional vulnerabilities. Under this theory, ego sores are rubbed raw by snubbing, ignoring, discounting a person's contributions, by-passing, reducing compensation, relocating to a smaller office, taking away perks without explanation, and countless other methods of supposedly motivating another through emotional intimidation.

Negative psychological intimidation has several advantages over physical intimidation. First, the cruelty is not visible; the bleeding is internal and comes much later. Second, the victim will not kick back since he has not actually been kicked. Third, since the number of psychological pains that a person can feel is unlimited, the impact may linger for hours or days. Fourth, the person administering the kick can appear to be perfectly innocent of any wrongdoing. Fifth, those who practice it receive some ego satisfaction (one-up-manship). Finally, the employee who does complain can always be accused of being paranoid since there is no tangible evidence of an actual attack. However, negative psychological intimidation does have one thing in common with physical intimidation—it does not work. It does demonstrate how unscrupulous an unprincipled leader can be.

What does negative psychological intimidation accomplish? If a person is subjected to physical or psychological intimidation, who is motivated? The intimidator is motivated, the intimidated is not. Intimidation does not lead to motivation. It leads to movement. Alligators and snakes will get movement out of any sane individual. However, alligators and snakes will produce movement only as long as they are present. Even this is unreliable because some people tame the alligators and snakes. So you're left trying to find another way to frighten/intimidate employees into movement.

Positive Manipulation

Most leaders are quick to see that psychological or physical intimidation is not motivation. On the other hand, many continue to believe that positive manipulation is motivation. If the leader says to the employee, "Do this for the company, and in return I will give you a reward, an incentive, more status, a promotion, all the quid pro quos that exist in an organization," is this motivation? Many leaders would answer with a resounding "yes." The reality, however, is far different.

I have a Border Collie named Princess. Let's say that when Princess was a puppy and I wanted her to move, I kicked her in the rear and she moved. Now that I have finished her obedience training, I hold up a dog biscuit whenever I want her to move. In this example, who is motivated—me or the dog? Princess wants the biscuit, but I want Princess to move. I am the one who is motivated, and Princess is the one who moves. All I did was apply manipulation frontally; I exerted a pull instead of a push. When an organization wishes to use a positive manipulation, it has available a variety of dog biscuits to wave in front of the employee to get him to jump (move).

Perhaps, you are thinking, negative intimidation is a no-brainer. It is disruptive to the individual and the organization, and it moves people but does not motivate them. What is so bad about dangling a carrot in front of an employee? Positive manipulation gets people moving with no hard feelings whatsoever.

Intimidation is easily recognized and rejected because it is raw force. Positive manipulation seems harmless because it is seduction. However, in this context, it is worse to be seduced than to be intimidated. Intimidation is a sinister act carried out by a deviant. Both the victim and the culprit are easily identified. Seduction, on the other hand, means you were party to your own manipulation. The organization does not have to kick you; you kick yourself.

Alligators and Carrots versus Entrepreneurs

Manipulation, whether negative or positive, is not motivation. It is movement and only movement. If I kick my dog from the front or the rear, she will move. And when I want her to move again, I have to kick her again. In the same way, I can charge a person's battery, and then recharge it, and recharge it again. But it is only when the person has his own generator that he is motivated. The person then needs no outside stimulation. He *wants* to do it. Alligators and carrots generate movement. Ownership and pride of workmanship generate motivation. It is the team member as entrepreneur that creates motivation. The team member must have a compelling reason to ask and act on a single question: What would I do if this business were mine? How then, do leaders give team members a compelling reason to ask and answer that question? How do leaders create a sense of ownership? How do leaders make entrepreneurs (a company of one) out of the people on the line?

The motivational theorist Frederick Herzberg gives us a framework for answering these questions. First, what are often thought of as motivators are actually only satisfiers. A satisfier is anything in the work environment which assures a level playing field. It is any aspect of work which, when met, becomes a neutral issue in the work environment. It satisfies, but does not motivate. This is not to say that satisfiers are unimportant. They are very important inasmuch as they create an environment which management and employees find mutually beneficial.

Satisfiers include:

- Company policy & procedure

- Employee relationship with leaders

- Work conditions (safety, cleanliness, et cetera)

- Compensation

- Relationship with peers

- Status

- Security

- Participation in decision making

Much of the positive manipulation developed in an attempt to create motivation is not a motivator at all—it is a satisfier.

These bogus motivators (which are in fact, satisfiers) include:

- **Reducing time spent at work.** This is done in the belief that additional time away from work will motivate a person when at work. The fact is that while motivated people do not necessarily work longer hours, they do not watch the clock either.

- **Increased wages.** This satisfier only motivates people to seek the next increase. It rarely motivates a person to be a self-starter or to work smarter. Good pay is a satisfier and an important one.

- **Benefits.** This became a satisfier in the U. S. Corporate Culture more than forty years ago. Employees believe vacations, health insurance, retirement, etc. are an entitlement due them as members of the organization.

- **The Big Picture.** The belief that employees only need to see where they fit in the big picture to be motivated is bogus. A guy tightening a thousand bolts a day just needs to know he is building a Buick, and he will be motivated. While most employees welcome information about the organization, once again, they consider it their right to know such information. Therefore, information is a satisfier.

- **Sensitivity Training.** If leaders and employees only understood themselves better as individuals by going through individual or group therapy, they would be motivated. While any effort to enhance self-understanding and human relations skills is commendable (even necessary in some instances), sensitivity training is, at best, a satisfier. It is not a motivator.

In contrast to satisfiers, motivators engage the *magic of the human heart*. Motivators awaken the internal generator which enables employees to charge their own battery. Motivators create owners. Owners are entrepreneurs. An entrepreneur is a company of one. What then, are motivators? Motivators are few in number but critical in mass. One well-engaged motivator will impact performance more than a dozen of the most creative satisfiers.

Motivators include:

- **Achievement:** The personal satisfaction which comes from having set a goal and paid the price to reach it. A word of caution: This only works if the employee is a part of the goal-setting process.

- **Pride in Workmanship:** The enhanced self-esteem which comes from having done a job as well or better than anyone else (world class quality).

- **Ownership:** The responsibility for oneself and one's work. This includes the opportunity to try, to fail, to learn, and to move on—to be trusted to take responsible risks.

- **Growth:** The opportunity to become more than I am; the opportunity for greater achievement, responsibility, and recognition. Growth is knowledge that I can increase my value to myself and to the organization.

- **Recognition:** The affirmation of my value and contribution, to be appreciated, thanked, and respected for the contribution I have made. This includes, of course, the opportunity to benefit from my contribution.

You have probably noticed that in describing motivators we have also described the entrepreneurial spirit at its best! Achievement, pride of workmanship, and ownership drive and motivate the Team Member as Entrepreneur to ask and answer the big question: What would I do if this business were mine? The Motivation Continuum on page 92 illustrates how leaders create The Team Member as Entrepreneur.

Entrepreneurial team members will view themselves as a company of one. They will see the work to be done as "my work." They will accept responsibility for themselves and their work. The myth that only a few people in the organization are capable of self-management will have to be put aside. In order for the job itself to change, the content of the job must change. It is the content of the job which will create motivation. Attitudes about being involved or challenged, are important, but not as important as the content. The organization will have to trust itself to the competence of the entrepreneur as team member. Fundamentally, this is achieved through employee-centered leadership, as illustrated on page 92. The degree to which the employee is granted freedom/responsibility (horizontal scale) is the degree to which the employee will accept ownership (left vertical scale). In contrast, the degree to which the leader exercises control is the degree to which the employee abdicates responsibility/ownership and is demotivated.

The following principles demonstrate employee-centered leadership which creates ownership in an organization.

Employee-Centered Leadership Principle	Motivators Involved
1. Removing some controls while retaining accountability	Ownership and personal achievement
2. Increasing employee's accountability for his or her own work	Responsibility, recognition, and pride in workmanship
3. Giving a person a complete natural unit of work (module, division, area, etc.)	Ownership, achievement, pride in workmanship, and recognition
4. Granting additional authority in his or her budget	Ownership, achievement, and recognition.
5. Making periodic reports directly available to the employee.	Growth, recognition and pride in workmanship.
6. Introducing new and more difficult tasks not previously handled	Growth and recognition.
7. Assigning individuals specific or specialized tasks, enabling them to become experts.	Ownership, growth, pride in workmanship, and recognition.
8. Encourage and facilitate the employees' continuing education.	Achievement, growth and recognition.

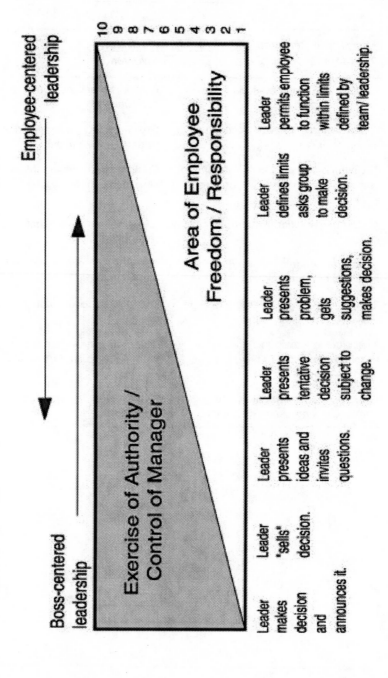

The Motivation Continuum

Finally, the argument for employee-centered leadership can be summed up as follows: The most effective way to motivate an employee is to grant the employee ownership of, and accountability for, meaningful work from which he can realize pride of workmanship. Employees can be pushed or pulled into movement by an alligator or carrot. However, people do their best for their own reasons. And people do their best for their own reasons because every person has a fundamental need to matter.

For most people, pride of workmanship and the opportunity to do meaningful work are expressions of their need to matter. Employees work for what their efforts will bring to themselves and to the people they love and care about. The leader who would lead others to lead themselves understands that work is not just work. A job well done and valued by the organization helps define the degree to which an employee will realize his or her need to be challenged, appreciated, and praised. Everyone has a heart they would gladly give to a place where they know they matter. This is motivation. This is the magic of the human heart.

10

Leaders Provide Performance Management

A leader is candid.
A leader tells the truth with compassion.

Once upon a time there was a vice president of engineering named Leo. Leo's company made fine-quality capital goods equipment. He had been with the company for thirty-five years. Leo was a good engineer who knew the product inside and out, and through the years he had come to know the customers as well. He felt proud of and personally involved in the installation of the product. It was not unusual to see him coatless and with his tie loose, perched on a stool before a drafting board surrounded by young engineers, digging at a tough installation problem. While some thought Leo did too much himself, others felt that with him on the job the customer would be satisfied.

One day, however, the company became a wholly owned subsidiary when the president, whose family owned the company, sold it to a large corporation. One allied product line was acquired, then another. Finally, Leo's department was asked to do the engineering work for several subsidiaries not set up to do their own.

Now Leo's job had changed, subtly but surely, and trouble began to brew for Leo because he couldn't seem to change with the situation.

Psychologically, Leo saw himself as a one man department (with assistants as trainees) who personally engineered the product for the customer, his friend. He resisted the impersonality of working on the engineering problems of sister companies whose customers and products he barely knew and cared less about. The new-fangled system of a home office staff engineering vice president seemed just another unnecessary complication. Nothing worked the way it used to. Leo saw himself bypassed by progress and change, and he did not like it.

So, unconsciously, Leo began to resist and to fight. His yearning for the good ole days forced him into a fast run to know more customers and more product lines, to work more evenings, and to press new systems into the form of old procedures. And, of course, he began to slip. Gradually, Leo came to be viewed by his superiors as good ole Leo. The idea now voiced by his superiors was, "Let's not let Leo in on this matter or he'll take it over himself and we'll get bogged down!" His direct reports considered Leo a fine fellow but a bit old-fashioned.

Fortunately, before the situation forced a major organizational shift, Leo took stock of his situation and really saw himself as he was. His self-image of a personal engineer was no longer applicable to the corporation's greatly expanded needs. And right then with this new glimpse of himself and the courage and self-honesty to face it, he began to change. He started by focusing on how his years of experience could be applied to the coaching of his direct reports. He consciously placed himself in the shoes of staff vice president of engineering. He began to understand how to better mesh gears with the new reality of the world around him. He stopped resisting the newfangled data processing and automation procedures. Leo began the most challenging re-engineering job of his career—changing Leo. In the process, Leo gained a powerful professional insight: The more realistic one's view of self, the greater the degree of personal effectiveness.

As Leo thought through this discovery, he realized that what he needed to do with Leo was what he had always done with equipment and processes: Be doggedly committed to the truth. Leo needed to apply to his self-concept the same capacity to critique which he routinely applied to his work. Leo realized that his image of himself functioned like a filter. Without self-critique, self-concept screens out what each person does not want to hear and see, and allows through only the information the person wants to see and hear. Utilizing his excellent problem-solving skills, Leo accurately concluded that you cannot (will not) fix what is broken until you admit that it is broken. Nothing changes until it becomes what it is.

However, this was only the beginning of Leo's new insight. With his greater capacity to self-critique, Leo acquired greater control over the thing he wants most to have control over: his destiny. Through self-critique, Leo could take charge of his own development and, therefore, take charge of his future. Even more exciting was Leo's recognition that the capacity to self-critique had important implications for his team, a concept he was learning to understand and use. Self-critique can lay the groundwork for insight, without which growth or change will not occur. Feedback (critique) from superiors, peers, and team members can provide the same level of growth and development born of shared insight.

Admitting that he could not do everything was tough for Leo. Accepting the fact that he was not right was even tougher. How does one gain such insight? How do individuals discover that not only can they change but they should change? Unfortunately, for those who like recipes and formulas, such questions are always bothersome because there is no one best way. There are, however, many excellent sources of insight. These sources are, as Leo recognized, the people we live and work with.

In an organizational context, a superior constructively pointing out a leader's need for growth can be a great source of insight. The emphasis, of course, is on the word constructive, which means helpful and insightful as opposed to a ceremonial or judgmental appraisal.

Opportunities for honest, constructive feedback from peers and team members can have a similar effect. The leader practiced in the art of self-critique and in the habit of being honest with himself will self-correct. Those who are unable to self-critique find it very nearly impossible to hear the critique of others.

A further source of insight can be perceptive spouses. For example, perceptive wives have unique ways of tugging husbands with distorted self-images back to reality. However, the feedback must be honest and constructive.

The problem, as you have probably recognized by now, is how to make feedback or critique a fundamental part of living and doing business, whether it is self-critique or feedback from others. As mentioned above, there are no formulas, but there are insights which many have found helpful. Before listing those insights, we need to recognize that they fall into two closely related categories: 1) The capacity to solicit and accept constructive feedback and 2) The capacity to provide constructive feedback.

Accepting Constructive Feedback

Our ability to deal responsibly with constructive feedback will often make or break us. No one is 100 percent right 100 percent of the time. We need the reality checks the people around us provide when they believe we value their insight. If the people around us believe we don't want or need their insights, they will often allow us to fail even when they hold in their hand the critical bit of information which might have produced success. Interestingly enough, the insight is usually not withheld because they don't want to help. It is withheld because we have consciously or unconsciously let them know we don't want their feedback.

So, how do we go about building relationships which invite honest, constructive feedback? Here are some insights many have found helpful.

1. **Understand the difference between constructive and destructive feedback.**

   Constructive feedback is usually presented in a positive, helpful, and civil manner. Destructive feedback is frequently negative, sarcastic, and rude. The constructive critic is concerned about issues. The destructive critic wants to focus on personalities. The constructive critic has the best interest of the organization and its people at heart. The destructive critic is driven by a personal, often hidden agenda. Recognizing constructive criticism will help you be more receptive when you are offered feedback.

2. **Don't take yourself too seriously.**

   This includes the ability to laugh at yourself although it goes deeper than a healthy sense of humor about one's own fallibility. Others will offer feedback much more willingly if they know the messenger will not be shot. Approach constructive feedback with an open mind which says: "Yes, I have a position on this issue. However, I am willing to be proven wrong or shown a better way."

3. **Look first at the critic, then at the criticism.**

   Is the critic someone who has earned your trust? Is he or she someone who has provided honest, constructive feedback in the past? If the answer to both these questions is "yes," it is a good idea to give the person a thoughtful hearing. After all, adverse criticism from a wise man is more desirable than the enthusiastic approval of a fool.

4. **Check your attitude toward the person providing feedback.**

   A negative, defensive attitude toward the critic can be more destructive than feedback itself. Giving someone the impression that you are more important than they are and therefore do not have to give them a hearing can damage more than the relationship with that one individual. You could, unintentionally, give others the impression you don't really have to listen to them either.

5. **Remember that the very best people are criticized.** This fact has at least three implications: A) The only way to ensure you won't be criticized is to do nothing; B) No matter who you are there is always room for improvement; C) No one is one hundred percent right one hundred percent of the time.

6. **Keep physically and mentally in shape.** Physical and/or mental exhaustion can have a tremendous effect on the way we act and react. Exhaustion distorts the way we see and handle the world around us. When we become overly tired, we become overly critical. The result is that we are less able to handle feedback whether it is constructive or destructive.

7. **Don't just see the critic; see if there's a crowd.** The following story illustrates this point. Mrs. Jones invited a great and well-known violinist to entertain at her afternoon tea. When it was over everyone crowded around the musician, "I've got to be honest with you," said one of the guests, "I think your performance was absolutely terrible." Hearing this criticism, the hostess tried to ease the sting, "Don't pay any attention to him. He doesn't know what he's talking about. He only repeats what he hears."

8. **Concentrate on your mission.** Especially in the face of destructive criticism and sometimes, even in the face of constructive criticism, it is easy to lose sight of our objective. Maintaining a big-picture perspective is critical to remaining focused. It is equally critical in evaluating the feedback we receive. Some things are simply not worth our time or attention. They do not contribute to our objectives, or the objectives of the organization. Constructive feedback, however, may keep us on course.

Providing Constructive Feedback

Responding gracefully to feedback builds strong professional relationships. Superiors, peers, and team members all appreciate the person who values their constructive input. Accepting feedback is only half of the Feedback Loop, though. The other half is the ability to provide constructive feedback. Every team member is both a receiver and sender. In effective teams, feedback flows in at least two directions and, ideally, in an unlimited number of directions. Therefore leaders/team members must develop effective feedback skills.

On the following pages you will discover some helpful insights for sharpening your feedback skills. Effective feedback skills will enhance your participation in the feedback loop.

1. **Check your motive.** The goal of constructive feedback is to help. Feedback which has a hidden agenda such as settling a score or punishing another will not bring about a positive change in behavior. Two questions will assist you in checking your motives. One, is the feedback motivated by personal or business considerations? If the answer is "business," mentally list the organizational issues you are concerned about. If you cannot list specific concerns, chances are you are acting out of the wrong motive. Two, am I out to make myself look better? Cutting another person down in order to make myself look good is the lowest form of self-gratification. It creates more than resentment. It creates animosity.

2. **Self-critique should come first.** Prior to putting others in their place, put yourself in their place. Look at things from the other person's perspective. Given the same situation, would you have done the same? What would you have done differently?

3. **Take care not to undermine the person's self-confidence.** Try to identify at least one area in which you can offer genuine praise before exposing the problem. Avoid all-inclusive statements like, "You always…" or "You never…" Your confidence in the person's ability to solve the problem should be evident.

4. **Be hard on the issue and easy on the person.** Deal with the issue at hand. When feedback becomes a personal attack, you destroy

your credibility. Constructive feedback leaves the person with a clear understanding of the issue and a sense of hope that it can be turned around.

5. **Don't compare one team member with another.** Relate to people as individuals. Asking individuals to beat their personal best is far less threatening than comparisons between team members. Comparisons cause resentment. Resentment almost always creates hostility.

6. **Be specific.** Constructive criticism will often be interpreted as destructive, personal, or petty when it is non-specific. Say exactly what you mean, and provide examples to back up your concerns. Don't beat around the bush. Aim carefully. Shoot straight. Use a rifle, not a shotgun.

7. **Be sure the time is right.** The ideal time to provide feedback is as soon as you become aware of a problem. However, this is not always the best time. Consider what you know about the individual's personal life. Is the person working through some personal issue such as divorce, grief, or illness? What about the amount of feedback they are trying to assimilate? Don't pile one issue upon another. Most people can effectively deal with only one to two issues at a time. The right time to provide feedback is when the person is able to hear it, not necessarily when you are ready to provide it.

8. **Ask for feedback on your feedback.** Once you have shared your concerns, ask the other person to respond. Make sure they heard what you were trying to say. Sometimes, what we believe we said clearly is not what the other person heard. In addition, reach a consensus about a course of action and offer to help. The offer to invest in the person's success is the most convincing evidence that the criticism is constructive, not personal or petty.

Accepting and providing feedback are opposite sides of the same coin—and the coin is self-critique. Leo refused delivery on feedback from others until he recognized the need to self-critique. Granted, Leo is unusual in that he came to this conclusion on his own. Most of us continue to pound our heads against the wall long after it is obvious to others we need to change. Once Leo was willing to self-critique, his ability to accept and provide constructive feedback paved the way for further professional success.

11

Leaders Manage Conflict

A leader is a peacemaker and a coalition builder.

Once upon a time there was a young man who lived in a second story apartment over a fried fish shop. It just so happens that he was a student and that he did not have much money. He had so little money that all he could afford to eat each day was a single bowl of rice. But each day, when he got ready to eat his bowl of rice, he would open all the windows of his second story apartment and allow the aroma of fried fish from the restaurant below to drift upward. And it was almost like he had fish to eat with his bowl of rice.

One day the young man was standing in front of the fried fish shop talking with a friend. He explained that his financial situation only allowed him a single bowl of rice to eat each day, but he opened all the windows of his apartment to allow the smell of the fish to drift upward. It was almost like he had fried fish to eat. As the young man was talking to his friend, the owner of the fried fish shop ran out onto the sidewalk. The owner grabbed the young man by the arm and said, "You can't be smelling the aroma of my fish frying without paying me something. I think I'm owed something for the smell of my fish." The young man looked at him in amazement and said, "You must be kidding. If I had money to pay for the smell, I'd buy the fish." They argued back and forth for a while, the young man insisting he would not pay; the owner of the fried fish shop insisting he should pay.

Finally, the owner of the fried fish shop said, "Okay, if you won't pay me, I'll sue you." And he did and they landed in court. They each explained their position to the judge. The owner of the fried fish shop said, "He's been smelling the aroma of my fish and I feel I'm owed something for it." The young man said, "Judge, if I could afford to pay for the smell, I'd buy the fish." The judge said, "Let me think about it for a moment." He went into his chambers and after about twenty minutes came out. The judge turned to the owner of the fried fish shop and said, "I've decided you're due something for the smell of your fish." Then he turned to the young man and said, "Do you have any money, any money at all?" And the young man said, "Well, I have just these few coins I've been saving to pay my tuition." And the judge said, "Let me have them." So the young man gave them to the judge who took the coins and dropped them several times from one hand to the other. The coins made the kind of tinkling sound that coins make when they bump together. Then the judge handed the coins back to the young man he had taken them from. The owner of the fried fish shop protested. "Judge, I thought you said I was due something for the smell of my fish." And the judge responded, "I did and you've been paid. I've decided that the price of the smell of fish is the sound of his money."

No doubt the owner of the fried fish shop did not get what he wanted. However, he got what most of us get when we attempt to create a win-lose relationship. The owner of the fried fish shop made a common mistake by allowing his disagreement with the young man to become a competition of wills. And when it became a competition of wills, he was determined that it would end in a win-lose. He, the owner of the fried fish shop would be the winner, and the young man would be the loser. The reality is that the best resolution for conflict is for everyone to win. That is, if you want to have a long-term relationship with the person with whom you are in conflict.

Close on the heels of the myth that a win-lose conflict creates a constructive relationship is the belief that I can win because I'm the boss.

The reality is that any time I win a disagreement only because I'm the boss I have, in fact, lost. Over time, conflict has gotten a bad reputation, to be sure. All our lives we've heard messages such as don't fight, love one another, and be nice. As a result, we see conflict as a sign that somebody (usually the other side) is bad or wrong. Therefore, we try to avoid conflict and sometimes simply pretend it doesn't exist. Ironically, this is precisely the attitude that creates more conflict.

While conflict can be painful, it is a natural, even healthy, part of life. That may be difficult to accept, but once you do, you're free from having to blame a conflict on someone (whether yourself or others). Therefore, you are able to manage it more rationally and productively.

Here's what I mean by dealing with conflict. First, minimize the amount of conflict in your life. Certain behaviors attract conflict like a magnet. When you identify and eliminate them, your life can become a whole lot easier. Examples of conflict magnets would be an arrogant attitude, a condescending manner, or an inappropriate aggressiveness. We have to be careful here to separate aggressive behavior from assertive behavior. Assertiveness is a good thing. It means that I will not allow others to control me—I will control me. Aggressiveness, on the other hand, is the desire to control others. Assertiveness does not create conflict. Aggressiveness does create conflict. Any attempt to gain unreasonable or unacceptable control over the will or behavior of another will result in conflict.

Second, minimize the severity of your conflicts. Not every conflict needs to escalate into World War III. Good conflict managers often find easy, painless resolutions to potentially explosive situations. Sometimes things are small, and they should remain small.

Third, it's possible to win more conflicts. This requires a new definition of winning. As mentioned earlier, normally for there to be a winner there also has to be a loser; that's true in sports, politics, and war. But conflict management includes finding a solution by which both sides can win. The downside is that you don't always get one hundred percent of what you want. Remember, however, that under the old win-lose rules, you often got one hundred percent of nothing. The best reward for handling conflicts confidently is the way you feel about yourself. We have a choice in life to have conflicts with other people or with ourselves. People who avoid external conflicts by complying or pretending to be someone they're not usually end up raging with conflict inside. By bringing conflicts out in the open and dealing with them, we develop honest, forthright, and loving relationships with ourselves and others. We turn heat into light. Here are some suggestions for doing just that.

1. **Choose the time and place carefully**. Never, ever initiate a conflict in a public setting or where uninvolved people are present. Also, be careful about confronting people after a hard day, before an event where they have to be at their best (such as a presentation or performance review), when they are dealing with a mistake or a loss, or when they are working under a deadline. Sensitivity to the other person's circumstances is important in any one-on-one communication, but in a conflict, it is critical.

2. **Change behaviors, not people**. There are two directions you can choose in facing a conflict: 1) You can fix the problem or 2) You can fix the blame. The first is by far more productive. If you make it your goal in a conflict to convince the other person that he or she is wrong, you will almost certainly fail. The reality is that you cannot argue someone out of an emotion, and by the time a conflict escalates, it is almost surely an emotional event. How much better it is simply to change that person's negative behavior, and by changing it, demonstrate to them how change is in their best interest. Or over time, lead them to the appropriate conclusion, that is, allow them to discover it for themselves. Here's an example. If you have a typist who consistently misspells words, you may be tempted to point out that good typists would never make these mistakes, a claim that would certainly be right. Two more productive resolutions, however, would be to buy your typist a speller's

dictionary or better yet, buy a word processor that identifies misspelled words. The key is to keep your eye on the solution, not on the problem.

3. **Agree on something**. Restating your agreement on basic goals makes it easier to discuss your disagreements. It reminds both sides that the relationship is solid which instantly minimizes insecurity and defensiveness and sets the stage for cooperation and problem solving. You're on the same side instead of being adversaries. Here are a couple of ways to state your agreement on basic goals. One is, "I'm bringing this up because I believe in you and want you to succeed here. "We agreed that we need to get this project done by the end of the month" also restates a goal.

4. **Use "I" language**. "I" language means stating your case in terms of your own feelings. For instance, instead of telling someone, "You broke our agreement," you would say, "I'm not happy with the way things are going with our agreement." Notice how the first comment, "you" language, naturally leads to defensiveness. It is, after all, an attack. The second statement may not be welcomed by the other person, but it is far more likely to be accepted. Make "I" language your approach even on minor issues. For instance say, "I didn't understand what you said," instead of "You didn't explain that clearly." By keeping your argument to the facts and preventing personal attacks, "I" language serves all three conflict management fronts: it reduces the number of conflicts, minimizes their severity, and leads more easily to winning solutions.

5. **Figure out where you went wrong.** Define how you may have contributed to the conflict and admit it. Difficult as this is, owning up to your mistakes is one of the most important aspects of conflict resolution. Did your rushed directions contribute to your coworkers mishandling of an issue? If so, admit it early on and you'll free the other person to admit his or her part in the problem.

When appropriate, there's no better way to begin a confrontation than to say, "I know I'm partly responsible for this situation."

6. **Criticize with precision**. A lot of conflict is the result of sloppy and vague criticism. Suppose you tell one of your peers, "You're unprofessional." Unless that person knows what you mean by unprofessional, there's not much he or she can do about it except feel bad, resentful, unmotivated, spiteful—you get the picture. How much better it is to point out specifically, "Punctuality is important to me, and you were twenty minutes late this morning and ten minutes late for this appointment." Conversely, when someone gives you vague criticism, ask that it be clarified. "What am I doing that makes you think I'm unprofessional? I'd like to change it." Think about this the next time you tell someone or someone tells you, "You have a bad attitude," "Your performance isn't up to par," or any one of the many vague criticisms that we hear every day.

7. **When someone attacks, agree**. On occasion, you may find yourself dealing with someone whose goal is to hurt you or to embarrass you in public. Trying to find a win-win solution will not work because the goal is to make you lose. In a case like this, some creative sidestepping may be in order. For example, if someone says "Your tie clashes with your suit," your response might be, "You're right, my tie *does* clash with my suit." By refusing to acknowledge the sniper's implicit attack—you don't how to dress, you're unprofessional, you don't belong here, etc., you have deflected it. In fact, your implied message is, "So what?" a response your attacker will rarely counter.

Another way to handle the person who insults in public is to simply look him or her in the eye for a second or so, then move on. Your implied message is, "I heard what you said, and I'm not going to deal with it." Not dealing with it is a right you can exercise most effectively to leave the insult in the sniper's lap where it belongs. Be careful that you don't pretend you didn't hear the insult; that's powerless behavior. Make sure the eye contact is strong and confident before you move on.

8. **Bow out for a while**. Giving yourself time is a good rule of thumb in all conflicts, but it's particularly important in highly emotional situations. Time allows the emotions to cool and enables both sides to move more easily from the blame phase to the solution stage. Imagine that you have discovered to your outrage that a co-worker has overstepped his or her bounds and caused a big problem for you. Instead of confronting your co-worker immediately, force yourself to wait a few hours or even a day. This doesn't mean you shouldn't have a strong confrontation, just that you'll be more effective once the first rush of anger has subsided.

9. **Have more conflicts**. Many people, believing that conflicts are a sign of a major breakdown in a relationship, strive to have conflict-free relationships. It is a good idea to have conflict-free relationships to the extent that you don't want to have destructive conflict. But you do want to have constructive conflict. Avoiding conflict builds resentment either slowly undermining the positive aspects of the relationship or instantly causing a blowup. How much better it is to bring up problems and annoyances, even minor ones, as they occur. Some people may find this behavior odd at first, but they will come to appreciate the result: a relationship where honesty prevails and neither side keeps an account against the other.

10. **Find the third option**. The minute emotions flair, the natural inclination is for both sides to lock into their positions automatically. The goodwill is gone, and the goal is no longer to resolve the conflict: it is to win. This is a critical juncture and how you handle it determines whether you win or lose at managing conflict. The challenge is to break out of the win-lose pattern.

Two married friends of mine tell of the evening when it was the husband's turn to cook. He didn't feel like cooking so he suggested that they go out to dinner. His wife was tired, and she refused. Just as each was getting into how selfish and insensitive the other was, their four-year old daughter suggested having a pizza delivered. End of argument. Creative solutions are often embarrassingly easy to find. Be open to them.

11. **Agree on the future**. Just as it is helpful to keep your conflict focused on the specifics of the problem, it pays to keep the resolution focused on the specific action that will be taken. For instance, your boss confronts you about exceeding your budget on a project. Instead of saying something like, "I'll be more careful next time," you might suggest that you will present weekly budget updates on your next project. Agreeing to this specific course of action, instead of just stating your good intentions, demonstrates your commitment to solving the problem and dramatically decreases the chance of it happening again.

12. **Work it out on paper**. A tool that integrates the principles I've just presented is reproduced below. It's a simple conflict analysis system that I use in some of my seminars. The beauty of the system, as with all good systems, is its simplicity. If you invest the two minutes it takes to complete this, you are far more likely to get positive results in your next conflict.

    A. Describe the results of the other person's negative behavior. Either describe your feelings ("I get angry") or the bottom line effect in terms of time, money, morale, etc. ("It causes us all to miss our deadlines.")

    B. Describe the other person's negative behavior. Remember to focus on the behavior, not the person. ("When you miss your deadlines" or "When you raise your voice," not "When you act like a jerk.") Remember to be specific and nonjudgmental.

C. Make a request. Identify the preferred behavior, and ask the person to use it. ("Would you please be more realistic about your deadlines?")

D. Describe the positive effect of cooperating. This is the benefit to the person if he or she changes the negative behavior. ("I'm sure we could work together a whole lot better.")

E. Describe the negative effect of not cooperating. This is optional. ("I'm going to have to give you a written warning next time you're late.") Be specific about the follow through then, do it. However, don't make promises you can't keep or don't intend to keep.

The owner of the fried fish shop had a narrow view of the world. He believed that in order to receive what he wanted (payment for the smell of the fish) the young man would have to lose, creating a win-lose relationship. His effort resulted in what we all get when we try to win at the expense of another—nothing but bad feelings. Wise leaders know that while it takes effort to fashion a win-win relationship; it is more than worth the effort.

12

Leaders Create Consensus

A leader is a team player who can follow as well as lead.
A leader understands the task of team building.

Once upon a time there were six blind men. The six blind men sat around a table talking about things they would like to see if, in fact, they could see. As they talked, they all agreed that one of the things they had always wanted to see was an elephant. It just so happens that as they came to this agreement, they heard what they believed to be the sound of an elephant outside the house where they were seated. Together, in single file, they got up and went out into the street and began to examine the elephant the only way blind men can examine an elephant—they began to touch the elephant.

One blind man took hold of the elephant's tail and said to himself, "Who would have thought it? An elephant is nothing more than a rope, just a rope." The second took hold of the elephant's massive hind leg and said to himself, "Who would have thought it? An elephant is just a tree trunk, just a great big tree trunk." The third ran his hands along the massive side of the elephant and said to himself, "What a strange animal. An elephant is just a wall, just a big wall." The fourth blind man took hold of the elephant's ear and holding the elephant's ear between his hands said to himself, "Hmm, quite interesting. An elephant is like a carpet, just a carpet you would put on the floor." And then the fifth man took hold of the elephant's tusk and, running his hands along the tusk, thought to himself, "This must be the most unusual animal in the world. It's just a spear, just like any other spear that a soldier would throw in battle." And finally, the sixth man took hold of the elephant's trunk as it wiggled about. He thought to himself, with a bit of humor, "Who would have imagined that an elephant is nothing more than a fat snake."

Having examined the elephant, the six blind men filed back into the house and sat down around the table and began to share their observations. The first blind man said, "I suppose you guys were kind of surprised to find that an elephant is just a rope—a rope like you would use to tie up a bundle of sticks." And the second man said, "I don't know where you were, but the elephant I had hold of was like a tree trunk." And the third one said, "Both of you are wrong. The elephant is like a wall." The fourth one spoke up and said, "I have no idea where you guys were, but the elephant I had hold of was like a carpet, that's all. Just a carpet you would lay out on the floor." And the fifth one said, "It's hard to believe that all four of you could be so wrong. An elephant is like a spear. I suspect everybody knows that, or anyone who had ever touched an elephant anyway." And finally, the sixth man said, "This is interesting. Apparently there were other animals out there. Because the elephant that I examined was nothing like the animal you've described. To me an elephant is just a big fat, wiggling snake."

And so they began to argue, each one in turn pushing his perspective, insisting that he was right and the others were wrong. After a while a sighted friend came by and the blind men called him over. "Come here, we need you to settle an argument for us. We've just examined an elephant and we want to know which one of us is right."

The first one told of his experience, "An elephant is like a rope." The second, "An elephant is like a tree trunk." The third, "An elephant is like a massive wall." The fourth, "An elephant is like a carpet." The fifth, "An elephant is like a spear." And finally, the sixth man insisted that an elephant is "like a fat, wiggling snake." After listening to each of the six blind men's argument as to what an elephant is like, the sighted friend thought for a moment and this was his response. "Individually, you are all wrong. Together, you are all right."

What was true for the six blind men is true for all would-be teams. Different perspectives are both the strength and the weakness of the team. And, as with the six blind men and the elephant, all would-be teams have a choice. Do we find a way to benefit from our different perspectives and insights, or do we falter because of our different perspectives and insights?

Over the years, we have identified the four stages of team development. These are four stages most would-be teams pass through. They are stages which enable the team to benefit from its diversity.

The first stage is the *forming* stage and occurs when individuals are just learning to deal with one another. This is typically a stage in which little work gets done. The second stage is the *storming* stage and this is a time of stress and trial. Here, the terms under which the team will work are being negotiated. The third stage is the *norming* stage. This is the stage in which roles are accepted. The team begins to feel like a team, and relationships become comfortable and spontaneous. Then the fourth and final stage is the *performing* stage. Optimal levels are finally realized—optimal levels of productivity, quality, decision making, and most of all, constructive interaction.

All successful teams go through all four of these stages. Sometimes a team gets lucky and its mix of personalities or the kinds of leadership that emerges among its members brings the group from forming to performing with a minimum of struggle and in record time. But no team goes directly from forming to performing. Struggle and adaptations are not only critical and difficult, but a necessary part of team development. A good place to begin moving your team from one stage to the next with minimal resistance is to identify where the team currently exists. Understanding these four stages often distinguishes successful teams from failed teams.

I. The Forming Stage

Forming is that stage in the team's development when everything is up for grabs. It is a team in the loosest sense of the word. The talent may all be right there in front of you—good engineers, good planners, good production people, good finance staff, but like a drill sergeant surveying his newest platoon on the first day of boot camp, you've never seen such a rag-tag bunch of individuals in all your born days.

Did you ever, as a kid, transfer to a new school? Remember what that first day felt like? Walking to school, you had one burning desire—to fit in. What mattered most was being accepted by all these strangers. They were going to be an important part of your life for the foreseeable future, and you wanted them to like you. That overwhelming need to fit in, meanwhile, was met with a certain naive opposition to adapting. No one wants to run up the white flag, unconditionally surrendering his or her personal identity. We all want to remain ourselves even as we struggle to fit into a group. We want more information on what we've gotten ourselves into. We want to know who's in charge, and what they're likely to require of us. It's exactly the same with being a team member. We don't want to plunge in; we need to know how cold the water is. That is the ambivalent mind-set we bring to joining new teams. One of the signs of a team at the forming stage is an over-weaning politeness, bending over backwards to be pleasant, not to offend, not to ruffle feathers. Everyone has fifteen seconds of self introduction then sits down, eyes darting nervously. This is understandable when you consider that manners are generally instituted to keep strangers from frightening one another. The hand extended in friendship is an ancient way of demonstrating that one is bringing peaceful intentions to the relationship, not a sword or a club.

This eagerness to appear non-threatening is really a key to how threatening the forming stage usually is. People getting together for the first time have all sorts of unanswered questions. Why are we here? What are we supposed to do? Who has power? Will power be shared?

And, along with their questions, people bring their doubts, prejudices, and insecurities to the team as well.

Amid these unsettling feelings, people cast about anxiously for something, anything, to form temporary alliances. It can be something as simple as two people smoking the same brand of cigarettes, a preference for the same vein of humor, or having worked together in the past: anything that a person can use to feel more comfortable in the larger group. Forming, by the way, is the birthplace of the clique.

During the forming stage, potential teammates identify expectations and desired outcomes, agree on the team's purpose, and identify possible resources and skills sets. They get to know each other, begin to bond, evaluate trust levels, and communicate personal needs. The challenge of forming is the challenge of helping a group of people who has no reason to work together to find a reason to work together. Here are some questions which must be answered in the forming stage:

- Why was I asked to participate on this team?

- Whose idea was the formation of this team?

- Why were we formed?

- Who are the other members and what are their strengths?

- How am I going to find out what they're good at and also let them know what I'm good at?

- How large should the team be?

- How and when are we to bring needed resources to the team and get rid of them when they're no longer needed?

People placed in a new role cast about desperately for common ground. All too typically, they settle on the organization and poke fun at the company for bringing them together to begin with. Within moments of being put together, they can be hard at work fashioning a caricature of the company they work for. Like the drawings of teachers that got them in trouble in the fourth grade, the decision to poke fun at the company is the team's first act of consensus. Someone or something must pay the price and serve as the safety valve for the tension in the group just getting together.

In addition to team size and configuration, other issues must be resolved early on. Who owns the team? Does management own us or do we own ourselves? By ownership, we mean commitment. Typically a new group has a weak sense of purpose and, therefore, has a hard time feeling a sense of ownership. In forming, ownership is virtually all management's. But before a team comes full circle, it will reverse that proportion. Team members will feel a bond of commitment so strong that it will have at least a few insecure people in top management scratching their heads. The team must eventually belong to the team, not to management.

One of the greatest dangers of all is that someone in the group, a quick study, will want to push forward too quickly. The quick study may feel that there is no time to waste and much progress to be achieved by sprinting to the finish line, vaulting over storming and norming directly into performing. But there are no short cuts to team development. The most important job now for this team is to orient itself not to build a better rocket or to double productivity. Its job is to orient itself to itself.

II. The Storming Stage

Forming and storming, together, are usually the most time consuming stages of team development. There is a phrase in industrial psychology called the dynamics of storm and stress, and it refers to an exaltation of individual sensibilities. In other words, it is somewhat necessary for people to experience both disagreement and some measure of stress as they learn to understand each other and to work together successfully. This certainly applies to the storming stage. It is the pathway to team building for sure, but it is replete with individual emotion, group conflict, and change. Storming is not for the squeamish. The best that can be said is that it is necessary and it clears the air. Any issues a team fails to settle during storming will surely return later. Unresolved issues may even drag the team, kicking and screaming, to the eye of its own storm.

All teams are tested in the storming phase. Storming always comes as a surprise, no matter how well one prepares for it. The best one can hope for is that it does not drag on forever as a gruesome war of attrition where no faction can win.

Here are some guidelines that teams still in formation need to consider. Leadership is of paramount importance. The leader who allows the new team unlimited time to sort out individual conflicts will not be successful. This may be the time for stepping in, explaining limits, offering suggestions, keeping a lid on the inevitable anarchy. You do not want storming to outgrow the office, spill over into the lunch room, and finally head down the street, torches ablaze, pitchforks poised for an all out riot.

During forming, the leader's role is to provide direction. He or she points out where people are headed until the group can get its own bearings. During storming, the leader continues to direct traffic, but he or she takes on the additional role of the coach—the person who not only defines the destination, but helps with suggestions on how to get there. Coaching is critical because storming is where the most important dimensions of a team are worked out—its goals, its roles, its relationships, and its likely barriers to long-term team success. Together with its goals which the team began establishing during forming, clarifying and implementing these other three elements comprise the entire agenda of teaming. The coach is there to help, not to interfere. It is a delicate tightrope act to perform. Morale may dip to new lows, and hostilities will emerge and demand a response.

One rule which storming team members often try to encourage in each other is the idea that you can say just about anything. This is true, yet it is not true. It is true that each person must feel free to speak. However, sniping, blaming, and belittling remarks are poison, not only to the targeted individual, but also to the sense of trust necessary for the team to function as a whole. When you first see signs of personal poison bubbling to the surface, that's when to call time out. People have work to do. Tormenting one another is not merely wrong, it's destructive to the team's mission.

As with forming, there are questions during storming that the group must answer to make progress. Those questions include the following:

- What are we supposed to accomplish as a team?

- What are our roles and responsibilities as they relate to accomplishing the goal?

- Who do each of get information from?

- To whom does our information go in order to complete our goal?

- Who's in charge? Will that change from day-to-day, from one phase of the team's process to the next?

- How does one adapt to change in leadership?

- How will we arrive at decisions?

- What happens when we fight?

- How do we increase our ability to take risks until we get to the most direct and most creative level?

- How can we focus our strengths to influence activities outside our own team?

- When will we meet and how—large groups, small groups, one-to-one, etc?

- How can we make ourselves more accessible in order to complete our goals in a timely manner?

A team that answers these questions in the early stages of storming will minimize the pain of a necessarily painful process. Remember that storming takes as much time as there are issues in need of resolution. It is not a difficult task for teams made up of like-minded individuals, all design engineers for example. Cross functional teams are, by nature, made up of unlike-minded individuals.

Leaders should understand the signs of storming. Storming is hope mingled with a large dose of fear. During storming, some team members wonder if they are respected by other team members. Some members will be hostile or overzealous. Some will be intimidated. Pulses will race. Sleep will be lost. Jealousy and infighting, competition and polarization are the order of the day. Alliances that seem solid one day come crashing down the next. Some individuals will rush too soon into the caldron and offer to be boiled down into teams. Others will resist membership as if their lives depend on it.

The worst news for leaders is that storming extracts a terrible toll from them personally. Among the many occurrences in midstorm is a rash of blaming that generally trashes leadership at all levels. Suddenly, you're the reason the group can't get itself together. You're the reason deadlines aren't met. You're the reason individuals feel unfulfilled and misunderstood. As team members wrestle with their identity and direction, leaders are led out for judgment, sometimes gagged and bound. I have seen leaders go white knuckled with rage at the accusations trumped up as part of the team's right of passage. "You weren't there when we needed you," is a common refrain. "You only care about yourself," they say. These can be bitter words to a leader who may have lost sleep every night for a year while grappling with how to intervene, or whether to intervene. Like all developmental stages, there is no alternative to riding out the storm. If it is any comfort, I offer solace that what at first sight appears to leaders a personality conflict is nothing of the sort. And that may be the saving grace of storming. It truly is about team formation and only superficially about personalities.

Storming is the stage in which a few people will decide to stonewall. They will show up for work, and they may still communicate with other team members. But if you look closely at their behaviors, it becomes clear that the team at hand is not the team they wanted, so they have decided against being enthusiastic members. Sometimes an entire team graduates from storming except for one individual, yet it finds itself unable to go on to the next stage. The holdout has them all by the shirttail, keeping them in place while storming on. For an individual like this, there are only two sensible options—get with the team or get out. At the same time, the team and the company owe each member a second chance, maybe even a third chance to reconsider and join the team.

The best analogy for storming is that it is like internal combustion. If you place a teaspoon of gasoline on a sidewalk, it quickly disperses, more or less harmlessly. Compressed in an engine cylinder, however, its vaporized particles begin to bounce into one another at supersonic speeds. Ideally, a controlled explosion occurs and a vehicle many thousands of times the weight and size of the teaspoon of fuel begins to move. When that happens with the team, the storm has broken: roles clarify, a team style materializes, the sun returns to the sky, and a calmer, new day dawns for everyone, best of all, for the team.

III. The Norming Stage

With the passing of the storm comes a new alignment and acceptance of roles within the team. The success experienced during the norming stage is a success marked by contradiction. The group becomes stronger as individuals let down their defenses, acknowledge weaknesses, and ask for help from people with compensating strengths. The norming stage is defined by acceptance of the very roles that storming raged against. Relationships that began in the forming stage as superficial events, coincidences of cigarette brands, favorite jokes, and alma maters have the opportunity to deepen during norming. What's more, the group itself can finally be said to have a relationship with itself. It can show affection for individual members in the storm of banter and repartee and genuine consideration. During norming, the ragged edges of conflict begin to subside, tension ebbs, and individuals now poke their heads out like forest creatures after a summer downpour. They realize it is okay to come out of hiding and to be a part of the team.

What has happened is that the hidden agendas covertly advanced by members during storming—"I want to lead," "I want to be left alone," "I deserve the right to disagree on any subject at anytime"—have been unmasked or have diminished in importance. A person's need to assert control over the group, whether actively or passively, shrinks in proportion to the growth of knowledge about the group. As the group becomes less threatening, individual members mount fewer threats against it. Even individuals who are still conflicted try to keep conflict from affecting other people's work. People take care not to derail or sabotage the hard-won feeling of team hood the group now enjoys.

As group members become more agreeable, the group as a group gains focus and unity. A splendid dynamic occurs in which every dismantled individual defense is used to shore up the group instead. Weaknesses are reconstituted as strengths, information is freely shared, and the group conducts periodic agenda checks to remind itself of its goals and to take note of its progress. During forming, leaders were critical in getting the group going. During storming, leaders were the sacrificial victim as struggling teams groped to achieve consensus at the leader's expense. Now during norming, formal leadership fades as important data is no longer exclusive to leadership. In the next stage, performing, leadership becomes a part of everyone's job and mutual interdependence becomes the order of the day. For the first time, the group may be pictured as a great hulking beast able to move in a single direction, if only haltingly. Before long, the great beast will be doing the dance of dances, the dance that is necessary when people of different perspectives and different understandings work together successfully. For the first time, the group will become a true team.

IV. The Performing Stage

There's no guarantee that your team will make it as far as performing. As Hamlet said in his reverie on team playing, "Tis a consummation devoutly to be wished." The work force of America is riddled with teams that never emerge from storming and continue to batter or ignore one another. They may call what they are doing every day from eight to five performing, but the numbers are never there and neither is the feeling. Performing is not "workaholism." In a way, it's the opposite because it is the admission by every member of the team that he or she cannot do the job alone. This is a level of genuine commitment to company goals and objectives, and it may be new to individual team members. Workaholics work every weekend and think they are indispensable because the rest of the world are morons. Therefore, workaholics cannot be part of the team because no one is as competent as they are.

Performers know the real worth of everyone they work with. Performing team members don't get bent out of shape if they're called over the weekend to help solve a pressing problem. Performing means being sufficiently in touch with one's own needs and requirements. It means one can fashion a work schedule that assures progress on team projects without twisting one's own priorities beyond recognition. Performing is a time of great personal growth among team members. With the sharing of the experiences, feelings, and ideas of other team members comes a new level of conscientiousness. It is the sense of knowing where other team members are, a sense of fierce loyalty, even to members who may not be friendly, and the willingness to find a way through any challenge that arises.

Performing means that the team becomes fly-eyed—seeing with many eyes instead of two just as the six blind men were able to see with six different touches or perspectives. This means a reduction in blind spots. It means that the team encountering an elephant, even if the team is blindfolded, will be able to identify exactly what it is, an elephant.

Performing means caring. With performing, members may move beyond the locker room banter of playful teasing into a dimension of communicating that is less self conscious and less afraid. The humor may linger on, but the little missiles we fire at one another throughout the work day will be disarmed or even go away altogether. The humor reflects a lesser degree of veiled aggression and a greater degree of caring. Conflict does not filter into the upper atmosphere during performing; it is more in evidence than ever. Perhaps it is because conflict is put on the table and not reshuffled into the deck that performing works so well. Disagreements are confronted, discussed, considered, and adjudicated.

What seemed destructive during storming (people at odds over projects and turf) seems to be healthy and positive during performing. Once the argument is resolved, team members resume working together. Losing an argument doesn't mean you get roasted. Winning doesn't mean you get to scorch the loser. The order of the day during performing is a good clean fight. The atmosphere is one of enthusiasm and esprit de corps. Best of all, the team is going strong and deadlines are being met. Production is up to par. And, the speed of information flow defies the usual mechanism of memo routing, weekly meetings, and quality checks. People are getting their work done properly on time and in coordinated sequence. And the word goes out throughout the company: "They're onto something over in department X—something called team work."

The Role of the Leader

Forming, storming, norming, and performing are, as I have indicated, an inevitable part of the team building process. The question often asked about these stages is this: What is the role of the leader? The answer is that the leader must be, throughout the process, an adult. The leader is the center of gravity for everyone else who is willing to do the right thing, not only for individual team members, but for the team as a whole. Thus, it is critical for the leader to be an individual who is focused first and foremost on modeling desired behaviors. The leader must provide an example for all in the way he or she manages his or her own behavior. This will establish a foundation of trust. The team leader must seek to be, whether it is acknowledged or not, an extraordinarily trustworthy individual. Thus the question arises: How does a leader build trust? First, the leader must trust others, a critical step during each stage of forming, storming, norming, and performing. Beyond that, here are some steps that a leader can take to demonstrate trust in others.

1. **Spend time with your team**. It's important to spend time with your people if you don't accomplish anything other than being present to talk about what's going on with their families or with their favorite sports team.

2. **Listen to your people without judgment or critique**. Just give people a good listening to. Don't give them a good talking to.

3. **Permit others to influence your decisions rather than dismissing their opinions**. When someone shares what is clearly a good idea, thank them for it. Integrate it into what you're doing.

4. **Reveal and share relevant information with your people.** Let them know everything they need to know and more. Begin with the assumption that all information should be shared unless there is some self-evident reason why information should not be shared.

5. **Be willing to depend on your people rather than keeping total control in your hands**. Don't be a workaholic. Let your people know that just as they need the team to be successful, you need the team to be successful as well.

6. **Give the complex a common sense edge**. Do all that is within your power to make what may seem like a fairly complex process

or idea quite simple. You can often give an issue a common sense edge if, in fact, it is realistic or practical. And if it cannot be given a common sense edge, it may be one indication that it is not practical or reasonable.

7. **Teach your people**. Engage in a process of sharing both your knowledge and experience in a non-threatening manner.

8. **Ask your people to help you identify obstacles to their success and then remove those obstacles quickly**. When an obstacle cannot be removed, be sure to explain why.

These eight steps are an important center of gravity for the leader who would be trusting and trustworthy through each of the four stages. It is essential that the leader be trusting and trustworthy in the forming, storming, norming, and performing stages of team development. It is critical that leaders establish trustworthiness by leading themselves well.

13

My Leader's Code

Once upon a time there were three stonecutters in a large courtyard, each cutting stones with a chisel. A stranger wandered up to them and asked what they were doing. The first one replied curtly, "Can't you see? I'm cutting stones." The stranger quickly moved away and approached the second stonecutter. He again asked, "What are you doing?" The second man replied warmly, "I'm working so that my family can live and grow." The stranger then queried the third cutter, who replied with a swelling sense of pride, "I'm building a cathedral. Each stone I cut goes into a house of worship that will last far beyond my lifetime."

Each worker performed the same task, but how very different the work felt to each of them. The first man felt tired, exhausted, and bored by his work because he was unable to see the larger picture. The second man felt satisfaction, even enthusiasm, because he could see what his work would bring to the people he cared about. The third stonecutter saw his work connected to a larger whole, full of spiritual meaning and significance. His mundane task was energized by a vision of what his stones would become and how they would enrich other people's lives. This cutter was connected to his inner mission with a vision of why he was working.

All the previous chapters of this book have been a preparation for asking the following questions: Which of the three stonecutters are you most like at present, and which of the three matches the inner vision you have for your life in your best moments? What is the personal meaning of your own work? What comes to mind when you think about the vision you have for your life? Are you just a teacher, or are you one who touches the future? Are you just an engineer, or are you one who builds roads which enhance the safety of others? Are you just a cook, or are you one who provides nourishing food for the well-being of others?

People who follow a dream or have a deep sense of purpose about their work are rewarded with an almost inexhaustible supply of energy. They use this energy to reach their goals and to enrich their lives and the lives of others. Such people understand that the future is not a gift; it is an achievement. They know that when you add up a person's yesterdays, they always equal a person's today's. Therefore, they work today with a vision of what they want tomorrow to be.

In the following pages you will find a *Gallery of Classic Morals* (Morals are principles to live by—bits of wisdom which help us realize our best self). This gallery of classic morals is divided into six sections, each section identified by one of the segments from the life wheel shown on the following page. Once you made your way through the gallery, follow the paradigm on pages 136–144 and write your own personal mission statement. Look in your heart and select the vision or dream which energizes you to become the stonecutter you can be.

The Life Wheel

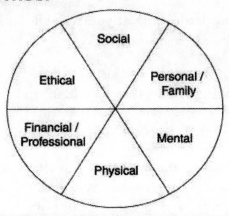

ETHICAL

1. **Live your own life.** Lead your own life. Do not allow others to determine your principles or your priorities. Assume full responsibility for where you've been, where you are, and where you are going.

2. **Laugh often, particularly at yourself.** Life is short; time passes quickly. Decide to enjoy the journey.

3. **Define your vision.** Clearly identify what you want your life to have been when you look back on it in the end. Never allow yourself to forget that if you don't know where you are going, you might end up where you are headed.

4. **Look a person in the eye when you shake hands.** Project an image of mutual worth, courtesy and goodwill. Treat others with esteem, courtesy, and goodwill. Insist on being treated with esteem, courtesy and goodwill.

5. **Be a loyal friend, associate, spouse.** Value relationships over professional success. Be there for people in good times and bad.

6. **Merit divine help.** Live an honorable life. Expect God's help only when doing the right thing and after you have demonstrated a willingness to help yourself.

PERSONAL AND FAMILY

1. **Live a balanced life.** Remember, no individuals ever looked back over their life and wished they had spent less time with a spouse, a child or a friend. Work some, play some, laugh some, and rest some every day.

2. **Love your family and friends unconditionally.** Establish high expectations of honesty and achievement, but love them beyond your disappointments and their failures and mistakes.

3. **Explain to your children where and how you are investing your life.** Take your children to work with you occasionally. Give them a sense of your personal pride of workmanship.

4. **When a friend or family member hurts you, assume that they are also hurting…you will be right most of the time.** Look beyond the friend or family member's anger and try to discover what pain or disappointment is behind the behavior. Then, focus on healing the pain or disappointment.

5. **Let your children know you consider it an honor to be their mom or dad.** Listen to your children. Spend time with your children. Respect your children as persons in their own right. Discipline your children in a way that guides but does not demean.

6. **Celebrate your family and friends.** Remember birthdays, anniversaries, graduations, weddings, bar mitzvahs and baptisms. Beyond these, look for opportunities to celebrate the accomplishments of those closest to you. For example, celebrate a home run, an award, or a recital.

SOCIAL

1. **Be honorable and discreet with the life and reputation of another.** Do not allow a careless word or a word spoken in anger to diminish the life of another. Do not steal from others their good name.

2. **Listen to what people don't say.** People are complex. They frequently expect their friends to listen for what is behind the words they speak—tone, emotion, cries for help.

3. **Salute other people's parades.** Enjoy the enjoyment of others. Allow others the sense of satisfaction and achievement you would claim for yourself. Applaud when their parade passes by.

4. **Treat others with courtesy.** Listen attentively. Speak with humility. Wait with patience. Refuse to patronize. Lace your language and actions with sincere expressions of "please" and "thank you."

5. **Respect the conscience of others.** No matter how different a person's life view, if there is consistency in his beliefs, words and actions, he has integrity. Allow others the dignity of being their own persons and living their own life.

6. **Forgive people for being stupid.** Sooner or later the best and brightest do dumb things. It is part and parcel of being human. Forgive others their human failings, as you would have them forgive yours.

MENTAL

1. **Tell yourself the truth.** Mental health requires a dogged commitment to reality. Self-deception is the first step in personal or professional self-destruction.

2. **Maintain intellectual integrity.** Knowing what you know inspires confidence. Knowing what you don't know, and the integrity to admit it, inspires trust.

3. **Invest in a program of life-long learning.** Discipline yourself to read. Know what is going on in the world and its potential impact on your world. Make time for professional seminars. Give wise men and women a thoughtful hearing.

4. **Admit when you are wrong and do it quickly.** Owning up to your mistakes builds credibility. By doing it quickly, you establish a reputation for accepting responsibility for yourself.

5. **Listen more than you speak.** When you know what others are thinking as well as what you are thinking, you have two sources of information. When you know only what you are thinking, you are at a disadvantage.

6. **Focus on what you can do, not on what you cannot do.** Pour your intellectual energy into the problems at hand. Avoid hand-wringing over problems beyond your control.

PHYSICAL

1. **Protect your most valuable asset.** Unless you are independently wealthy, your greatest financial asset is your capacity to work. Protect your health. Protect your most valuable asset.

2. **Rest and begin again.** The most responsible thing a tired person can do is rest. Exhausted people rarely bring significant change to their world or the world of others.

3. **Listen to your body.** When something about your physiology does not feel right, check it out. Most diseases or injuries can be cured or healed when detected early.

4. **Practice safe living.** Wear safety belts. Buy cars with air bags. Approach stairs with caution. Respect electricity, especially lightning. When a sign says "warning" or "caution," act accordingly.

5. **Play often.** Having fun renews the body, the mind and the soul. Find something which restores your sense of joy and do it often.

6. **Be quiet and still.** Make time to keep in touch with yourself by being still and quiet. The world around you has its own agenda. Only you can protect your vision. Personal moments of stillness and quiet are your best strategy.

FINANCIAL AND PROFESSIONAL

1. **Begin with the end in mind.** Focus on the big picture. Financial and professional success is never a single event. Keep your eye on your destination. Do not allow any single event or person to sidetrack your vision.

2. **Know your strengths and weaknesses.** No one person can know everything. No one person is good at everything. If you need help managing your money, get help. When you need assistance in resolving a professional concern, ask for help. Asking for help is a sign of wisdom and strength.

3. **Don't burn bridges.** Conduct yourself with integrity and grace. You never know what past actions will come back to haunt you.

4. **Disagree without being disagreeable.** Feedback and competing views are essentials of personal and organizational life. After all, no one is 100 percent right 100 percent of the time. How you present your views will determine how you are perceived by others.

5. **Make requests rather than issuing orders.** Unless you are in the military, orders are not usually well received. People want to be asked. A request invites participation and strengthens collegiality.

6. **Invest in the success of others.** Long-term success is almost always the result of win-win partnerships built over a long period of time.

A PARADIGM
FOR DEVELOPING
A PERSONAL MISSION STATEMENT

Follow these suggested steps and you will be able to write a **Personal Mission Statement** that will inspire you and will provide direction for your life. As you work though the paradigm, keep in mind that a Personal Mission Statement is as much a journey as a creation. Don't rush it or set rigid timetables for yourself; rather, work consistently through the paradigm, ask yourself the right questions, and think deeply about your dreams and aspirations.

A meaningful Personal Mission Statement contains two essential elements.

The first element is what you want to accomplish—what your goals are, what contributions you want to make.

The second element is how you would like to be remembered by family, friends and associates—what character strengths you want to have, what virtues you want to develop.

Step One
Define what you want to accomplish and be remembered for.

Some of the elements I would like to have in my Personal Mission Statement are:

What I'd like to accomplish:	*What I'd like to be remembered for:*
_____	_____
_____	_____
_____	_____
_____	_____
_____	_____
_____	_____
_____	_____
_____	_____
_____	_____
_____	_____
_____	_____
_____	_____
_____	_____
_____	_____

Step Two
Identify an influential person.

To help you focus on what you want to accomplish and be remembered for, identify an influential individual in your life. This person may be a parent, a work associate, a friend, family member, or neighbor. Answer the following questions, keeping in mind the personal goals you want to accomplish and be remembered for.

Who has been one of the most influential people in my life?

_____

_____

_____

Which of his or her qualities do I most admire?

_____

_____

_____

What qualities have I gained (or hope to gain) from that person?

_____

_____

_____

Step Three
Define your life roles.

You live your life in terms of roles—not in the sense of role-playing—but in the sense of authentic parts you have chosen to fill. You may have roles in work, in the family, in the community, and in other areas of your life. These roles become a natural framework to give order to what you want to accomplish.

You may define your family role as simply family member. Or, you may choose to divide it into roles such as wife and mother or husband and father. Some areas of your life, such as your profession, may involve several roles. For example, you may have one role in administration, one in marketing, and one in long-range planning.

<u>EXAMPLES</u>
Wife/Mother; Manager, New Products; Manager, Research; Manager, Staff Development; United Way Chairperson; Friend.

Husband/Father, Sales Manager, Budget Administration, Sunday School Teacher, Friend.

Define up to six life roles and then write these roles in the boxes provided. Next, project yourself forward in time and write a brief statement of what you would most like to accomplish and be remembered for in each particular role.

By identifying your life role you will gain perspective and balance. By writing these descriptive statements you will visualize what you want to accomplish and how you want to be remembered. You will also identify the core principles and values you want to live by.

Role	Statement
Mother	I want my children to think of me as one who has both time and energy for them

My Life Roles

Step Four
Write a draft of your Personal Mission Statement

Now that you have identified your life roles and have defined what you want to accomplish, you are prepared to begin working on your Personal Mission Statement.

In the space provided below write a rough draft of your Personal Mission Statement. Draw heavily upon the thinking you've done in the previous three steps. Carry this draft with you and make notes, additions, and deletions before you attempt another draft.

_____

_____

_____

_____

_____

_____

_____

_____

_____

_____

_____

_____

_____

_____

_____

_____

_____

_____

_____

Step Five
Evaluate

It is important that you keep your Personal Mission Statement up to date. Periodic review and evaluation can help you keep in touch with your own development and keep your statement in harmony with your dreams. Ask yourself these questions on a regular basis:

Is my personal mission based on timeless, proven principles? Which ones?

_____

_____

_____

_____

_____

Do I feel this represents my best?

_____

_____

_____

_____

_____

During my best moments, do I feel good about what this statement represents?

_____

_____

_____

_____

_____

Do I feel direction, purpose, challenge, and motivation when I review this statement?

_____

_____

_____

_____

_____

Which strategies and skills will help me accomplish what I have written?

_____

_____

_____

_____

_____

What do I need to start doing now to be where I want to be tomorrow?

_____

_____

_____

_____

_____

Step Six
Write a final draft

I recommend that you keep a rough draft of your Personal Mission Statement for a while to revise and evaluate. Be sure it inspires the best within you.

When you do have a final copy, review it frequently. I strongly recommend that you commit it to memory and display it prominently so that you keep your vision and your values clearly in mind.

_____

_____

_____

_____

_____

_____

_____

_____

_____

_____

_____

_____

_____

_____

_____

_____

_____

_____

_____

_____

The Next Level: New Economic Realities

In the past few decades there have been major developments in the national and global economy. These developments have made a high level of self-esteem more urgent for everyone, from the leader of an enterprise to entry-level personnel. The following examples illustrate key developments affecting economic progress:

- The shift from a manufacturing to an information economy entailing the diminishing need for manual or blue-collar workers and the rapidly growing need for knowledge workers with advanced verbal, mathematical, and social skills.

- The escalating explosion of new knowledge, new technology, and new products and services, all of which keep raising the requirements of economic viability.

- The emergence of a global economy of unprecedented competitiveness, yet another challenge to our ingenuity and belief in ourselves.

- The increasing requirement at every level of a business enterprise, not just at the top, but throughout the system, for self-management, personal responsibility, self-direction, and a commitment to innovation and contribution.

- The rise of the entrepreneurial model as central to our thinking about economic adaptiveness.

- The emergence of the mind as the dominant force in all economic activity.

In an agricultural economy, wealth is identified with land. In a manufacturing economy, it is identified with the ability to make things: capital assets and equipment, machines, and various materials used in industrial production. In either of these societies, wealth is understood in terms of matter, not mind; physical assets, not knowledge and information. Intelligence is the guiding force behind economic progress in a manufacturing society, to be sure, but when people think of wealth they think of raw materials such as nickel and copper, and physical property, such as steel mills and textile looms. Wealth is created by transforming the materials of nature to serve human purposes—transforming a seed into a harvest, transforming a waterfall into a source of electricity; transforming iron ore into steel; and transforming steel into the girders of apartment buildings.

If all wealth is the product of mind and labor, of thought directing action, then one way to understand the transition from an agricultural to an industrial society is to say that the balance between mind and physical effort is profoundly altered. Physical labor begins to slide along a declining arc of importance, while mind begins to climb. As an extension of human intelligence, a machine substitutes the power of thought for the power of muscles. Machines make physical labor less demanding and more productive. As technology evolves, the ratio shifts in favor of mind. And as mind becomes more important, self esteem becomes more important.

The climax of this process of development is the emergence of an information economy in which material resources mean less and less, while knowledge and new ideas account for almost everything. The value of a computer, for instance, lies not in its material components, but in its design—in the thinking and knowledge it embodies—and in the quantity of human effort it makes unnecessary. Microchips are made out of sand; their value is a function of the intelligence encoded within them. A copper wire can carry forty-eight telephone conversations; a single fiber-optic cable can carry more than eight thousand conversations. Yet fiber-optic cables are cheaper, more efficient, and much less energy consuming to produce than copper.

Each year since 1979, the United States has produced more with less energy than the year before. The worldwide drop in the price of raw materials is a consequence of the ascendancy of mind in our economic life. The mind always has been our basic tool of survival. For most of our history, this fact has not been understood. Today it is obvious.

In an economy in which knowledge, information, and creativity—and their translation into innovation—are clearly the source of wealth and competitive advantage, there are distinct challenges both to individuals and to organizations.

Individuals, whether employees or self-employed professionals, face the following challenges:

- Acquiring appropriate knowledge and skills and committing oneself to a lifetime of continuous learning made mandatory by the rapid growth of knowledge.

- Working effectively with other human beings: developing written and oral communication skills, participating in non-adversarial relationships, building consensus through give and take, and being willing to assume leadership and motivate co-workers.

- Managing change and responding appropriately.

- Cultivating the ability to think for oneself—for without this ability, innovativeness is impossible.

Such challenges entail the need to bring a high level of consciousness to one's work. This consciousness demands the acquisition of knowledge and skill and to provide opportunities for growth and self-development. A commitment to life-long learning is a natural expression of the practice of living consciously.

In relating to other people, one needs the self-respect that underlies respect for others; freedom from gratuitous fear, envy, or hostility; the expectation of being dealt with fairly and decently; and the conviction that one has genuine value to contribute. Again we are led to the importance of self-esteem. Moreover, the success of cooperative endeavors rests on the willingness of participants to be accountable, a corollary of the practice of self-responsibility. Such endeavors rely on the willingness of people to keep their promises, honor their commitments, think about the consequence of their actions on others, and manifest reliability and trustworthiness—all expressions of the practice of personal integrity. Self-esteem is far from being the only asset one needs—let there be no mistake about this—but without it one is severely impaired and is, in effect, at a competitive disadvantage.

To organizations, the challenges include the following:

- Responding to the need for a constant stream of innovation by cultivating a discipline of innovation and entrepreneurship into the mission, strategies, policies, practices, and reward system of the organization.

- Designing a culture in which initiative, creativity, self-responsibility, and contribution are fostered and rewarded.

- Recognizing the relationship between self-esteem and performance. Implementing policies that support self-esteem is a challenge that demands recognizing and responding to the employees' need for a sane, intelligible, non-contradictory environment that a mind can make sense of; for learning and growth; for achievement; for being listened to and respected; for being allowed to make responsible mistakes.

When prospective employees ask themselves, "Is this an organization where I can learn, grow, develop, and enjoy my work?" they are implicitly asking, whether they recognize it or not, "Is this a place that supports my self-worth or a place that injures it?"

Conditions of a High Self-Esteem Organization

An organization whose people operate at a high level of consciousness, self-acceptance (and acceptance of others) self-responsibility, self-assertiveness (and respect for the assertiveness of others), purposefulness, and personal integrity will be an organization of extraordinarily empowered human beings. These traits are supported in an organization to the extent that the following conditions are met:

- *People feel safe:* They are secure that they will not be ridiculed, demeaned, humiliated, or punished for openness and honesty or for admitting, "I made a mistake" or for saying, "I don't know, but I'll find out."

- *People feel accepted:* They are treated with courtesy, listened to, invited to express thoughts and feelings, and dealt with as individuals whose dignity is important.

- *People feel challenged:* They are given assignments that excite, inspire, test and stretch their abilities.

- *People feel recognized:* They are acknowledged for their individual talents and achievements and rewarded monetarily and non-monetarily for extraordinary contributions.

- *People receive constructive feedback:* They hear how they can improve performance in non-demeaning ways that stress positives rather than negatives and build on their strengths.

- *People see that innovation is expected:* Opinions are solicited, brainstorming is invited, and new ideas are welcomed.

- *People are given easy access to information:* Not only are they given the information (and resources) they need to do their job properly, they are also given the wider context in which they work—the company's goals and progress—so they can understand how their work relates to the organization's overall mission.

- *People are given authority appropriate to their accountability:* They are encouraged to take initiative, make decisions, and exercise judgment.

- *People are given clear-cut and non-contradictory rules and guidelines:* They are provided with a structure their intelligence can grasp and rely on, and they know what is expected of them.

- *People are encouraged to solve their own problems:* They are expected to resolve issues close to the action rather than pass responsibility for solutions to higher-ups—and they are empowered to do so.

- *People see that rewards for success are far greater than any penalties for failure:* Too many companies make the penalties for mistakes much greater than the rewards for success, and people are afraid to take risks or express themselves.

- *People are encouraged to learn and are rewarded for learning:* They are encouraged to participate in internal and external courses and programs that will expand their knowledge and skills.

- *People observe congruence between an organization's mission statement and professed philosophy, on the one hand, and the behavior of leaders and managers on the other:* They see integrity exemplified, and they feel motivated to model what they see.

- *People experience fair and just treatment:* They feel that the workplace is a rational universe they can trust.

- *People take pride in the value of what they produce:* They perceive the result of their efforts as genuinely useful; they perceive their work as worth doing.

The extent to which these conditions are operative in an organization will be the extent to which an organization is a place where people with high self-esteem will want to work. It will also be one in which people of more modest self-confidence will find their self-confidence increased.

Creating a High Self-Esteem Organization

For leaders who want to build a high-performance/high self-esteem organization, I would structure a different but inevitably overlapping list of proposals that go to the heart of what such an organization requires:

- *Work on your own self-esteem:* Commit yourself to raising the level of consciousness, responsibility, and integrity you bring to your work and your dealings with people—staff, reports, associates, higher-ups, customers, and suppliers.

- *When you talk with your people, be present:* Make eye contact, listen actively, offer appropriate feedback, give the speaker the experience of being heard. Be empathic: let the speaker know that you understand his or her feelings as well as statements—which is a way of giving the speaker an experience of being visible.

- *No matter who you are speaking to, maintain a tone of respect:* Do not permit yourself to speak in a condescending, superior, sarcastic, or blaming tone.

- *Keep work encounters task-centered, not ego-centered:* Never permit a dispute to deteriorate into a conflict of personalities. The focus needs to be on reality. What is the situation? What does the work require? What needs to be done?

- *Give your people opportunities to practice self-responsibility:* Give them space to take the initiative, volunteer ideas, attempt new tasks, and expand their range.

- *Speak to your people's understanding:* Give reasons for rules and guidelines (when they are not self-evident); explain why you cannot accommodate certain requests; do not merely hand down orders from on high.

- *If you make a mistake in your dealings with someone, if you are unfair or short-tempered, admit it and apologize:* Do not imagine (like an autocratic parent) that it will demean your dignity to admit taking an action you now regret.

- *Invite your people to give you feedback on the kind of leader you are:* I agree with someone who once said, "You are the kind of leader your people say you are." So check it out, and let your people see that you are open to learning and self-correction. Set an example of non-defensiveness.

- *Let your people see that it is safe to make a mistake or say "I don't know, but I will find out:"* To evoke fear of error or ignorance is to invite deception, inhibition, and an end to creativity.

- *Let your people see that it is safe to disagree with you:* Convey respect for differences of opinion. Do not punish those who disagree

- *Describe undesirable behavior without blaming:* Let someone know if his or her behavior is unacceptable, communicate consequences and what kind of behavior is expected, and refrain from character assassination.

- *Let your people see you talk honestly about your feelings:* When you are hurt or angry or offended, say so with honesty and dignity and give everyone a lesson in the strength of self-acceptance.

- *If someone does superior work or makes an excellent decision, invite him or her to explore how it happened:* Do not limit yourself simply to praise. By asking appropriate questions, help raise the person's consciousness about what made the achievement possible, and thereby increase the likelihood that they will repeat the behavior in the future.

- *If someone does unacceptable work or makes a bad decision, practice the fore-going principle:* Do not limit yourself to corrective feedback. Invite an exploration of what made the error possible, thus raising the level of consciousness and minimizing the likelihood of repetition.

- *Provide clear and unequivocal performance standards:* Let people understand your nonnegotiable expectations regarding the quality of work.

- *Praise in public and correct in private:* Acknowledge achievements within the hearing of as many people as possible while letting a person absorb corrections in the safety of privacy.

- *Let your praise be realistic:* Like parents who praise their children's every accomplishment extravagantly, you weaken your positive acknowledgments if they are not calibrated to the reality of what has been accomplished.

- *When someone's behavior creates a problem, ask him or her to propose a solution:* Avoid handing down solutions. Give the problem to the responsible party, thereby encouraging responsibility, self-assertiveness, and self-awareness.

- *Convey in every way possible that you are not interested in blaming—you are interested in solutions—and exemplify this policy personally:* When we look for solutions, we grow in self-esteem; when we blame (or alibi), we weaken others' self-esteem.

- *Give your people the resources, information, and authority to do what you have asked them to do:* Remember that there can be no responsibility without power, and nothing so undermines morale as assigning the first without giving the second.

- *Remember that a great leader is not one who comes up with brilliant solutions, but one who sees to it that his people come up with brilliant solutions:* A leader, at his or her best, is a coach, not a problem solver for admiring children.

- *Take personal responsibility for creating a culture of self-esteem:* No matter what is said, reports are unlikely to sustain the kind of behavior I am recommending if they do not see it exemplified by higher ups.

- *Change aspects of the organization's culture that undermine self-worth:* Avoid over-directing, over-observing, and over-reporting. Excessive managing (micro-managing) is the enemy of autonomy and creativity.

- *Plan and budget appropriately for innovation:* Do not ask for people's innovative best and then announce there is no money (or other resources)—creative enthusiasm may dry up and be replaced by low morale.

- *Ask your people what they need in order to feel in control of their work, and if possible, give it to them:* To promote autonomy, excitement, and a strong commitment to goals—empower, empower, empower.

- *Stretch your people's abilities:* Assign tasks and projects slightly beyond their known capabilities.

- *Educate your people to see problems as challenges and opportunities:* This perspective is clearly shared by high achievers and people with high self-confidence.

- *Support the talented individualist:* In addition to the necessity for effective teamwork, there should be a place for the brilliant hermit who moves to different music; team players benefit from this respect for individuality.

- *Teach that mistakes are opportunities for learning:* "What can you learn from what happened?" is a question that promotes self-worth; it also prevents repeating mistakes, and sometimes it points the way to a future solution.

- *Challenge the seniority tradition, and promote from any level on the basis of merit:* Recognition of ability inspires self-respect.

- *Set a standard of personal integrity:* Keep your promises, honor your commitments, deal with everyone fairly (not just insiders, but suppliers and customers as well), and acknowledge and support this behavior in others; your people will take pride in working for a principled leader.

I doubt there is one principle listed here that thoughtful leaders are not already aware of—in the abstract. The challenge is to practice them consistently and weave them into the fabric of daily procedures.

In conclusion, the higher the self-confidence of the leader, the more likely it is that he or she can inspire others. A mind that distrusts itself cannot evoke the best in the minds of others. Nor can leaders inspire the best in others if their primary need arising from their insecurity is to prove themselves right and others wrong.

It is a fallacy to say that a great leader should be egoless. A leader needs an ego sufficiently healthy that it does not feel itself on the line in every encounter—the leader is free to concentrate on tasks and results, not self-promotion or self-protection.

If degrees of self-confidence are placed on a scale from one to ten, with ten representing optimal self-confidence and one the lowest imaginable, then is a leader who is rated a five more likely to hire a seven or a three? Very likely, this leader will feel more comfortable with the three since insecure leaders often feel intimated by others more confident than themselves. Multiply this example hundreds of times and project the consequences for an organization.

Leaders often do not fully recognize the extent "who they are" affects virtually every aspect of their organization. They do not appreciate the extent to which they are role models. Their smallest behaviors are noted and absorbed by those around them, not necessarily consciously, and reflected via those they influence throughout the organization. If a leader has unimpeachable integrity, a standard is set that others feel drawn to follow. If a leader treats people with respect—associates, reports, customers, suppliers, shareholders—that behavior tends to translate into a company culture. For these reasons, a person who wants to develop leadership ability should work on self-confidence as an expression of self-esteem.

Can the right organizational environment transform a person of low self-esteem into one with high self-esteem? Not very likely, although a good leader can establish in a person a foundation for improved self-respect. Clearly there are troubled individuals who need more focused professional help, and it is not the function of a business organization to be a psychological clinic. For the person of average self-esteem, an organization dedicated to the importance of the individual has immense potential for doing good at the most intimate and personal level—even though that is not, of course, its purpose for being. And in doing so, it contributes to its own life and vitality in ways that are not remote and ethereal but, ultimately, bottom line.

The policies that support self-esteem are also the policies that make money. The policies that demean self-esteem are the policies that sooner or later cause a company to lose money. When you treat people with disrespect and frustrate ego energy, you cannot possibly hope to get their best. And in today's fiercely competitive, global economy, nothing less than their best is good enough.

The Next Level:
What Is Self-Esteem?

Most of us are children of dysfunctional families. I do not mean that most of us have alcoholic parents or were sexually, physically, or otherwise abused or that we grew up in an atmosphere of physical violence. I mean that most of us grew up in homes characterized by conflicting signals—denials of reality, parental lying, and lack of adequate respect for our mind and person. I am speaking of the average home.

Let me give you an example of the kind of craziness with which so many of us grew up. Imagine a scene involving a child, a mom, and a dad. Seeing a look of unhappiness on the mom's face, the child asks, "What's the matter, mommy? You look sad." Mom answers, her voice tight and tense, "Nothing is the matter. I'm fine." Then dad says angrily, "Don't upset your mother!" The child looks back and forth between mother and father, utterly bewildered. Unable to understand the rebuke, the child begins to cry. The mom cries to the dad, "Now, look what you've done."

I like this story because of its ordinariness. Let's take a closer look at it. The child correctly perceives that something is troubling mother and responds appropriately. Mother acts by invalidating the child's [correct] perception of reality. Mother lies, though you could argue that was not her intention. Perhaps mother does so out of the misguided desire to "protect" her child, or perhaps she herself does not know how to handle her unhappiness.

If she had said "Yes, mommy is feeling a little sad right now, thank you for noticing," she would have validated the child's perception. By acknowledging her own unhappiness, simply and openly, she would have reinforced the child's compassion and taught something important concerning a healthy attitude toward pain. She would have taken the catastrophe out of the situation.

Father, perhaps to "protect" the mother or perhaps out of guilt because mother's sadness concerns him, scolds the child, thus adding to the incomprehensibility of the situation. If the mother is not sad, why would a simple inquiry be upsetting? If she is sad, why is it wrong to ask about it and why is mommy lying?

Now to confound the child still more, mother screams at father, rebuking him for reproaching their child. Contradictions compound and incongruities mount. How is the child to make sense out of this situation?

The child may run outside, frantically looking for something to do or someone to play with, seeking to erase all memory of the incident as quickly as possible, repressing feelings and perceptions. And if the child flees into unconsciousness to escape the terrifying sense of being trapped in a nightmare, do we blame her well-meaning parents for behaving in ways that encourage her to feel that sight is dangerous and that there is safety in blindness?

A Story Without Villains

No one is likely to imagine that the parents are motivated by destructive intentions. But in choosing to deny simple reality, they give the child the impression that she exists in an incomprehensible world where perception is untrustworthy and thought is futile. Multiply that incident by a thousand, more or less like it, none of which the child is likely to remember in later years, but all of which will almost certainly have a cumulative impact on the child's development.

If the child does draw the conclusion that her mind is powerless, how can a good self-esteem develop? And without it, how can she face life?

Complex Factors Determine Our Self-Esteem

I do not wish to imply that how our parents treat us determines the level of our self-esteem. The matter is more complex than that. We have a decisive role of our own to play. The notion that we are merely pawns, shaped and determined by our environment, cannot be supported scientifically or philosophically. We are all causal agents in our own right, active contestants in the drama of our lives, originators and not merely reactors or responders.

Clearly, however, the family environment can have a profound impact for good or for ill. Parents can nurture self-trust and self-respect, or place appalling roadblocks in the way of learning such attitudes. They can convey that they believe in their child's competence and goodness, or they can convey the opposite.

They can create an environment in which the child feels safe and secure or they can create an environment of terror. They can support the emergence of healthy self-esteem, or they can do everything conceivable to subvert it.

Obstacles to the Growth of Self-Esteem

Parents throw up severe obstacles to the growth of a child's self-esteem in the following ways:

1. Convey that the child is not "enough."

2. Chastise the child for expressing "unacceptable" feelings.

3. Ridicule or humiliate the child.

4. Convey that the child's thoughts and feelings have no value or importance.

5. Attempt to control the child by shame or guilt.

6. Overprotect the child and consequently, obstruct normal learning and increase age appropriate self-reliance.

7. Raise the child with no rules at all, and thus, no supporting structure. Or else, institute rules that are contradictory, bewildering, un-discussable, and oppressive. In any case, inhibiting normal growth.

8. Deny a child's perception of reality and implicitly encouraging the child to doubt his or her mind.

9. Treat evident facts as unreal, thus shaking the child's sense of rationality. For example, when an alcoholic father stumbles to the dinner table, misses the chair, and falls to the floor as the mother goes on eating or talking as if nothing has happened.

10. Terrorize a child with physical violence or the threat of it, thus instilling acute fear as an enduring characteristic at the child's core.

11. Treat a child as a sexual object.

12. Teach that the child is bad, unworthy, or sinful by nature.

Today, millions of men and women who have come out of such childhood experiences are searching for ways to heal their wounds. They recognize that they have entered adult life with a liability, a deficit of self-esteem.

Whatever words they use to describe the problem, they know they suffer from some nameless sense of not being "enough" or some haunting emotion of shame or guilt or of generalized self-distrust or a diffusive feeling of unworthiness. They sense their lack even if they do not know precisely what self-esteem is, let alone, how to nurture and strengthen it within themselves.

A Definition of Self-Esteem

As teachers and parents, we seek to fan a spark in those we work with and seek to raise, that innate sense of self-worth that presumably is our human birthright. But that spark is only the anteroom to self-esteem. If we are to do justice to those we work with and we seek to raise, we need to help them develop that sense of self-worth into the full experience of self-esteem.

Self-esteem is the experience that we are equipped for life and the requirements of life. More specifically, self-esteem is characterized by these two qualities:

1. Confidence in our ability to think and cope with the challenges of life.

2. Confidence in our right to be happy, the feeling of being worthy, deserving, entitled to assert our needs and wants, and to enjoy the fruits of our efforts.

A Powerful Human Need

Self-esteem is a powerful human need. It is a basic human need that makes an essential contribution to the life process. It is indispensable to normal and healthy development. It has survival value.

Lacking positive self-esteem, our psychological growth is stunted. Positive self-esteem operates as, in effect, the immune system of consciousness, providing resistance, strength, and a capacity for regeneration.

When self-esteem is low, our resilience in the face of life's adversities is diminished. We crumble before life's challenges, challenges that a healthier sense of self could vanquish. We tend to be more influenced by the desire to avoid pain, than to experience joy. Negatives have more power over us than positives.

Addiction and Self-Esteem

These observations help us to understand addictions. We either become addicted to alcohol, drugs, or destructive relationships, with conscious inattention invariably to ameliorate anxiety and pain. What we become addicted to are tranquilizers and anything that can ease our pain. The "enemies" we are trying to escape are fear and pain. When the means we have chosen do not work and make the problems worse, we are driven to take more and more of the poison that will eventually kill us.

Addicts are not less fearful than other human beings. They are more fearful. The pain is not milder, it is more severe. We cannot drink or drug our way into self-esteem any more than we can buy happiness with toxic relationships. We do not attain self-esteem by practices that evoke self-hatred. If we do not believe in ourselves, neither in our efficacy nor in our goodness, the universe is a very frightening place.

Valuing Ourselves

This does not mean that we are necessarily incapable of achieving any real values. Some of us may have the talent and drive to achieve a great deal in spite of a poor self-concept. Like the highly productive workaholic who is driven to prove his worth, to a father who predicted he would amount to nothing.

But it does mean that we will be less effective, less creative than we have the power to be and it means that we will be crippled in our ability to find joy in our achievements. Nothing we do will ever feel like "enough."

If we have realistic confidence in our mind and value, if we feel secure within ourselves, we tend to experience the world as open to us and to respond appropriately to the challenges and opportunities. Self-esteem empowers, energizes, motivates. It inspires us to achieve and allows us to take pleasure and pride in our achievements. It allows us to experience satisfaction.

In their enthusiasm, some writers today seem to suggest that a healthy sense of self-value is all we need to assure happiness and success. The matter is far more complex than that. We have more than one need and there is no single solution to all the problems of our existence.

A well-developed sense of self is a necessary condition of our well being, but not a sufficient condition. Its presence does not guarantee fulfillment, but its lack guarantees some measure of anxiety, frustration, or despair.

Self-esteem proclaims itself as a need by virtue of the fact that its [relative] absence impairs our ability to function. This is why we say it has survival value, and never more so than today. We have reached a moment in history when self-esteem, which has always been an extremely important psychological need, has also become a supremely important economic need—an attribute imperative for adaptiveness to an increasingly complex, challenging, changing, and competitive world.

Psychological Resources for the Future

The shift from a manufacturing society to an information society, the shift from physical labor to mind work as the dominant employee activity in the emergence of a global economy characterized by rapid change, accelerated scientific and technological breakthroughs, and an unprecedented level of competitiveness create demands for higher levels of education and training than were required of previous generations. Everyone acquainted with business culture knows this. But what is not equally understood is that these developments also create new demands on our psychological resources. Typically, these developments ask for a greater capacity for innovation, self-management, personal responsibility, and self-direction. This is asked not just "at the top," but also at every level of the corporate enterprise from senior management to first-line supervisors, and even entry-level personnel.

A modern business can no longer be run by a few people who *think* and a great many people who *do* what they are told [the traditional military command and control model]. Today organizations need not only an unprecedently higher level of knowledge and skill among all those who participate, but also a higher level of personal autonomy, self-reliance, self-trust, and the capacity to exercise initiative. In a word, everyone needs higher self-esteem.

This means that people possessing a decent level of self-esteem are now needed economically in large numbers. Historically, this is a new phenomenon.

Intelligent Choices Require Healthy Self-Esteem

In a world where there are more choices and options than ever before, and frontiers of limitless possibilities face us in whatever direction we look, we require a higher level of personal autonomy. This means a greater need to exercise independent judgment, to cultivate our own resources, and to take responsibility for the choices, values, and actions that shape our lives, a greater need for self-trust and self-reliance, and a greater need for a reality-based belief in ourselves.

The greater the number of choices and directions we need to make at a conscious level, the more urgent our need for healthy self-esteem. To the extent that we are confident in the efficacy of our minds, confident of our ability to think, learn, and understand, we tend to persevere when faced with difficulties or complex challenges.

Persevering, we tend to succeed more often than we fail, thus confirming and reinforcing our sense of efficacy. To the extent that we doubt the efficacy of our minds and lack confidence in our thinking, we tend not to persevere, but to give up. Giving up, we fail more often than we succeed, thus confirming and reinforcing our negative self-assessment.

High self-esteem seeks the stimulation of demanding goals and reaching demanding goals nurtures good self-esteem. Low self-esteem seeks the safety of the familiar and undemanding. And confining one-self to the familiar and undemanding serves to weaken self-esteem.

The higher our self-esteem, the better equipped we are to cope with adversity in our careers or in our personal lives. The quicker we are to pick ourselves up after a fall, the more energy we have to begin anew.

The higher our self-esteem, the more ambitious we tend to be. Not necessarily in a career or financial sense, but in terms of what we hope to experience in life emotionally, creatively, even spiritually. The lower our self-esteem, the less we aspire to and the less we are likely to achieve. Either path tends to be self-reinforcing and self-perpetuating. The higher our self-esteem, the more disposed we are to form nourishing rather than toxic relationships.

Like is drawn to like, health is attracted to health, and vitality and expansiveness in others are naturally more appealing to people with good self-esteem than emptiness and dependency.

Attraction to Those Whose Self-Esteem Matches Our Own

An important principle of human relationships is that we tend to feel more comfortable, most "at home" with people whose self-esteem level resembles our own. High self-esteem individuals tend to be drawn to high self-esteem individuals. Medium self-esteem individuals are typically attracted to medium self-esteem individuals. Low self-esteem seeks low self-esteem in others.

The most disastrous relationships are those between two persons, both of whom think poorly of themselves. Predictably, the union of two abysses does not produce a height.

I once knew a woman who grew up feeling she was bad and undeserving of kindness, respect, or happiness. She married a man who "knew" he was unlovable and felt consumed by self-hatred. He protected himself by being cruel to others before they could be cruel to him. She did not complain about his abuse, since she "knew" that abuse was her destiny. He was not surprised by her increasing withdrawal and remoteness from him since he "knew" no one could ever love him.

They had spent twenty years of torture together "proving" how right they were about themselves and about life. When I commented to the wife that she had not known much happiness, she looked astonished and said, "Are people ever really happy?"

The higher our self-esteem, the more inclined we are to treat others with respect, benevolence, goodwill, and fairness since we do not tend to perceive them as a threat and since self-esteem is the foundation of respect for others. It is, after all, simply an expression of the respect we have for ourselves.

The Time Bomb of Poor Self-Esteem

While an inadequate self-esteem can severely limit an individual's aspirations and accomplishments, the consequences of the problem need not be so obvious. Sometimes the consequences show up in more indirect ways.

The time bomb of a poor self-concept may tick silently for years, while an individual, driven by a passion for success and exercising genuine ability may rise higher and higher in his or her profession. Then, without real necessity, he or she starts cutting corners, morally and/or legally in his or her eagerness to provide more lavish demonstrations of their mastery. Then, they commit more flagrant offences still, telling themselves that this is "beyond good and evil" as if challenging the fates to bring them down. Only at the end when life and career explode in disgrace and ruin, can the individual see how for many years they have been moving relentlessly toward the final act of an unconscious life script that they began writing at the age of three.

Self-Efficacy and Self-Respect

Self-respect has two interrelated aspects

1.   A sense of personal efficacy [self-efficacy].

2. A sense of personal worth [self-respect].

As a fully realized psychological experience, self-respect is the integrated sum of these two aspects. Self-efficacy means confidence in the functioning of my mind, in my ability to think, and the processes by which I judge, choose, and decide. It is confidence in my ability to understand the facts of reality that fall within the sphere of my interests and needs, cognitive self-trust, and cognitive self-reliance.

Self-respect means assurance of my value, an affirmative attitude toward my right to live and be happy, comfort in appropriately asserting my thoughts, wants, and needs; the feeling that joy is my natural birthright.

Consider that if an individual felt inadequate to face the challenges of life, if an individual lacked fundamental self-trust, confidence in his or her mind, we would recognize the presence of a self-esteem deficiency, no matter what other assets he or she possessed.

Or, if an individual lacked a basic sense of self-respect, felt unworthy or undeserving of the love and respect of others, unentitled to happiness, fearful of asserting thoughts, wants, or needs again, we would recognize a self-esteem deficiency no matter what other positive attributes he or she exhibited.

The Dual Pillars of Self-Esteem

Self-efficacy and self-respect are the dual pillars of healthy self-esteem. Lacking either one, self-esteem is impaired. They are the defining characteristics of the term because of their fundamentality. They represent not derivative or secondary meanings of self-esteem, but its essence.

The experience of self-efficacy generates the sense of control over one's life that we associate with psychological well being—the sense of being at the vital center of one's existence as contrasted with being a passive spectator and a victim of circumstances.

The experience of self-respect makes possible a benevolent, nonneurotic sense of community with other individuals, fellowship of independence and mutual regard as contrasted with either alienated estrangement from the human race on the one hand, or a mindless submergence into the tribe on the other.

Within a given person, there will be inevitable fluctuations in self-esteem levels, much as there are fluctuations in all psychological states. We need to think in terms of a person's average level of self-esteem.

How Do We Experience Our Self-Esteem

While we sometimes speak of self-esteem as a conviction about oneself, it is more accurate to speak of a disposition to experience oneself a particular way. What way? To recapitulate:

1. As fundamentally competent to cope with the challenges of life, thus trust in one's mind and processes—self-efficacy.

2. As worthy of success and happiness thus the perception of one's self as someone to whom achievement, success, respect, friendship, and love are appropriate—self-respect.

A Formal Definition of Self-Esteem

To sum up in a formal definition, self-esteem is the disposition to experience one's self as competent to take on the challenges of life and deserving of happiness.

Note that this definition does not specify the childhood environmental influences that support healthy self-esteem [for example, physical safety, nurture, etc.], nor the later internal generators [the practice of living conscientiously, self-responsibly], nor emotional or behavioral consequences [compassion, willingness to be accountable, etc.].

It merely identifies what the self-evaluation concerns and consists of. Am I suggesting that the definition of self-esteem I offer is written in stone and can never be improved on? Not at all. Definitions are by nature contextual. They relate to a given level of knowledge. As knowledge grows, definitions typically become more precise.

The concept of "competence" as used in my definition is metaphysical, not "western." That is, it pertains to the very nature of things, to our fundamental relationship to reality. It is not the product of a particular culture. There is no society on earth, no society even conceivable whose members do not face the challenges of fulfilling their needs, who do not face the challenges of appropriate adaptation to nature and to the world of human beings. The idea of efficacy in this fundamental sense [which includes competence in human relationships] is not a "western" idea as I have heard suggested on some occasions. It is, instead, a universal need.

We delude ourselves if we imagine there is any culture or society in which we will not have to face the challenge of making ourselves appropriate to life. Every person in every culture in every part of the world struggles to discover meaning in life. For every single person, that meaning, to some degree, is met through self-esteem.

The Next Level:
Why Do We Need Self-Esteem?

To understand self-esteem, we must ask the following question: Why do we need self-esteem? For lower animals, the question of the efficacy of their consciousness or the worthiness of their being does not exist. Only human beings wonder: Can I trust my mind? Am I competent to think? Am I adequate? Am I enough? Am I a good person? Do I have integrity; that is, is there congruence between my ideals and my practice? Am I worthy of respect, love, success, and happiness?

It is not self-evident why such questions should even occur. Our need of self-esteem is the result of two basic facts, both intrinsic to the human experience.

The first is that we depend for our survival and our successful mastery of the environment on the appropriate use of our consciousness. Our lives and well-being depend on our ability to think.

The second is the right use of our consciousness is not automatic. It is not "hard wired" by nature. In the regulating of its activity, there is a crucial element of choice, therefore, a personal responsibility.

The Mind is the Basic Tool of Survival

Like every other species capable of awareness, we depend for our survival and well-being on the guidance of our distinctive form of consciousness, the form uniquely human, our conceptual faculty—the faculty of abstraction, generalization, and integration. This form of consciousness is what I understand by the term "mind." Its essence is our ability to reason, which means to grasp relationships. Our lives and well-being depend on the appropriate use of our minds.

Mind is more than immediate, explicit awareness. It is a complex architecture of structures and processes. It includes more than the verbal, literal, analytical processes popularly, if misleadingly, described sometimes as "left brain" activity.

It includes the totality of mental life, including the subconscious, the intuitive, the symbolic, all of which is sometimes associated with "right brain." Mind is all the means by which we reach out and apprehend the world.

The Process of Thought

To learn to grow food, to construct a bridge, to harness electricity, to grasp the healing possibility of some substance, to allocate resources so as to maximize productivity, to see wealth-producing possibilities where they had not been seen before, to conduct a scientific experiment, to create, all require a process of thought. To respond appropriately to the complaints of a child or a spouse, to recognize that there is a disparity between our behavior and our professed feelings, to discover how to deal with hurt and anger in ways that will heal, rather than destroy, all require a process of thought.

Even to know when to abandon conscious effort and problem solving and turn the task over to the subconscious. To know when to allow conscious thinking to stop or when to attend more closely to feelings or intuition [subconscious, perceptions, or integrations] require a process of thought, a process of rational connection.

To Think Or Not To Think—A Choice

This is the problem and the challenge. Although thinking is a necessity of successful existence, we are not programmed to think automatically. We have a choice.

We are not responsible for controlling the activities of our heart, lungs, liver, or kidneys. They are all part of the body's self-regulating system [although we are beginning to learn that some measure of control of these activities may be possible for us]. Nor are we obliged to supervise the homeostatic processes, which, for instance, maintain our more or less constant temperature. Nature has designed the organs and systems of our bodies to function automatically in the service of our life without our volitional intervention.

But our minds operate differently. Our minds do not pump knowledge as our hearts pump blood, when and as needed. Our minds do not automatically guide us to act on our best, most rational informed understanding, even when such understanding would clearly be beneficial.

We do not begin to think "instinctively" merely because non-thinking in a given situation becomes dangerous to us. Consciousness does not "reflexively" expand in the face of the new and unfamiliar. Sometimes, we contract it instead. Nature has given us an extraordinary responsibility with the option of turning the searchlight of consciousness brighter or dimmer. This is the option of seeking awareness or not bothering to seek it or actively avoiding it. The option of thinking or not thinking. This is the root of our freedom and our responsibility.

We Can Make Rational or Irrational Choices

We are the one species who can formulate a vision of what values are worth pursuing and then pursue the opposite. We can decide that a given course of action is rational, moral, and wise and then suspend consciousness and proceed to do something else.

We are able to monitor our behavior and ask if it is consistent with our knowledge, convictions, and ideals. And we are also able to evade asking that question—the option of thinking or not thinking.

If I have reason to know that alcohol is dangerous to me and I, nonetheless, take a drink, I must first turn down the light of consciousness. If I know that cocaine has cost me my last three jobs and I, nonetheless, choose to take a snort, I must blank out my knowledge, must refuse to see what I see and know what I know. If I recognize that I am in a relationship that is destructive to my dignity, detrimental to my self-esteem, and dangerous to my physical well-being; and I nonetheless choose to remain in it, I must drown out awareness, fog my mind, and make myself functionally stupid. Self-destruction is an act best performed in the dark.

Our Choices Affect Our Self-Esteem

The choices we make concerning the operations of our consciousness have enormous ramifications for our lives in general and our self-esteem in particular. Consider the impact on our lives and on our sense of self-entailment by the following options:

- Focusing versus non-focusing

- Thinking versus non-thinking

- Awareness versus unawareness

- Clarity versus obscurity or vagueness

- Respect for reality versus avoidance of reality

- Respect for facts versus indifference to facts

- Respect for truth versus rejection of truth

- Perseverance in the effort to understand versus abandonment of the effort

- Loyalty in action to our confessed convictions versus disloyalty to the issue of integrity

- Honesty with self versus dishonesty

- Self-confrontation versus self-avoidance

- Self-critique versus non-self-critique

- Receptivity to new knowledge versus closed mindedness

- Willing to see and correct errors versus perseverance in the error

- Concern with congruence versus disregard of contradictions

- Reason versus rationalism

- Respect for logic, consistency, coherence, and evidence versus disregard or defiance

- Loyalty to the responsibility of conscientiousness versus betrayal of that responsibility

If one wishes to understand the foundations of genuine self-esteem, this list is a good place to begin.

Consciousness, Responsibility, Moral Choices

The point is not that our self-esteem "should" be affected by the choices we make. But rather, by our nature, it must be affected. If we develop habit patterns that cripple or incapacitate us for effective functioning and that causes us to distrust ourselves, it would be irrational to suggest that we "should" go on feeling just as efficacious and worthy as we would feel if our choices had been better. This would imply that our actions have, or should have, nothing to do with how we feel about ourselves. It is one thing to caution against identifying oneself with a particular behavior. It is another to assert that there should be no connection between self-assessment and behavior.

A disservice is done to people if they are offered "feel good" notions of self-esteem that divorce it from questions of consciousness, responsibility, or moral choice. It is the fact that we have choices such as I have described. We are confronted by options encountered nowhere else in nature, and we are the one species able to betray and act against our means of survival. This creates our need for self-esteem, which is the need to know we are functioning as our life and well-being require.

Simply stated, our choices will enhance or harm our self-esteem. We have the option of "choice." Unfortunately, that "choice" does not include the capacity to divorce "choice" from consequence. We are the sum of our choices. Those choices either add up to healthy self-esteem or they do not. The choices we make are within our control—the consequences are not.

If our behavior [choices] devalues us, we cannot merely "choose" not to be devalued. Instead, we must learn to "choose" behaviors which build and sustain healthy self-esteem.

The Next Level:
Self-Esteem and Achievement

Self-esteem is not a free gift that we need only claim. To acquire healthy self-esteem is a true achievement that occurs only over time. To qualify as authentic self-esteem, the experience I am describing must be reality based. It is more than simply a matter of "feeling good about oneself." A state that, at least temporarily, can be induced in any number of ways from having a pleasant sexual encounter to buying a new outfit to receiving a compliment to ingesting certain drugs. Genuine self-efficacy and self-respect asks far more of us than this.

In a current magazine an article appeared that stated, "a standardized math test was given to thirteen year olds in six countries last year. Koreans did the best. Americans did the worst, coming in behind Spain, Ireland, and Canada. Now the bad news—besides being shown triangles and equations, the kids were shown the statement 'I am good at mathematics.' Americans were number one with an impressive sixty-eight percent in agreement. American students may not know their math, but they had evidently absorbed the lessons of the newly fashioned self-esteem curriculum wherein kids are taught to feel good about themselves."

Given the limits of this naïve understanding of self-esteem, the criticisms of "self-esteem curriculum," the author of this article goes on to make are justified. Therefore, when I write of self-efficacy or self-respect, I do so in the context of reality, not of feelings generated out of wishes or affirmations.

One of the characteristics of people with healthy self-esteem is that they begin to assess their abilities and accomplishments realistically, neither denying nor exaggerating them.

How can a student do poorly in school and yet have good self-esteem? Of course, there are any number of reasons why a particular boy or girl might not do well scholastically, including lack of adequate challenge and stimulation. Grades are hardly a reliable indicator of a given individual's self-efficacy and self-respect, though they are certainly an indication of knowledge on a particular subject. But rationally, self-esteeming students do not delude themselves that they are doing well when they are doing poorly.

Schools should, indeed, be concerned to introduce self-esteem principles and practices in their curriculum and there are some excellent programs now in place. But we do not serve the healthy development of young people when we convey that self-esteem may be achieved by reciting "I am special," everyday or by stroking ones own face while saying "I love me," or by identifying self-worth with membership in a particular group [ethnic pride] rather with personal character.

On this last point, let us remember that self-esteem pertains to that which is open to our volitional choice. It cannot properly be a function of the family we were born into or our race or the color of our skin or the achievement of our ancestors. These are values people sometimes cling to in order to avoid responsibility for achieving authentic self-esteem. They are sources of what below I call "pseudo self-esteem."

Can one ever take legitimate pleasure in any of these values? Of course. Can they ever provide temporary support for fragile, growing egos? Probably. But they are not substitutes for consciousness, responsibility, or integrity. They are not sources for self-efficacy and self-respect. They can, however, become sources of self-delusion.

But Is It Authentic?

Sometimes we see people who enjoy worldly success, who are widely esteemed, and who have a public veneer of assurance, yet, are deeply dissatisfied, anxious, or depressed. They may project the appearance of self-esteem, but do not possess the reality. How might we understand them?

Let us begin with the observation that to the extent that we fail to develop authentic self-esteem, the consequences are varying degrees of anxiety, insecurity, self-doubt. This is the sense of being, in effect, inappropriate to existence [although no one thinks of themselves in these terms, instead, one might feel something is "wrong" with me]. This state is extremely painful and because it is painful, we are motivated to evade it, to deny our fears, rationalize our behaviors, and fake a self-esteem we may not possess. We may develop what is often termed pseudo self-esteem.

Pseudo self-esteem is the illusion of self-efficacy and self-respect without the reality. It is a non-rational, self-protected device to diminish anxiety and to provide a spurious sense of security to assuage our need for authentic self-esteem by allowing the real causes of its lack to be evaded.

It is based on values that may be appropriate or inappropriate, but that in either case, are not intrinsically related to that which genuine self-efficacy and self-respect require. For example, instead of seeking self-esteem through consciousness, responsibility, and integrity, a person may seek it through popularity, prestige, material acquisition, or sexual exploits. Instead of valuing personal authenticity, we may value belonging to the right clubs or the right church or the right political party. Instead of practicing appropriate self-assertion, we may practice blind loyalty to a particular group. Instead of seeking self-respect through honesty, we may seek it through philanthropy [I must be a good person, I do good works].

Instead of striving for the power of competence, we may pursue the "power" of manipulating or controlling other people. The possibilities for self-deception are almost endless—all the blind alleys down which we can lose ourselves, not realizing that what we desire cannot be purchased with counterfeit currency.

Self-esteem is an intimate experience that resides in the core of my being. It is what I think and feel about myself, not what someone else thinks and feels about me. This simple fact can hardly be overstressed.

I can be loved by my family, my mate, and my friend, and yet not love myself. I can be admired by my associates, yet regard myself as worthless. I can project an image of assurance and poise that fools virtually everyone, and yet secretly tremble with the sense of my inadequacy. I can fulfill the expectations of others and yet fail my own. I can win every honor, yet feel I have accomplished nothing. I can be adored by millions, and yet wake up each morning with a sickening sense of fraudulence and emptiness.

To attain "success" without attaining positive self-esteem is to be condemned to feeling like an impostor, anxiously awaiting exposure.

Acclaim Is Not Self-Esteem

The acclaim of others does not create our self-esteem. Neither do knowledge, skills, material possessions, parenthood, philanthropic endeavors, sexual conquests, or face lifts. These things can sometimes make us feel better about ourselves temporarily, or more comfortable in particular situations, but comfort is not self-esteem.

Unfortunately, teachers of self-esteem are no less impervious to the worship of false gods than anyone else. I recall listening to a lecture by a man who conducts self-esteem seminars. He announced that one of the very best ways to raise our self-esteem was to surround ourselves with people who think highly of us. I thought of the nightmare of low self-esteem persons surrounded by praise and adulation, like rock stars who have no idea how they got where they are and cannot survive a day without drugs.

I thought of the futility of telling a person of low self-esteem, who feels lucky if he or she is accepted by anyone, that the way to raise self-esteem is to seek the company only of admirers. Clearly, it is wiser to seek companions who are the friends of ones self-esteem, rather than its enemies.

Nurturing relationships are preferable to toxic relationships, but to look to others as a primary source of self-esteem is dangerous. First, because it doesn't work, and second, because we run the risk of becoming approval addicts, which is deadly to mental and emotional well-being.

I do not wish to suggest a psychologically healthy person is unaffected by the feedback he or she receives from others. In fact, we should be impacted by it to some degree. We should factor it in. We are social beings, and certainly others contribute to our self-conceptions, but there are gigantic differences among people in the relative importance to their self-esteem of the feedback they receive. Persons for whom it is almost the only factor of importance and for persons for whom the importance is a good deal less. This is merely another way of saying there are gigantic differences among people in the degree of their autonomy.

Having worked for over twenty-five years with persons who are unhappily preoccupied with the opinions of others, I am persuaded that the most effective means of liberation is by raising the level of consciousness one brings to one's own experience. The more one turns up the volume on one's inner signals, the more external signals tend to recede into proper balance.

This entails, I believe, learning to listen to the body, learning to listen to the emotions, learning to think for oneself.

Authentic Pride

Self-esteem pertains to the experience of our fundamental competence and value. Pride pertains to the more explicitly conscious pleasure we take in ourselves because of our actions and achievements. Self-esteem contemplates what needs to be done and says, "I can." Pride contemplates what has been accomplished and says, "I did."

Authentic pride has nothing in common with bragging, boasting, or arrogance. It comes from an opposite root. Not emptiness, but satisfaction is its wellspring. It is not out to "prove," but to enjoy. Pride is the emotional reward of achievement. It is not a vice to overcome, but a value to be attained.

Does achievement always result in pride? Not necessarily as the following story illustrates:

The head of a medium-sized company consulted me because he said that although he had made a great success of his business, he was depressed and unhappy. He could not understand why. We discovered that what he had always wanted to be was a research scientist, but that he had abandoned that desire in deference to his parents who pushed him toward a career in business.

Not only was he unable to feel more than the most superficial kind of pride in his accomplishments, but he was also wounded in his self-esteem. The reason was not difficult to identify. In the most important issue of his life, he had surrendered his mind and values to the wishes of others, out of the wish to be "loved" and to "belong."

Clearly a still earlier self-esteem problem motivated such a capitulation. His depression reflected a lifetime of performing brilliantly, while ignoring his deepest needs. While he operated within that framework, pride and satisfaction were beyond his reach. Until he was willing to challenge that framework and to face the fear of doing so, no solution was possible for him.

This is an important point to understand because we sometimes hear people say, "I have accomplished so much, why don't I feel more proud of myself?" Although there are several reasons why someone may not enjoy his or her achievements, it can be useful to ask, "Who chose your goals, you or someone you were seeking to please?"

Neither pride nor self-esteem can be supported by the pursuit of second-hand values that do not reflect who we really are, or more importantly, how we truly feel about the world around us.

Volitional Choice—What We Are Willing To Do

As far as our own actions and behavior are concerned, our self-esteem depends to a very great extent, on what we are willing to do. I stress this aspect of volitional choice because there is reason to believe that we may come into this world with certain inherent differences that make it easier or harder to attain healthy self-esteem, differences pertaining to energy, resilience, disposition to enjoy life, and the like. I suspect that in future years, we will learn that our genetic inheritance is definitely part of the story, even to a greater degree than to which we understand it to be today. And certainly, upbringing can play a powerful role. No one can say how many individuals suffer such damage in the early years before the psyche is fully formed. But it is all but impossible for healthy self-esteem to emerge later, short of intense psychotherapy.

Research suggests that one of the best ways to have good self-esteem is to have parents who have good self-esteem and who model it. In addition, we need parents who raise us with love and respect, who allow us to experience consistent and benevolent acceptance, and who give us the supporting structure of reasonable rules and appropriate expectations. We need parents who do not assail us with contradictions, who do not resort to ridicule, humiliation, or physical abuse as a means of controlling us, who project that they believe in our competence and goodness, and then we have a decent chance of internalizing their attitudes and, thereby, acquiring the foundation for healthy self-esteem.

But no research study has ever found this result to be inevitable. Most studies clearly show that this is not the case. There are people who appear to have been raised superbly by the standards indicated above, and yet who are insecure, self-doubting adults. And there are people who have emerged from appalling backgrounds, raised by adults who did everything wrong, yet they do well in school, form stable and satisfying relationships, have a powerful sense of their own value and dignity, and as adults, satisfy any rational criteria of good self-esteem. It is as if they were put on earth to baffle and confound psychiatrists.

While we may not know all the biological and developmental factors that influence self-esteem, we do know a good deal about the specific [volitional] practices that can raise or lower it. We know that an honest commitment to understanding inspires self-trust and that an avoidance of the effort has the opposite effect. We know that people who live mindfully feel more competent than those who live mindlessly. We know that integrity engenders self-respect and that hypocrisy does not. We know all this implicitly, although it is astonishing how rarely such matters are discussed.

Supporting Self-Esteem

We cannot work on self-esteem directly, neither our own or anyone else's because self-esteem is a consequence, a product of internally generated practices, such as that of living consciously, responsibly, purposefully, and with integrity. If we understand what those practices are, we can commit to initiating them within ourselves and to dealing with others in such a way as to facilitate or encourage them to do likewise.

To encourage self-esteem in the family, the school, or the workplace, for instance, is to create an environment that supports and reinforces the practices that strengthen self-esteem.

How Does Self-Esteem Manifest

There are fairly simple and direct ways in which healthy self-esteem manifests itself in our being:

- A face, manner, way of talking and moving that projects the pleasure one takes in being alive.

- Ease in talking of accomplishments or shortcomings with directness and honesty since one is in friendly relationship with the facts.

- Comfort in giving and receiving compliments, expressions of affections, appreciation, and the like.

- Openness to criticism and comfortable about acknowledging mistakes because one's self-esteem is not tied to the image of "perfection."

- One's words and movement tend to have a quality of ease and spontaneity since one is not at war with one's self.

- Harmony between what one says and does and how one looks, sounds, and moves.

- Openness to and curiosity about new ideas, new experiences, and new possibilities.

- Feelings of anxiety or insecurity, if they present themselves, will be less likely to intimidate or overwhelm one since accepting them, managing them, and rising above them rarely feels impossibly difficult.

- An ability to enjoy the numerous aspects of life in one's self and others.

- Flexible in responding to situations and challenges, moved by a spirit of inventiveness and even playfulness since one trusts ones mind and does not see life as doomed or defeat.

- Comfort with assertive [not belligerent] behavior in oneself and others.

- Ability to preserve a quality of harmony and dignity under conditions of stress.

Then on the purely physical level, one can often observe characteristics such as these:

- Eyes are alert, bright, and lively.

- A face is relaxed and [barring illness] tends to exhibit natural color and good skin vibrancy.

- A chin is held naturally in alignment with ones body.

- Jaw is relaxed.

- Shoulders are relaxed, yet erect.

- Hands are relaxed, graceful, and quiet.

- Arms hang in a relaxed, natural way.

- Posture is relaxed, erect, well balanced.

- A walk that is purposeful without being aggressive or overbearing.

- Voice is modulated with intensity appropriate to the situation and with clear pronunciation.

Notice that the theme of relaxation occurs again and again. Relaxation implies that we are not hiding from ourselves and are not at war with who we are. Chronic tension conveys a message of some form of internal split, some form of self-avoidance, or self-repudiation, one aspect of the self being disowned or held on a very tight leash.

How Much Is Enough Self-Esteem?

Is it possible to have too much self-esteem? No it is not. No more than it is possible to have too much physical health. Sometimes self-esteem is confused with boasting or bragging or arrogance, but such traits reflect not too much self-esteem, but too little. They reflect a lack of self-esteem.

People of high self-esteem are not driven to make themselves superior to others; they do not seek to prove their value by measuring themselves against a comparative standard. Their joy is in being who they are, not in being better than someone else.

Engendering Resentment in the Less Secure

True enough, people with troubled self-esteem are often uncomfortable in the presence of high self-esteem people. They may even feel resentful and declare, "They have too much self-esteem," or use some other way to characterize what makes them uncomfortable.

Insecure men, for instance, often feel more insecure in the presence of self-confident women. Low self-esteem individuals often feel irritable in the presence of people who are enthusiastic about life. If one marriage partner has deteriorating self-esteem and sees the other partner's self-esteem growing, the response is sometimes anxiety in an attempt to abort the growth process. The sad truth is, whoever is successful in this world runs the risk of being a target. People of low achievement often envy, and resent people of high achievement. Those who are unhappy often envy and resent those who are happy. Those of low self-esteem sometimes like to talk about the danger of having "too much self-esteem."

The Next Level:
The Sources of Self-Esteem

I remember as a child being enormously bewildered by the behavior of adults. I was often baffled by what I perceived as the strangeness and superficiality of their values. I saw an incongruity between statements and feelings. I experienced an anxiety that seemed to saturate much of the atmosphere around me. It seemed to me that often the adults in my life did not know what they were doing, that they were lost and helpless, while at the same time, they pretended to be in complete control.

This experience was painful and at times, frightening. As a child, like most children, I wanted desperately to understand why human beings behaved as they did. Somewhere in my mind, at quite a young age, there must have been the conviction, that knowledge is power, safety, security, and serenity. Doubtless, this conviction played a significant role in my own personal and professional development.

All of us know times of bewilderment, despair, and a painful sense of impotence or inadequacy. The question is do we allow such moments to define us. It's not that people of healthy self-esteem do not suffer or sometimes know anxiety, but they are not stopped by such experiences. They do not identify themselves with their fear or pain, just as if they got sick, they would not identify themselves with their sickness. They do not see suffering as the essence of life.

Living Consciously, Responsibly, With Integrity

The need for self-esteem arises from the fact that the function of our consciousness is volitional, which confers upon us a unique task—that of making ourselves competent to cope with the challenges of life. We achieve this by living consciously, responsibly, and with integrity. We should judge ourselves by that which is in our volitional control, as I have already stressed. To judge ourselves by that which depends on the will and choices of others, is clearly dangerous to our self-esteem. The tragedy of millions of people is that this is just what they do.

Self-esteem pertains to the issue of our fundamental appropriateness to life and, therefore, to the mental operations that lie behind our behavior. If this is understood, we can readily appreciate the error of measuring our worth by such standards as our popularity, influence, affluence, material possessions, or good looks.

Since we are social beings, some measure of esteem from others is necessary. But tying our self-assessment to the good opinion of others is to place ourselves at their mercy in the most humiliating way. The desire to "please" and, therefore, to avoid disapproval, can lead us to do things that betray our self-esteem. And what are we to do when the people whose esteem we desire have different expectations so that to gain the approval of one's significant other would be to risk the disapproval of another.

There again, we may take pleasure in an attractive appearance, but to tie our self-esteem to our appearance is to be in growing terror with every passing year as the marks of age inevitably advance upon us. And if our good looks are superior to our behavior, they will hardly heal the psychic wounds inflicted by dishonesty, irresponsibility, or irrationality.

A Commitment to Awareness; the Will to Understand

Whenever we see men and women of high self-esteem, we see a high commitment to awareness as a way of life. They live mindfully. They are concerned to know what they are doing when they act, to understand themselves and the world around them, including the feedback they receive which informs them whether they are on course or off course with regard to their goals and purposes. This is what I think should be called the "will to understand."

The potential range of our awareness depends on the extent of our intelligence and the breadth of our abstract capacity, which means our ability to grasp relationships [to see the connection between things]. But the principle of commitment to awareness for the "will to understand" remains the same on all levels of intelligence. It entails the behavior of seeking to integrate, that which enters our mental field, as well as the effort to keep expanding that field.

The beginning of self-assertion is the assertion of consciousness itself—the act of seeing and of seeking to grasp that which we see, of hearing and of seeking to grasp that which we hear, or responding to life actively rather than passively. This is the foundation of healthy self-esteem.

The Bewildering World of Adults

Many children undergo experiences that place enormous obstacles in the way of the healthy development of this attitude. The child may find the world of parents and other adults incomprehensible, even threatening. The self is not nurtured, but attacked. After a number of unsuccessful attempts to understand adult policies, statements, and behaviors, some children give up and take the blame for their feelings of helplessness. Often they sense, miserably, desperately, and inarticulately, that there is something terribly wrong with their elders, or with themselves, or with something, which they cannot quite name.

What they often come to feel is "I'll never understand people. I'll never be able to do what they expect of me. I don't know what's right or wrong, and I'm never going to know."

Developing a Powerful Source of Strength

The child who continues to struggle to make sense out of the world and the people in it, however, is developing a powerful sense of strength, no matter what the anguish or bewilderment experienced.

Caught in a particularly cruel, frustrating, and irrational environment, he or she will doubtless feel alienated from many of the people in the immediate surrounding world, and legitimately so.

But the child will not feel alienated from reality; will not feel, at the deepest level, incompetent to live. The growing individual who retains commitment to awareness learns subjects, acquires skills, accomplishes tasks, and reaches goals. And of course, these successes validate and reinforce the choice to think. The sense of being appropriate to life feels natural. A commitment to awareness, a commitment to rationality, to consciousness, and a respect for reality as a way of life is both a source and expression of positive self-esteem.

Often we associate positive self-esteem only with the result—with knowledge, success, the admiration and appreciation of others, and miss the cause: all the choices that cumulatively add up to what we call a commitment to awareness, the will to understand. We thus can deceive ourselves about the actual sources of self-esteem.

The Will to Be Efficacious

When we see self-esteem, we see what I call "the will to be efficacious." The concept of the will to be efficacious is an extension of the will to understand. It places its emphasis on perseverance in the face of difficulties, continuing to seek understanding, and understanding does not come easily, pursuing the mastery of a skill or the solution of a problem in the face of defeat, maintaining a commitment to goals while encountering many obstacles along the way.

The will to be efficacious is the refusal to identify our ego or self with momentary feelings of helplessness and defeat. The will to be efficacious is the refusal of a human consciousness to accept helplessness as its permanent and unalterable condition.

Strategic Detachment—Knowing You Are More Than Your Problems

It is impressive to see a person who has been battered by life in many ways, who is torn by a variety of unsolved problems, who may be alienated from many aspects of the self, and yet who is still fighting, still struggling, still striving to find the path to a more fulfilling existence moved by the wisdom of knowing "I am more than my problems."

Children who survive extremely adverse childhoods have learned a particular survival strategy that relates to the issue we are discussing. I call it, "strategic detachment." This is not the withdrawal from reality that leads to psychological disturbance, rather an intuitively calibrated disengagement from noxious or poison aspects of their family life or other aspects of their world. They somehow know this is not all there is. They hold the belief that a better alternative exists somewhere and that someday they will find their way to it. They persevere in that idea. They somehow know mother is not all women, father is not all men, and this family does not exhaust the possibilities of human relationships. There is life beyond this neighborhood.

This does not spare them suffering in the present, but it allows them not to be destroyed by it. Their strategic detachment does not guarantee that they will never have feelings of powerlessness, but it helps them not to be stuck there. Whether as children or adults, having the will to be efficacious does not mean that we deny or disown feelings of inefficacy when they arise. It means that we do not accept them as permanent. We feel temporarily helpless without defining our essence as helplessness. We can feel temporarily defeated without defining our essence as failure. We can allow ourselves to feel temporarily hopeless, overwhelmed, while preserving the knowledge that after a rest, we will pick up the pieces as best we can and start moving forward again.

Our vision of our life extends beyond the feelings of the moment. Our concept of self can rise above today's adversity. This is one of the forms of heroism possible to a volitional consciousness.

Self-Esteem and IQ

No study, that I am aware of, has ever suggested that good self-esteem correlates with IQ. And this is not surprising. Self-esteem is a function, not of our natural endowment, but of our manner of using our consciousness—the choices we make concerning awareness, the honesty of our relationship to reality, the level of our personal integrity.

Self-esteem is neither competitive nor comparative. Its context is always the individual's relationship to self and to the choices of self. A person of high intelligence and high self-esteem does not feel more appropriate to life or more worthy of happiness than a person of high self-esteem and more modest intelligence.

An analogy may prove helpful. Two people may be equally healthy and physically fit, but one is stronger than the other. The one who is stronger does not experience a higher level of physical well-being. One can merely do some things the other cannot. Looking at them from outside, we may say that one enjoys certain advantages over the other, but this does not mean that there is a difference in the internal feeling of wellness and aliveness.

Thinking Independently

Intellectual independence is implicit in the commitment of awareness or the will to understand. A person cannot think through the mind of another. We can learn from one another, but knowledge entails understanding, not mere repetition or imitation. We can either exercise our own mind or pass on to others the responsibility for knowledge and evaluation and accept their verdicts more or less uncritically. The choice we make is crucial for the way we experience ourselves and for the kind of life we create.

Goals and Intentions Are Crucial

That we are sometimes influenced by others in ways we do not recognize does not alter the fact that there is a distinction between the psychology of those who try to understand things for themselves, think for themselves, judge for themselves, and those to whom such a possibility rarely occurs. What is crucial here is the matter of intention, the matter of an individual's goal.

I recall a person who once said to me, "I can't understand why I'm always relying on the opinions of other people." I asked her, "As you were growing up, did you ever want to be independent, and did you ever make independence your goal?" She pondered for a moment and then replied, "No." I said, "No need to be surprised then that you didn't arrive there."

To speak of "thinking independently" is useful because independency has value in terms of emphasis. Often what people call "thinking" is merely recycling the opinions of others. So we can say that thinking independently about our work, our relationships, the values that will guide our lives, and the goals we will set for ourselves is a generator of self-esteem. And healthy self-esteem results in a natural inclination to think independently.

Self-Esteem is Acquired, Not Given

Seeing only the tail end of the process I am describing, a person might say, "It's easy for him to think independently, look at how much self-esteem he has." But self-esteem is not given, it is acquired. One of the many ways self-esteem is acquired is by thinking independently when it may not be easy to do so or when it may be frightening. When the person doing the thinking struggles with feelings of uncertainty and insecurity and chooses to persevere nonetheless, the person's self-esteem will increase.

It is not always easy to stand by our judgment and if it has become easy, that itself is a psychological victory, because in the past, there were certainly times when it was not easy, when the pressures against independent thought were considerable and when we had to confront and endure anxiety. When a child finds that his or her perceptions, feelings, or judgment conflict with those of parents or other family members and the child must choose whether to heed the voice of self or to disown it in favor of the voice of others.

When a woman believes that her husband is wrong on some fundamental issue, she must choose whether to express her thoughts or to suppress them and thus protect the "closeness" of the relationship. When an artist or scientist suddenly sees a path that would carry him or her far from the consensual beliefs and values of colleagues, far from the mainstream of contemporary orientation and opinion, the artist must choose whether to follow that lonely path, wherever it leads, or to draw back. The issue and the challenge in all such situations remain the same—should one honor one's inner signals or disown them. Independence versus conformity, self-expression versus self-repudiation, self-assertion versus self-surrender.

The Heroism of Consciousness

While it may sometimes be necessary, we do not normally enjoy long periods of being alienated from the thinking and beliefs of those around us, especially those we respect and love. One of the most important forms of heroism is the heroism of consciousness, the heroism of thought, and the willingness to tolerate loneliness.

Like every other psychological trait, independence is a matter of degree. No one is perfectly independent and no one is hopelessly dependent all of the time. The higher the level of our independence and the more willing we are to think for ourselves, and then the higher our self-esteem will be.

Learning to Discriminate

No one can feel properly efficacious [that is, competent to cope with the basic challenges of life] who has not learned to differentiate between facts on one hand and wishes and fears on the other. The task is sometimes difficult because thoughts themselves are invariably touched or saturated with feeling.

Still, on many occasions, we can recognize that the desire to perform some action is not proof that we should perform it. For example, running out of the room in the midst of an argument when you become upset is not desirable. And the fact that we may be afraid to perform some action is not proof that we should avoid performing it. Going to a physician for a checkup when there are signs of illness is another example. If we make a purchase we know we cannot afford and avoid thinking about impending bills we will not be able to pay, we have surrendered our consciousness to our wishes.

If we ignore signs of danger in a marriage and then profess to be bewildered and dismayed when the bridge finally explodes, we have paid the penalty for sacrificing consciousness to fear.

Our Underlying Intentions

As far as self-esteem is concerned, the issue is not whether we are flawless in executing the task of distinguishing among facts, wishes, and fears, and choosing consciousness over some form of avoidance. Rather, the issue is one of underlying intention.

When we describe a person as "basically honest," in the sense meant here, we do not mean that he or she is impervious to the influence of wishes and fears, but rather that there is a pronounced and evident desire and intention to see things as they are. We cannot always know for certain whether or not we are being rational or honest, but we can certainly be concerned about it. We can certainly care. We are not always free to succeed in our thinking, but we are always free to try.

The accumulated sum of our choices in this matter yields an inner sense of basic honesty or dishonesty, the fundamental responsibility or irresponsibility toward existence. From childhood on, some individuals are far more interested in and respectful of such questions of truth than others.

Some operate as if facts need not be facts if we do not choose to acknowledge them, as if truth is irrelevant, and lies are lies only if someone finds them out. The bottom line is that to honor reality is to honor self-esteem.

Integrity

Where we see self-esteem, we see behavior that is consistent to the individual's professed values, convictions, and beliefs. We see integrity. When we behave in ways that conflict with our judgments of what is appropriate, we lose face in our own eyes. We respect ourselves less. If the policy becomes habitual, we trust ourselves less or cease to trust ourselves at all.

In their eagerness to disassociate themselves from philosophy in general and ethics in particular, psychologists are often uncomfortable with anything that sounds like a reference to morality in the context of psychotherapy or psychological well-being. In consequence, they can miss the obvious fact. Integrity is, in effect, one of the guardians of mental health. It is cruel and misleading to encourage people to believe that practicing "unconventional positive regard" toward themselves will bring them to self-love, irrespective of the question of their personal integrity.

Values, Principles, and Standards

Sometimes an individual seeks to escape from the burden of integrity by disavowing or professing to disavow all values and standards. The truth is human beings cannot successfully regress to a lower level of evolution. We cannot draw back to a time before thinking and principles and long-range planning were possible. We are conceptual beings. That is our nature and we cannot function successfully as anything less.

We need values to guide our actions. We need principles to guide our lives. Our standards may be appropriate or inappropriate to the requirements of our lives and well-being, but to live without standards of any kind is impossible.

A Code of Values

We may accept a code of values that does violence to our needs as living organisms. For example, certain religious teachings implicitly or explicitly condemn sex, condemn pleasure, condemn the body, condemn ambition, condemn material success, and condemn [for all practical purposes] the enjoyment of life on earth. This acceptance of life-denying standards is an enormous problem and one that I think we cannot escape if we are honest with ourselves.

Here, I will simply observe, that once we see that living up to our standards appears to be leading us toward self-destruction, the time has obviously come to question our standards, rather than simply resigning ourselves to living without integrity. We may need to summon up the courage to challenge some of our deepest assumptions concerning what we have been taught to regard as good.

Self-Acceptance

Where we see self-esteem, we see self-acceptance. High self-esteem individuals tend to avoid falling into adversarial relationships with themselves. If we are to grow and change, we must begin by learning self-acceptance. In my experience, self-acceptance is not an easy concept for most people to understand. The tendency is to equate self-acceptance with the approval of every aspect of our personality [or physical appearance] and with the denial that any change or improvement might be desirable.

To be self-accepting does not mean to be without a wish to change, improve, or evolve. It means not to be at war with ourselves, not to deny the reality of what is true of us right now, at this moment of our existence.

To accept ourselves is to accept the fact that what we think, feel, and do are all expressions of the self at the time they occur. If we cannot accept the fact of what we are at any given moment of our existence, if we cannot permit ourselves fully to be aware of the nature of our choices and actions, if we cannot admit the truth into our consciousness, we cannot change.

The Power of Self-Responsibility

Working with people from all walks of life, I am intrigued when I catch the moment at which growth suddenly seems to spurt forward. I often see that the most radical transformation occurs after the person realizes that "No one is coming to the rescue." Many people have said to me, "When I finally allowed myself to face fully my responsibility for my life, then I began to grow, I began to change, and my self-esteem began to rise."

In reality, we are responsible for our choices and actions. Not responsible as the recipient of moral blame or guilt, but responsible as the chief causal agent in our lives and behavior. I do not mean to imply that a person never suffers through accident or through the fault of others, nor that a person is responsible for everything in life that may happen to him or her. We are not omnipotent. But self-responsibility is clearly indispensable to good self-esteem.

Avoiding self-responsibility victimizes us with regard to our own lives. It leaves us helpless. It is just this view from which many people need to emancipate themselves if they are ever to evolve to a non-tragic sense of life. Self-empowerment comes in believing and declaring the following:

- I am responsible for the attainment of my desires and goals.

- I am responsible for my choices and actions.

- I am responsible for how I deal with people.

- I am responsible for the level of consciousness and conscientiousness I bring to my work.

- I am responsible for the decisions by which I live.

- I am responsible for my personal happiness.

Much more remains to be said about the conditions of successful self-esteem, more than can be covered in this writing alone. What I have offered here are some general observations concerning the fundamentals of self-esteem.

The Roots of Self-Esteem Are Internal

Self-esteem is rooted internally in mental operations rather than external successes or failures. This is an essential point to understand. The failure to understand this principle causes an incalculable amount of unnecessary anguish and self-doubt. If we judge ourselves by criteria that entail factors outside our volitional control, the result, unavoidably, is a precarious self-esteem that is in chronic jeopardy.

But our self-esteem need not be affected or impaired if, in spite of our best efforts, we fail in a particular undertaking, even though we will not experience the same emotion of pride that we would have felt if we had succeeded.

Further, we need to remember that the self is not a static, finished entity, but is continually evolving, creating, and unfolding in our choices, decisions, thoughts, judgments, responses, and actions. To view ourselves as basically and unalterably good or bad, independent of our present and future manner of functioning, is to negate the facts of freedom, self-determination, and self-responsibility. We always contain within ourselves the possibility of change. We need never be the prisoner of yesterday's choices.

The simple reality is that people change when they choose to change. And until they choose to change, they do not change. All else, that is, all else that appears to be change, is simply accommodation.

The Next Level:
Self-Esteem in the Workplace

Self-esteem may be the most important emotional resource we have to help us meet the challenges of the future. That challenge is especially evident in the workplace where it is becoming clear that self-esteem is not an emotional luxury, but a survival requirement.

Recent research is helping to clarify the important role that self-esteem plays in our ability to take risks, learn new skills, be creative, take feedback, deal with others fairly and benevolently, be productive, and assertive. We need to cultivate these important traits in order to function optimally in our families, organizations, and communities. We have reached a moment in history when self-esteem, which has always been a supremely important psychological survival need, has now become a supremely important economic survival need as well.

We have witnessed the shift from a manufacturing society to an information society—and from a domestic economy to a global economy. We live in a time of extraordinarily rapid change, of phenomenal scientific and psychological breakthroughs. Muscle work is becoming a smaller and smaller part of our economic activity. Mind work is on the rise. This is the day of the knowledge worker. New leadership techniques must be developed that are appropriate for leading a better educated, more independent and creative workforce. Even psychotherapists and counselors need greater awareness of these issues as they see more clients with job-related stress.

Developments in the workplace in this time of accelerated change, choices, and challenges demand a greater capacity for innovation, self-management, personal responsibility, and self-direction—all qualities of high self-esteem.

Trusting Yourself

The most fundamental meaning of self-esteem is trust in your own mind, your own mental processes. Therefore, trust in your ability to learn to judge and to decide. So the primary way we can think of self-esteem as a survival need is in the context of realizing that for humans, the mind or conscientiousness is the basic means of survival on which we rely to keep us in contact with reality and guide our behavior appropriately.

An individual who, at a core level, distrusts his or her own mind is at a severe disadvantage in coping with the choices and options that life presents.

Think of positive self-esteem as the immune system of consciousness, providing resistance, strength, and a capacity for regeneration in handling the challenges of life.

The Ability to Make Decisions

Studies conducted among top executives suggest that one of the leading causes of failure is the inability to make decisions. That inability is due to troubled self-esteem. That is, distrusting one's own mind and judgment.

In many situations, a great amount of information must be obtained and analyzed in order for leaders to make good decisions. And certainly the input of others is a contributing factor. Much has been written about the value of making "balanced" decisions, but that must mean more than merely gathering votes. Consensus thinking may actually lead away from innovative choice.

Guidelines for Making Decisions

In my view, decision-making is a matter of looking at the widest possible context when you make your decisions. It is the ability to ask yourself the following:

1. What are all the factors I know of that can conceivably bear upon my decision?

2. What are all of the foreseeable consequences of my decisions?

3. Who is likely to be affected and how?

   In other words, a highly conscious person is looking for the greatest amount of relevant input he or she can find to guide the decision-making process. It is not a matter of my decision versus someone else's. It is an issue of respect for fact, respect for truth. One of the hallmarks of healthy self-esteem is a strong reality orientation and then trusting your own mind for making the right decision.

   There will be contexts in which healthy self-esteem includes or even demands getting input from others, though that does not necessarily mean taking opinion polls. Someone may be far ahead of the other people involved and able to see things others are not able to see. The Wright Brothers, for example, did not bother to take a poll.

   The consensus model of decision-making has its place, but depends, to some extent, on the ability of innovators or visionaries to get their ideas across. Some are not able to articulate the vision clearly enough to get support for what might be the best decision. Some very important ideas are lost to this inability.

   For an innovator to put across a new product or technique or management method, a high level of self-esteem is of inestimable value.

Approaching Others in a Benevolent Spirit

People who are happy to be themselves, who trust themselves, and are at peace with themselves are free emotionally and psychologically to approach others in a benevolent spirit. Those with positive self-esteem tend to elicit cooperation, share enthusiasm and consensus more readily than people who are more self-doubting, insecure, and think in terms of a "you versus me or in a win-lose" model of human relationships.

Whenever you are thinking about people in the context of a large organization or in their personal lives, people who trust themselves tend to deal with others with much greater respect and benevolence than do those who do not—with predictable outcomes in terms of their ability to gain cooperation.

The Conviction That We Are Worthy of Success

This also relates to the worthiness component of self-esteem—that conviction that we are worthy and deserving of success, happiness, trust, respect, and love.

All of life consists of pursuing values. To pursue values, I have to value the beneficiary of my values, namely myself. If, at the core, I do not feel worthy of success or happiness, I most likely will not attain it, and if I do, I am unlikely to enjoy it. We often see people at work who feel capable, but not worthy. So they work and work and never feel entitled to rest and enjoy what they have accomplished.

People, who doubt their efficacy and worth, tend to experience fear of other people and, as a consequence, may tend to fall into adversarial relationships with them. Other people are perceived to be a threat.

If, in contrast, we have confidence in our efficacy and worth, we are much less likely to fall into a "you versus me" mentality. We are more likely to form cooperative relationships and be skillful at building consensus.

High Levels of Social Cooperation

People with high self-esteem are not driven to make themselves superior to others. They do not seek to prove their value by measuring themselves against a comparative standard. Their joy is in being who they are, not in being better than someone else.

Feeling As If You Make a Difference

I have worked with a number of unproductive teams over the years. One of the core causes is many of the individuals on such teams feel that they really did not have the capacity to make a difference. They did not think that their contribution was going to count for anything. The more they began to believe their input would matter, the more easily they cooperated with each other. It was clearly an issue of self-esteem.

It is a basic human desire to be visible to others, to be seen and appreciated for who we are. And it is natural to want to work in an environment which supports us, supports our self-esteem, supports the view that our contribution can and will make a difference.

Self-Esteem, Anchored in Our Ability to Learn

Because knowledge is exploding rapidly, all of us, to remain effective, need to have a commitment to life-long learning. For many, this represents a significant shift in attitude. It is not easy to take a more abstract approach in which self-esteem is anchored, not in what we have or know, but in our ability to learn. This is important not only in unstable economic times. Any unpredictable change can force the need to learn something new. It is our comfort level—the ease with which we continue to learn and grow—that drives our individual survival (success) in times of change.

For example, it is more helpful to ask, "How did I go from knowing nothing about engineering [or sales or teaching, etc.] to knowing quite a bit about it? What do I already know about learning unfamiliar things that I can bring to this new challenge?"

High Expectations for Success

Those in a position to coach or train others need to cultivate an appreciation for the ability to learn. In the workplace, leaders need to uphold high expectations for success in themselves and in those they lead, and at the same time, create an environment where it is safe to make responsible mistakes. It is very tricky to create a disciplined, risk taking, non-punitive environment. It can be difficult to hold people to higher levels of expectancy while allowing them to grow and learn. This is not a contradiction, but it does take a lot of careful thinking in order to implement.

You might start with the premise that they are going to have something worthwhile and interesting to say. And if you do not really believe that the person can think and their opinion is worth something, think about how you would act if you did believe it and then practice those behaviors for sixty to ninety days and see if you notice any changes.

Regarding setting high expectations when delegating work, ask the person if they can accomplish this task, if they are willing to be responsible for delivering it, etc. Work to get firm agreement about what has been promised and then review it after the task is done.

Goal Setting Responsibility

Whenever possible, it is best to have a team set its own expectations and goals within the framework of the organization's goals. It strengthens the experience of personal autonomy. And some research says that when groups set their own goals, they tend to set them higher than when others set the goals for them.

Leaders with positive self-esteem have less trouble giving up control of goal setting and other tasks. To implement such leadership techniques as shared goal setting it is probably worthwhile to bring in a self-esteem expert who can really make clear what kind of difference it will make in the workplace and why.

Once people understand how self-esteem operates in the human psyche, they will spot opportunities for application that an outsider would not.

A leader is not a psychotherapist and cannot be expected to be. It has never been my view that leaders should be. And furthermore, employees do not sign on for their leader's psychotherapy even if the leader were so disposed.

Challenge, Stimulate, and Stretch

Studies suggest that we get the best out of people when we ask a little more of them than they think they can do. In other words, we stretch them. We set our sights high, but not so high as to be paralyzing. I think the same high principle can be applied to ourselves. Leaders need to set their self-expectations realistically to be sure, but high enough to challenge, stimulate, and stretch. For every individual whose problem is that he overestimates his abilities, there are a hundred people who underestimate theirs.

No Shortcuts to Self-Esteem

There are no shortcuts to high self-esteem. We cannot cheat reality. If we do not live consciously, authentically, responsibly, and with high integrity, we may be successful, popular, wealthy, and belong to all the right clubs, but we will have only pseudo self-esteem. Self-esteem is always an intimate experience. It is what we think and feel about ourselves, not what someone else thinks and feels. In the final analysis, self-esteem is the reputation we get with ourselves.

0-595-29587-8

CPSIA information can be obtained at www.ICGtesting.com
Printed in the USA
LVOW130327120113

315462LV00001B/8/A

"Mike Brown's book *Has God Failed You?* is a ... So much packed into a short book. His answers to the objections to the picture of the God of the Old Testament and His laws are some of the best I have seen. Also, his empathy for doubters is touching and helpful. The exposition of Job? Wonderful. Do avail yourself of this fine book."

Daniel C. Juster, author, *Social Justice: The Bible and Applications for Our Times*

"I did not have 'valleys' as a part of my charismatic theology until I went through cancer, lost my dear wife to cancer, became a single dad, faced a mountain of medical debt and had to rebuild my life in front of a global community. So I know the narrative contained in this eye-opening book. I applaud my friend and colleague, Dr. Michael Brown, for tackling these complex and often overlooked subjects. We need real people who will tackle real issues and deliver the real truth! Michael Brown does it once again!"

James W. Goll, founder, God Encounters Ministries and GOLL Ideation

"My friend Dr. Michael Brown is one of the great Christian apologists of our time, and nowhere is that more evident than in his new book, *Has God Failed You?* His heart to reach the lost and those who have stepped away from the faith is one that I admire greatly."

Robert Morris, senior pastor, Gateway Church; bestselling author of *The Blessed Life*, *Beyond Blessed* and *Take the Day Off*

"Dr. Michael Brown is one of the most incredible men of God that I know. His knowledge of Scripture is unparalleled, and his Spirit-filled insights help the Scriptures come alive. Get ready to have your misunderstandings biblically understood as you read. I would highly recommend this book to anyone who has questions."

Todd White, president and founder, Lifestyle Christianity

"Dr. Brown has done it again. I always appreciate his thoughtful research and helpful insights. This book is a gem."

Josh D. McDowell, author

HAS
GOD
FAILED
YOU?

HAS GOD FAILED YOU?

Finding Faith When You're
Not Even Sure God Is Real

MICHAEL L. BROWN

Chosen
a division of Baker Publishing Group
Minneapolis, Minnesota

Published by Chosen Books
11400 Hampshire Avenue South
Bloomington, Minnesota 55438
www.chosenbooks.com

Chosen Books is a division of
Baker Publishing Group, Grand Rapids, Michigan

Printed in the United States of America

Library of Congress Cataloging-in-Publication Data
Names: Brown, Michael L., author.
Title: Has God failed you? : finding faith when you're not even sure God is real / Michael L. Brown.
Description: Minneapolis, Minnesota : Chosen, a division of Baker Publishing Group, [2021]
Identifiers: LCCN 2020052778 | ISBN 9780800762001 (trade paper) | ISBN 9780800762322 (casebound) | ISBN 9781493431359 (ebook)
Subjects: LCSH: Faith.
Classification: LCC BV4637 .B765 2021 | DDC 234/.23—dc23
LC record available at https://lccn.loc.gov/2020052778

To everyone who has lost their faith
or who finds it very difficult to believe
in an all-powerful, all-good God—
this book is for you.

Contents

Preface

If you are reading this book, you are most likely struggling with your faith, or you know someone who is struggling with his or her faith and you want to help. Whoever you are (even if you are a skeptic who is wanting to deride or ridicule), I am glad you have chosen to read the words that follow. I have written them with much prayer and with a sense of deep dependence on the Lord as I recognize my inadequacy. After all, these are issues of life and death, of hope and despair and of eternal destiny and purpose. Not a syllable was written without serious thought. I pray that you will find life-changing truths as you read.

I was approached initially by Jane Campbell, longtime editor at Chosen Books, who asked me to consider writing a book on the great falling away that Jesus spoke about in the New Testament (see Matthew 24:10–12). Are we in that period today? Is that why many are losing their faith?

As we continued to discuss the project, I felt my heart pulled toward the many who used to believe but no longer do, to those who were once vibrant in faith but now look back at those early days with scorn (or sadness), and to those who secretly struggle with doubt but have nowhere to go with their questions. I wanted to write a book for them—for you—because I have been challenged by serious questions about my beliefs since my first days in the Lord. (I will share more about that in the book.)

If our faith cannot withstand serious questions, how real is it? If our belief system cannot survive careful scrutiny, how deep is it? And if we cannot create an environment that welcomes doubters, seekers, questioners and cynics, how secure are we? Why must we be so fragile when it comes to serious questions of faith?

It is my hope and prayer that as you read this book your confidence will grow and that you will realize that God is real—and more wonderful than you could imagine. I pray that you will find deeply satisfying answers about your faith, and that you will encounter the Lord for yourself.

In the chapters that follow, I address what seem to be the biggest issues people have with the God of the Bible—the problems and objections that come up the most—and I do my best to do so with honesty and openness. I trust you will see that I dodge no issues and that I speak with candor. I can do this because after almost fifty years as a follower of Jesus, with my faith challenged from scores of directions over these decades, I have certainty that God *is* true, that His Word *is* reliable and that He *will* keep His promises as we humble ourselves in His sight. While your own experience may have been very different from mine—perhaps what you have suffered and lost is immeasurably more than I have—our Father remains the same.

So, please read with a prayerful heart and an open mind. Be assured that many are praying for you as you read. May you experience the faithfulness of God in a lasting way!

My appreciation again to Jane and her team at Chosen, including Deirdre Close, Kate Deppe and Mycah McKeown, and to Lori Janke for her careful editorial work. I am also deeply indebted to Nancy, my best friend since 1974 and my bride since 1976. She became an atheist at the age of eight only to have a radical conversion experience at the age of nineteen. Over the years, she has helped me understand how many atheists think, how they perceive some of our best arguments and answers, and what it can feel like to be unsure if God even exists. Her heart of compassion for a suffering world has also helped sensitize me to the pain that dominates the lives of so many people who are loved by God and for whom Jesus died. May they, too, find everything they need in Him.

one

You Are Not a Statistic

We hear the same statistics over and over again. More and more Americans are leaving organized religion and are identifying as "nones." Generation Z (speaking of people born in the late 1990s or early 2000s) has the highest percentage of atheists of any living generation. Young people are dropping out of Church. Faith in God is on the decline. The statistics are striking and scary.[1]

If you are one of those people, you are not simply a statistic. You have your own unique story and your own distinctive journey. You have a life, and your life matters—to you, to people who love you, to people like me who do not know you personally and, above all, to the Lord. Yes, the God you are struggling to trust (or whose existence you question or outright deny) cares deeply for you. In fact, I believe it is by His will and plan—not a coincidence or a stroke of luck—that you are reading these pages right now.

That is why I have written this book. It is for you—not for some number on a chart or some dot on a graph. And with every page I have written and every verse of the Bible that I quote, I have had someone's story in mind. I wrote to a real person who has experienced real pain, who has lived with doubt and unbelief, who has endured deep disappointment, who has been hurt or who has questions that will not go away. And as I wrote, I often saw faces—the faces of those who are struggling and the faces of those who have given up the struggle.

Could it be that some of those stories are your stories or that one of those faces is your face? If so, I encourage you strongly to keep on reading.

Perhaps, just perhaps, the pages that follow will change your life. Perhaps the pages that follow will answer some of your deepest questions or resolve some of your deepest tensions. Better still, perhaps the pages that follow will lead you into a wonderful, fresh, life-transforming encounter with the living God. That is why I wrote this book—for you, with the hope that you would find something of eternal value as you read.

But I want to be candid with you. Although I have written more than forty books, I felt deeply inadequate when I began to write this book. The issues are so personal and so weighty that they are often matters of life or death—literally. And your questions have no easy answers.

What makes me think that I could possibly help you? What "magic" formula could I supply? What could I tell you that you have not already heard? Maybe you suffered a devastating loss, something that was almost impossible to bear. But what made things even worse was that you felt abandoned by God.

With tears of anguish you cried out, "Where are You!?" To this day, you still wonder, "Where was God when I was hurting? Why didn't He let me feel His presence? Why didn't He speak to me or send help my way when I needed Him the most? What kind of God is that—if He even exists? Or was there something wrong with me?"

There are no easy answers or trite responses to questions such as those. To offer cheap answers is to insult you more than help you, and they often minimize the pain you endured. Yet there *are* answers. And you are still here. You are even reading this book.

Of course, you might be reading to prove me wrong. You could believe that there are no answers and that you are going to prove it to yourself by reading this. You might believe that this whole Bible, faith or God thing is one big myth. You might have once believed in the inspiration of Scripture, but the more that you studied, the more you believed that it was like any other ancient book.

Yet still, you are reading this, and that encourages me. I have been praying for you even though we have never met. In fact, many people have been praying for you. Perhaps God has a good plan for you after all!

That is why I put no trust in myself as I wrote this book. I put all my trust in the wisdom and goodness of God. Only with His help can I help you. That is why I am kneeling by the side of my bed in deep dependence on Him as I write these words. We really need Your help, Lord!

There is a remarkable verse in Isaiah where the prophet says, "Truly you are a God who has been hiding himself, the God and Savior of Israel" (45:15). Isaiah calls the Lord the God of Israel and says that He is the Savior. Yet at the same time, he says this God sometimes hides Himself for protracted periods of time. In my heart, I am confident that this same God is your Savior, too, even if He seemed to hide Himself from you for a time.

But my words will never be enough. You must experience God for yourself. When you do, the doubts will disappear, and the pain will find an outlet. Healing and restoration will flow, and questions will be answered and resolved. This cannot be manufactured. The Lord must do it, and I am confident that He will. It is our heavenly Father who stirred me to write, and He did so because He is jealous for you—jealous to see you whole, to see you full of joy, to see you strong, to see you restored and to see you walking closely with Him. What seems far-fetched or even impossible to you is possible with Him. I can feel His faithfulness as I write!

A Short Personal Word

Before we go on this journey together, may I share a little about my own faith walk so that we can get to know each other better? I was born in a Jewish home in New York City in 1955, and I celebrated my bar mitzvah at the age of thirteen. But we were not religious Jews, and I got caught up in the whole counter-cultural revolution of the 1960s. I became a rock drummer and heavy drug user from the ages of fourteen to sixteen. Then, in 1971, two of my best friends became born-again Christians. I decided to attend their church with the goal of pulling them out. Their lives were changing, and I did not like it.

But God had other plans, and by the end of 1971, I, too, was gloriously born again. I was immediately delivered from drugs (which at that point included shooting heroin) and experienced deep satisfaction in the Lord. I found myself meeting with a local rabbi, then with other rabbis, all of whom wanted to turn me away from my new faith in Jesus. Jews should not believe in Him! My beliefs were being challenged within weeks of my newfound faith. Those challenges continued for many years thereafter, right through earning a Ph.D. in Near Eastern Languages and Literatures from New York University.

But I need to be candid with you. Over the course of these last fifty years, I have not been tormented with long-term doubt.

I have had some very intense battles with serious doubt, but those battles were short. I have had some very challenging seasons in my walk with the Lord as the oppressive battles raged on month after month, and I have known what it has been like to be under extreme spiritual pressure, even for a period of years. I have suffered real losses, as all of us ultimately do. But I have not experienced some of the pain and inner turmoil that you might have encountered. How, then, can I help you find your way if I have not experienced what you have lived through?

That is a question I have wrestled with, too, but I believe that as you read the pages that follow, you will find empathy and understanding rather than cheap, superficial clichés. That is because I have listened carefully to those who have lost their faith, to those who find the idea of trusting God to be difficult, if not impossible, and to those who can make a strong case for their unbelief. I have listened, and my heart has become burdened deeply, which has driven me to my knees in prayer. Your pain became my pain and your unbelief became my unbelief. God has sensitized my heart.

In fact, as I worked on the chapters within this book, I felt strangely drawn into some of what I can imagine are your own experiences. I felt the pain, the questions and the doubt. I felt the sting of unbelief. I wrestled with the question of where was God when I needed Him most. I saw things, at least in part, from the perspective of someone who no longer believed. This, too, drove me to prayer and dependence on God. I knew that my own thoughts would solve nothing or help no one. I also knew that one word from God can change someone forever. I pray there will be many such words in the pages that follow.

I have also been helped immensely by the endless hours I have spent talking with my wife, Nancy. When we met at the age of nineteen in 1974, she was a staunch atheist. To this day, almost five decades later, she can articulate to me the mindset of an atheist and the struggles of a doubting believer. She can also cut through a superficial argument the way a sharp knife cuts through softened butter. I trust that her influence, though unseen, will be felt throughout the pages that follow.

In addition, I believe that the focus and research that I spent working on a biblical commentary on the book of Job helped prepare me to write this book for you. Job was a godly, prosperous man who lost his wealth, his ten children, his reputation and his health in a matter of days as he found himself in the middle of a wager between God and Satan. After praising God at the beginning of his calamities, he ended up challenging God after being provoked by his friends. Yet his act of challenging was also an act of faith. In the end of the book, the Lord appeared to him with an unexpected message—a message I will share with you later. Living with Job these many years has made me more sensitive to suffering, pain, unbelief and doubt.

But there is another reason I felt called to write this book. Even if a doctor has not experienced a sickness, he can still prescribe a cure. Even if a mechanic has not had his own car break down, he can still fix someone else's broken down car. A coach can help an athlete become a champion even if the coach has never played professional sports. Put another way, truth is truth and healing is healing. Since I know the God of whom I speak and I know the truth of His Word, I can—with His help—share that life-giving, transformative and healing truth with you.

You see, Jesus understands our weaknesses, our temptations, our trials and our pains. He was subject to weakness as we are. He has perfect compassion, complete empathy, endless mercy and infinite hope. If I can point you to Him, He will take things from there (see Hebrews 4:14–16).

Be assured that people are praying for you. An army of inter-cessors is asking God to help you. As the flicker of faith begins to rise, do not snuff it out. It is not too late for you. You are not beyond hope, and in Jesus, your future is as bright as the promises of God.[2]

two

What If There Is No God?

The title of this book, *Has God Failed You?*, was meant to be provocative, to get your attention and to draw you in. From one perspective, though, this is a self-contradictory question. If the God of the Bible truly exists, then He cannot fail anyone, ever. As an old Gospel chorus proclaims, "God can do anything but fail."[1] We may fail Him, but He will never fail us. The point of the book's title was to ask, "Do you feel as if God has failed you? Do you believe that God has let you down?"

Maybe for you, though, the title falls short. It is possible that at this point in your life you are not even sure that God exists. Maybe you feel sure that there is no God, declaring yourself an atheist rather than an agnostic. Can I speak with you directly for a few minutes? What if there was no such thing as God—meaning the Creator of the universe, an eternal, all-powerful, all-knowing, perfectly good being who personally cared for you? What if such a God did not exist?

If God did not exist, we would have a whole new set of problems to deal with, including:

1. How could nothing create everything?
2. How did life begin?
3. How did human life develop on earth?
4. How do we account for the computer coding (DNA) in our cells?
5. How do we explain human consciousness?[2]

But these are not the issues I want to focus on. Let's ask some more practical, down-to-earth questions instead. If there is no God, can there truly be a sense of purpose, destiny, calling or greater meaning in our day-to-day existence? The answer is obviously no. This world would be completely natural with no spiritual significance of any kind. In this godless scenario, since nothing would have been planned or ordered by an outside force, there would be no particular meaning or destiny involved in any of our lives.

Think of it like an endless game of craps in which someone throws a pair of dice onto a table. One time the dice come up with two ones, totaling two. Another time, the result is a three and a four, totaling seven. And on and on it goes. If a pattern emerges over time, it is nothing but chance. And in the end, there is no meaning to it at all.

Of course, contrary to a pair of dice, we have free will and can make choices about our lives. True enough. Still, if there is no God, there can be no specific destiny for our lives. We cannot say, "I feel as if God put me here for such a time as this," or "I have a deep sense of destiny, knowing that there is a specific purpose to my life." There is no purpose, no destiny or no divine calling if there is no God. We are simply the haphazard products of an unguided, random evolutionary process. We are the ones who somehow made it thus far through the survival of the fittest. And if a fitter race emerges from among us at the expense of our race, so be it. That is evolution.

This does not mean that atheists cannot have joy in their lives, pursue a hobby or enjoy a career. This does not mean that they do not love their families or that they cannot be decent, kindhearted people. It simply means that there is no deeper meaning to any of their actions, decisions and lives. We are here for a period of time and then we are gone. There is no life after death. There is no eternal righting of wrongs. And there is nothing else to look forward to. Those are stark realities for a consistent atheist.

A few years back I was flying to Germany to speak at a conference. I sat next to a Russian American man who owned a company that specialized in cardiac care. It turned out that this man had been raised in the atheistic Soviet Union, and he and his family were all atheists. I asked him the same question I have posed in this chapter.

"Do you have any sense of purpose or destiny in your life?"

He immediately answered, "No."

He had a successful business that was helping to save lives. He had moved to America, had started a new life and was raising his family here. And yet he had no sense of destiny or purpose.

"But," he continued, "I recently discovered something that has given me some sense of purpose in life. It may sound silly, but it gives me something to look forward to as I travel around the world."

He had discovered ballroom dancing. As he traveled to different cities, he would meet up with other dancers. It was even better when he met another good dancer who could partner with him any time that he was in town.

I did not demean him or belittle his ballroom dancing hobby, of course, but my heart broke as he shared his new discovery with me. This was as close as he could get to having a sense of purpose or destiny.

You might say to me, "I'm an atheist, and sometimes I feel compelled to help someone in need. Don't tell me I can't experience a sense of purpose in doing this. I know that I can make a positive difference while I'm here."

But that is not what I am saying. My point is that these feelings are either the result of your own evolutionary process—in other words, there is nothing volitional about it; it is the way your carbon material evolved—or these are choices you decide to make. No intelligent being outside of you fashioned you for this moment. No one outside of you has guided the development of your life to prepare you for this mission. You are no more destined to help a person in need than a rock is destined to lay on the ground. In fact, you may not even have a free will at all. As the title to an article that is posted on a prominent atheist website, RichardDawkins.net, states, "There's No Such Thing As Free Will." As the author, Stephen Cave, explains,

> The sciences have grown steadily bolder in their claim that all human behavior can be explained through the clockwork laws of cause and effect . . . . our ability to choose our fate is not free, but depends on our biological inheritance . . . . In recent decades, research on the inner workings of the brain has helped to resolve the nature-nurture debate—and has dealt a further blow to the idea of free will. Brain scanners have enabled us to peer inside a living person's skull, revealing intricate networks of neurons and allowing scientists to reach broad agreement that these networks are shaped by both genes and environment.[3]

Interestingly, an article on the *Psychology Today* website called out Richard Dawkins, one of the most influential atheists of our generation, for being inconsistent on this topic. The article was written by philosophy-professor Tamler Sommers, who made reference to a five-minute video that accused Richard Dawkins of being inconsistent in his belief that free will and moral responsibility is justified, but belief in God is unjustified.

Sommers explained:

> In response to a questioner, Dawkins concedes that if you take a deterministic or mechanistic view of the universe, it seems absurd to think we have free will and that we can go around blaming criminals and praising distinguished authors. The whole idea of blame and praise seems to go out the window. It's like [someone] blaming his car for not running properly. And since there's likely no one alive who takes a more mechanistic view of human behavior than Dawkins, he should stop going around affirming free will and blaming and praising people. But when asked why he doesn't stop, he says first, that it seems to us that have free will and second, that life would be intolerable if we believed otherwise. . . . Let's grant Dawkins those claims. Dawkins concludes that "this is an inconsistency we have to live with" and so we may continue to believe in free will and moral responsibility, and blame and praise people accordingly. (In his defense, he does seem slightly uncomfortable about the tension.)[4]

How interesting. The learned Professor Dawkins must admit to being inconsistent. But, of course, he must. After all, how can there be blame and praise when the process of evolution has locked everything into place? As expressed by Pastor J. D. Greear:

> If all we are is biology and chemistry, then our behavior in any situation is solely due to what our genes and chemicals in us compel us to choose. Even when we think we're acting freely,

it's only because some chemical construct in our minds pushes us to act that way, because there is no "us" behind it all. There is only our flesh.[5]

Not only so, but,

If you deny God's existence—or if you are one of the "Nones" straddling the fence by waffling on God's existence—you've got to wrestle with *this*. The implications of a closed system, in which biology and chemistry are all that there is, lead to frightening conclusions when you apply them to human action.

If there is no freedom for us to act against our sinful instincts, then there is no free will. That means that every decision you've ever made is an illusion. *You* might think you "chose" to marry your wife or quit smoking or move to Raleigh. But remember, without God there isn't really any *you* to speak of. Your biology made you do those things, and your mind just tricked you into thinking it was voluntary.[6]

In fact, if atheist philosopher Daniel Dennett is correct, then even the sense of consciousness that you experience (as in "I think, therefore I am") is an illusion. As he famously wrote, "What we think of as our consciousness is actually our brains pulling a number of tricks to conjure up the world as we experience it. But in reality, it's all smoke, mirrors, and rapidly firing neurons."[7]

As explained by Anna Buckley on BBC News,

From an evolutionary perspective, our ability to think is no different from our ability to digest, says Dennett. Both these biological activities can be explained by Darwin's Theory of Natural Selection, often described as the survival of the fittest. We evolved from uncomprehending bacteria. Our minds, with all their remarkable talents, are the result of endless biological experiments. Our genius is not God-given. It's the result of millions of years of trial and error.[8]

In the words of Steven Pinker, a psychology professor at Harvard and an outspoken atheist, "Computation has finally demystified mentalistic terms. Beliefs are inscriptions in memory, desires are goal inscriptions, thinking is computation, perceptions are inscriptions triggered by sensors, trying is executing operations triggered by a goal."[9] Or, we might add, even feelings of love can be reduced to a mathematical process in the brain.

As an atheist, you might not accept all of these arguments, but you must accept some of them to be consistent. Does that bring you a sense of hope or a sense of despair? And consider the fact that without a God who can intervene, whichever way the world is going it will continue to go. Nothing can change or alter that. How does that make you feel?

Christian author Randy Alcorn illustrates the difference between an atheistic worldview and a Christian worldview. First, the atheistic worldview:

> You are the descendant of a tiny cell of primordial protoplasm washed up on an empty beach three and a half billion years ago. You are the blind and arbitrary product of time, chance, and natural forces. You are a mere grab-bag of atomic particles, a conglomeration of genetic substance. You exist on a tiny planet in a minute solar system in an empty corner of a meaningless universe.[10]

You are, therefore, "a purely biological entity," similar to a microbe, virus, or amoeba. You do not exist outside of your physical body. You are entirely a material being. When you die, you cease to exist—you came from nothing and are going nowhere. Would you say this is a fair assessment?

Next, here is the Christian worldview. According to Alcorn, you have been designed and fashioned by a God who is powerful and good. Not only this, but He has created you in

His own image, meaning that you can think, you can love, you can hate, and you can worship. This means that you are different from the rest of the earthly creation, different from trees and animals and different from parasites and fish. But better still, "Your Creator loves you so much and so intensely desires your companionship and affection that He has a perfect plan for your life. In addition, God gave the life of His only son that you might spend eternity with Him."[11] And if you will humble yourself before Him and receive forgiveness through His Son, you can become His child with divine destiny inside of you and a beautiful forever with Him.

In response to this, Dinesh D'Souza asks,

> Now imagine two groups of people—let's call them the secular tribe and the religious tribe—who subscribe to these two worldviews. Which of the two tribes is more likely to survive, prosper, and multiply? The religious tribe is made up of people who have an animating sense of purpose. The secular tribe is made up of people who are not sure why they exist at all. The religious tribe is composed of individuals who view their every thought and action as consequential. The secular tribe is made up of matter that cannot explain why it is able to think at all.[12]

Obviously, someone who believes in the Christian worldview has much more reason for hope. They have more reason to believe in the possibility of transformative change, to feel loved (by something outside of themselves) and to feel chosen and special. None of this can exist for a consistent atheist. Could that also be why atheists, on average, have lower birthrates than people of faith?[13]

But maybe all of this sounds too philosophical. Allow me to return to a more practical and down-to-earth issue. Perhaps you were once a committed believer, happily married, churchgoing and blessed with three amazing children. Then, your middle child, your precious four-year-old daughter who was so full of life, energy and had an ever-present sparkle in her eyes was stricken with leukemia. How could this be?

In addition to getting her the best medical treatment available, you fasted, prayed and cried out to God asking Him to have mercy on your little one. Surely, if He was who the Bible said He was He would not allow her to suffer. He would not allow her to die. But suffer she did until the pain was too great and that sparkle left her eyes. Then, she was gone. With her death your faith died, too. You concluded that God simply did not exist.

Honestly, I cannot imagine living through something like that. Even though this did not happen to me, I feel a knot in the pit of my stomach and have to fight back the tears. Watching your own small child die must be indescribably agonizing. And how helpless it must feel!

But if atheists are right and there is no God, then what happened to the daughter in this scenario was also the random process of the arbitrary forces of evolution. It was a ruthless act of nature, without meaning or significance, and her parents will never see her again. And from the viewpoint of a vast, uncaring universe, the daughter's life had no larger purpose at all. There is no design and there is no Designer. For that matter, there is no devil either, so personified evil cannot be factored in. No God, no explanation, no hope.

But if God really does exist, even though He did not answer the prayers for healing, everything changes. He can use the daughter's death to work a profound change in her parents that can help many others in their suffering and pain. He can explain to the parents one day why their daughter was taken from them. And perhaps, out of the parents' intense hatred for sickness and disease, He can use them to bring healing to other children. At the very least, they can look forward to being with their daughter forever in the world to come, a world far more real and enduring (and perfect) than this current, broken world.

My point here is not to say that we should conjure up a belief in God and fool ourselves into being in a state of temporary happiness. Perish the thought. I am a realist to the core of my being. Rather, my point is that if you believe there is no God, I want you to consider the implications of atheism. Are you sure that you are sure? Are you certain that your life has no eternal meaning or significance? And when you watch a beautiful sunset, is it nothing but natural phenomena? Is there not the slightest bit of awe inside of you?

The bottom line is that if there is no God, then there is also no afterlife, no eternal reward for sacrifice, no punishment for wrongdoers who escaped justice in this life, and no ability to freely determine the direction of your life. Even what you consider reality and what you relate to as good, bad, truth or lies is merely the result of neurons firing in your brain. Is there really such a thing as absolute truth or definable goodness? Consistent atheism must say no.

But if God exists, then everything can change dramatically—and I mean dramatically. Suddenly, there can be vistas of hope, redemption, purpose, meaning, fulfillment and life that never ends. Suddenly, when we factor our Creator and Designer and Redeemer back into the picture, everything changes. Suddenly, there is bright, wonderful light shining in the darkness.

The exciting thing is that God is absolutely real and is infinitely more wonderful than we could ask for or imagine. It is by His plan and purpose that you are reading this book. That is why my heart is filled with hope for you, wherever you find yourself on this journey. Your future is about to look much brighter than it has in years.

three

Does Prayer Really Work?

It seems simple. God, our Father, makes promises and gives directives. You hold Him to His promises and follow His directives, but nothing happens. So you come up with all kinds of rationalizations and explanations until you arrive at a frightening conclusion: This whole prayer thing is not working. "I've kept my end of the bargain," you say to yourself, "but God hasn't kept His end of the bargain. Why should I go on with the charade? He's obviously not really there. Or if He is there, He certainly doesn't care." Can you relate to this?

Let's consider some of the Bible's wonderful promises and exhortations concerning prayer. Jesus said,

> "Ask and it will be given to you; seek and you will find; knock and the door will be opened to you. For everyone who asks receives; the one who seeks finds; and to the one who knocks, the door will be opened. Which of you, if your son asks for bread, will give him a stone? Or if he asks for a fish, will give him a snake? If you, then, though you are evil, know how to give good gifts

to your children, how much more will your Father in heaven give good gifts to those who ask him!"

Matthew 7:7–11

"Very truly I tell you, whoever believes in me will do the works I have been doing, and they will do even greater things than these, because I am going to the Father. And I will do whatever you ask in my name, so that the Father may be glorified in the Son. You may ask me for anything in my name, and I will do it."

John 14:12–14

Anything means anything. "Again, truly I tell you that if two of you on earth agree about anything they ask for, it will be done for them by my Father in heaven. For where two or three gather in my name, there am I with them" (Matthew 18:19–20).

Why were your prayers for healing not answered? Why were your prayers for provision, help, guidance or deliverance not answered as well? Perhaps it was right to conclude that the Bible was untrue or that God did not exist. In a following chapter, we'll take up the question of holding to a wrong theology. In this chapter, we'll focus on the issue of prayer.

I certainly agree that there are many promises concerning prayer that appear to be black and white. They seem to say that you pray, and God responds. You ask, and God answers. It's like putting money in a vending machine. You put the money in, and your product comes out. But is it really that simple? If we read the Bible correctly, is this the conclusion to which we should come?

The Call to Persevere

"Then Jesus told his disciples a parable to show them that they should always pray and not give up" (Luke 18:1). Other transla-

34

tions render the last words as "not lose heart" (NKJV) and "not be discouraged" (TLV).[1] What is Jesus telling us? He is telling us that sometimes the answer will not come quickly. Sometimes, we will be tempted to lose heart and quit. Sometimes we will want to throw in the towel. The Lord, Himself, is speaking these words.

Prayer is not simply pushing a button, and it is not always answered instantaneously or according to our own time frames. Often, we need to persevere, refusing to quit or lose hope. To illustrate this, Jesus shared a parable:

> "In a certain town there was a judge who neither feared God nor cared what people thought. And there was a widow in that town who kept coming to him with the plea, 'Grant me justice against my adversary.' For some time he refused. But finally he said to himself, 'Even though I don't fear God or care what people think, yet because this widow keeps bothering me, I will see that she gets justice, so that she won't eventually come and attack me!'"
>
> And the Lord said, "Listen to what the unjust judge says. And will not God bring about justice for his chosen ones, who cry out to him day and night? Will he keep putting them off? I tell you, he will see that they get justice, and quickly. However, when the Son of Man comes, will he find faith on the earth?"
>
> Luke 18:2–8

What a sobering lesson. This widow had to persevere against all odds, but it was her perseverance that procured her victory. And notice that Jesus speaks of "a judge who neither feared God nor cared what people thought." There was no possible way this widow could have influenced him other than by her perseverance.

Is Jesus comparing His heavenly Father—and our heavenly Father—to a wicked, heartless judge? Certainly not. But He is telling us that in some cases it may feel as if God does not care or is not listening. With that in mind, let's look more deeply into this amazing parable from the Lord.

First, Jesus speaks about God's children crying out to Him day and night. That is serious prayer. That is heartfelt prayer. That is sacrificial prayer. That is persistent prayer. And it sounds similar to God's exhortation to Jerusalem, "On your walls, O Jerusalem, I have set watchmen; all the day and all the night they shall never be silent. You who put the LORD in remembrance, take no rest, and give him no rest until he establishes Jerusalem and makes it a praise in the earth" (Isaiah 62:6–7 ESV).

Take no rest for yourselves and give God no rest until He answers your prayers for Jerusalem. That is the spirit of prayer. Those are the kinds of prayers that will be answered. But how many times will we be tempted to cave in and quit along the way? God is saying, "Don't stop praying. I will certainly answer."

Jesus asks this pointed question about God's response to His children's prayers, which He immediately follows up with a decisive answer. "Will he keep putting them off? I tell you, he will see that they get justice, and quickly" (Luke 18:7–8).

God *will* act, and "quickly"—but that "quickly" might not seem so quick at the moment. Otherwise, why would Jesus give a parable about the need for perseverance? Why would He teach us to pray always and not give up, lose heart, cave in or faint? This is underscored by the penetrating words that close out this teaching. "However, when the Son of Man comes, will he find faith on the earth?" (Luke 18:8). In other words, despite the promise that God will bring justice quickly for His people who cry out to Him day and night, many will lose faith along the way.

Perhaps Jesus is speaking directly to you right now. Perhaps you are feeling a ray of hope when previously you felt only despair or downright disgust. Perhaps you are starting to see that you gave up the journey with the destination still in sight.

Maybe Just One Big Game?

At this point, you might be asking, "So, is this just one big game? God tells us to pray, and He promises to answer our prayers, but then He turns around and says, 'Of course, many times your prayers won't be answered. But keep on believing and trusting! One day an answer might come.'"

Actually, your line of thinking makes sense except for two things. First, we need to interpret Scripture with Scripture. There are many verses, stories and illustrations in the Bible that communicate clearly that prayer is not simply a push-button exercise. God is not our heavenly concierge service. He is not a magic genie who lives in our personalized bottle. We need to put the wonderful prayer promises in biblical context, indicating there is more to the story than "pray for anything, and you will always receive an instant answer."

Common sense tells us this cannot be the case. Otherwise, we could lay in bed all day and pray for all of our needs to be met. Maybe we could ask for breakfast in bed, too! Obviously, that is not real life, nor would such a scenario help us grow as human beings. Nothing gets handed to us on a silver platter, and sometimes it takes a while for our prayers to be answered.

The Bible records that "Isaac was forty years old when he married Rebekah daughter of Bethuel the Aramean from Paddan Aram and sister of Laban the Aramean. Isaac prayed to the LORD on behalf of his wife, because she was childless. The LORD answered his prayer, and his wife Rebekah became pregnant" (Genesis 25:20–21).

Boom. It seems as if in a moment of time the answer came. Isaac cried out and the Lord answered. No muss, no fuss, no sweat, no tears. But that is not how it happened. When you read the rest of the text, you find out that Isaac was sixty years old when Rebekah gave birth (see Genesis 25:26). That is twenty years from when they got married. That is twenty years of questions, frustrations, doubts and feelings of rejection. This was hardly an overnight answer. But it was a God-sent answer, nonetheless.

That is the next point we need to emphasize. The Bible records scores of miraculous answers to prayer, answers that only the loving Creator of the universe could produce. And throughout history, there are countless millions of answers to prayer—dramatic answers, supernatural answers, mind-blowing, awe-inspiring answers, undeniable and God-birthed answers.

We cannot deny that God *does* answer prayers, and we cannot deny that not all of our prayers are answered when we would like them to be. But rather than this being some kind of cruel game, it is something wonderful, something beautiful and something glorious. God is at work in our lives even when we do not see it or feel it. He is building a deeper relationship with us, teaching us to trust Him and making us into better people in the process. Prayer is much more than simply asking and receiving.

Over the years of leading different ministries and schools, I have often come under extreme financial pressure in which there was no way for us to pay our ministry team or faculty. There was no money for us to pay our mortgages. We were working hard, even sacrificially, but funds were nowhere to be found.

On one occasion at FIRE School of Ministry, we needed $50,000 for school salaries and pressing bills, and we needed it immediately. But we had no way of getting it. We called for a day of prayer and fasting with our student body without specifically mentioning any of the financial needs. It was April 24,

2003, and I recorded this in my journal: "I led the last 2 1/2 hours of corporate fasting and prayer, with a focused outcry for the release of funds." That was it. At one point during our time of prayer and fasting I cried out to God for the release of funds—and the Lord knew the amount.

What happened? This was my journal entry for the very next day, April 25. "A check for $48,220 was sent to FIRE today! Ha!! GOD IS WITH US!!" A company that had been giving us money for some time felt prompted to overnight this check to us, having no earthly clue that we had been praying. Out of the blue on the day we were praying, they sensed that we might have a need, and they sent us the money. Talk about a dramatic answer to prayer! We were able to make payroll and cover some other pressing needs. But more importantly, we grew in faith. Had things not happened the way they did, we would never have grown the way we did.

One year earlier, my personal ministry was under tremendous pressure. Along with that, my wife and I were under severe pressure. It was not a pleasant time. But on July 11, 2002 at 11:13 p.m., I emailed one of my close friends, saying, "God has really been moving on me/us today, and I can say with total confidence and without any natural evidence at all that breakthroughs are coming! Finances are coming! Release is coming! I know it."

Here is my journal entry from the next morning: "Ha! Ha! Yes! J—calls with the news that there's mail from K—with a check for $30,000 for ICN [that was our ministry name, standing for Israel, the Church and the Nations]. Plus, today—not yesterday—FIRE also received $9,000 from some regular supporters."

Somehow, without any earthly evidence, I knew the night before that funds were on the way. In fact, they had already been sent and were about to arrive the next day. What an amazing experience. And although it was a tremendous blessing to receive these much-needed funds, the greater blessing was my encounter with the Lord. My whole being was shouting, "You are faithful, Lord!"

But without the trials and the delays and what felt like unanswered prayer until then, the dramatic breakthrough would not have been as dramatic. That is one of the reasons Jesus taught us not to cave in. We have to persevere until the answer comes. And when it does come—wow!

The Trying of Our Faith Brings Rich Rewards

There are times when God tries our faith intentionally, but He does it for our good. He wants to teach us to trust Him and to lean on Him. Sometimes He does not answer a small prayer because He has much bigger plans for our lives, and those plans require a much stronger faith foundation. He withholds the lesser because He wants to give us the greater, and because He wants to make something better out of us.

Look at what Peter says about the trying of our faith. After speaking about our great salvation and the inheritance waiting for us in heaven, he writes:

> In all this you greatly rejoice, though now for a little while you may have had to suffer grief in all kinds of trials. These have come so that the proven genuineness of your faith—of greater worth than gold, which perishes even though refined by fire—may result in praise, glory and honor when Jesus Christ is revealed.
>
> 1 Peter 1:6–7

Perhaps you quit in the midst of a trial thinking God had abandoned you. Perhaps you concluded that Christianity was not working for you just as the Lord was trying to deepen you as a person and stretch you as a believer. Perhaps—to use a sports analogy—you fired your coach because he let some golden opportunities pass you by, not realizing that his plan was to make you hungrier and more determined so that you would one day become a world champion.

You see, the Lord has each of us in a process, and the goal of this process is far greater than anything we could ask for or imagine. That is why Jacob (James) wrote, "Consider it pure joy, my brothers and sisters, whenever you face trials of many kinds, because you know that the testing of your faith produces perseverance. Let perseverance finish its work so that you may be mature and complete, not lacking anything" (James 1:2–4).

And, he added, "Blessed is the one who perseveres under trial because, having stood the test, that person will receive the crown of life that the Lord has promised to those who love him" (James 1:12).

If only we will endure the test and not drop out and quit. If only we will keep praying, believing and trusting. The rewards in this life and in the life to come will be indescribable.

Paul addresses this as well.

Therefore, since we have been justified through faith, we have peace with God through our Lord Jesus Christ, through whom we have gained access by faith into this grace in which we now stand. And we boast in the hope of the glory of God. Not only so, but we also glory in our sufferings, because we know that suffering produces perseverance; perseverance, character; and character, hope. And hope does not put us to shame, because God's love has been poured out into our hearts through the Holy Spirit, who has been given to us.

Romans 5:1–5

Jacob (James) says that we should count our difficult trials as pure joy. Paul says that we glory in our sufferings, knowing what they will produce in our lives, namely, perseverance, character and hope. I will trade some quick-fix answer to prayer for the qualities of perseverance, character and hope any day of the week. I will take the long-term, glorious blessing over the momentary deliverance, even if it takes some time for the answer to come—even if it means getting stretched and tested, and even if it means some pain. The gain makes it all worth it.

Here, again, we need to look at the big picture. Sometimes God has a good reason for not answering a particular prayer, and it is not because He is indifferent or uncaring. Instead, it is because He wants to make something better out of us so that in the long run we will be blessed. Sometimes we do not receive the good because our Father wants to give us the great.

And as we cultivate an intimate relationship with Him, rather than allowing this to breed frustration, anger or unbelief, it can breed love and trust. That is also why we have verses in the Bible such as the following:

> Have mercy on me, LORD, for I am faint; heal me, LORD, for my bones are in agony. My soul is in deep anguish. How long, LORD, how long? Turn, LORD, and deliver me; save me because of your unfailing love. Among the dead no one proclaims your name. Who praises you from the grave? I am worn out from my groaning. All night long I flood my bed with weeping and drench my couch with tears. My eyes grow weak with sorrow; they fail because of all my foes.
>
> Psalm 6:2–7

How long, LORD? Will you forget me forever? How long will you hide your face from me? How long must I wrestle with my thoughts and day after day have sorrow in my heart? How long will my enemy triumph over me? Look on me and answer, LORD my God. Give light to my eyes, or I will sleep in death, and my enemy will say, "I have overcome him," and my foes will rejoice when I fall.

Psalm 13:1–4

These passages are in the same Bible that promises that God answers our prayers. This is because the Lord wants us to know that sometimes it will look as if He has not come through. Sometimes it will look as if He did not keep His word. And He knows we will feel like that, asking, "How long, Lord?"

But He also knows the end of the story, as these same psalms proclaim: "The LORD has heard my cry for mercy; the LORD accepts my prayer" (Psalm 6:9). And, "I will sing the LORD's praise, for he has been good to me" (Psalm 13:6). The psalmist lived to tell the story. As another psalm declares, "For his anger lasts only a moment, but his favor lasts a lifetime; weeping may stay for the night, but rejoicing comes in the morning" (Psalm 30:5).

Sometimes we do not know why an answer was delayed. We simply know that in the end, and often just in time, it came through. God had not forgotten about us after all.

Answers to Prayer Are Not Unconditional

At the same time, the Lord never promised to answer all of our prayers indiscriminately. Jacob (James) addresses some reasons for unanswered prayer, and he does it without pulling any punches.

What causes fights and quarrels among you? Don't they come from your desires that battle within you? You desire but do not have, so you kill. You covet but you cannot get what you want, so you quarrel and fight. You do not have because you do not

ask God. When you ask, you do not receive, because you ask
with wrong motives, that you may spend what you get on your
pleasures.

James 4:1–3

One reason we do not have is because we do not ask. Another reason we do not have is because we ask with wrong
motives. Or, we ask wrongly to spend it on our passions. This
means that if I ask God for a million dollars because I am
greedy, carnal and want to spend the money on drugs and
drink, my prayer will not be answered. That should be pretty
obvious. But many times our prayers have wrong motives that
are more subtle. God will not answer those either, and we have
no right to blame Him for failing to answer a selfish, carnally
motivated prayer.

Our Father really has our best interests in mind, which is why
getting in harmony with Him is the key to seeing our prayers
answered. "Take delight in the LORD, and he will give you the
desires of your heart" (Psalm 37:4). Or, in the words of Jesus, "If
you remain in me and my words remain in you, ask whatever
you wish, and it will be done for you" (John 15:7). God is saying
that when we find our delight in Him, we can ask whatever
we want, and He will answer—because our prayers will be in
harmony with His will.

Perhaps we sometimes focus on the "ask whatever you wish"
part and neglect the part where He says, "Remain in Me and My
words in you." Perhaps we expected God to give us the desires
of our heart without first yielding our hearts to Him.

That is why 1 John 5:14-15 states, "This is the confidence we
have in approaching God: that if we ask anything according to
his will, he hears us. And if we know that he hears us—whatever
we ask—we know that we have what we asked of him." When
we truly love Him and honor Him, our desires will align with

His, and what we pray will be in harmony with His will. When we pray according to His will, we receive wonderful and amazing answers.

We also have to remember that our prayers for other people will not always be answered instantly because they have a free will, too. In other words, if you are praying for the salvation of your neighbor, God will work in your neighbor's heart, but your neighbor has a choice to make. That is why we often pray for years for someone to come to faith. Over that period of time, the Lord is convicting and calling as He did with us in our own lives.

Thank God He does not give us control over other people's lives in prayer. That is witchcraft and manipulation more than true prayer. And remember that if you have that kind of power over others, then they have that kind of power over you.

Like Chopping Down a Giant Tree

Years ago, as I was thinking about this subject and was asking myself if my prayers really mattered or if they made a difference in the lives of those for whom I prayed, this picture came to mind. There was a lumberjack standing next to a giant tree swinging away with his ax. One swing. Two swings. Ten swings. Twenty swings. One hundred swings. Finally, the giant tree came tumbling down.

The lesson was clear: Every swing made a difference. Every swing weakened the resistance. Every swing brought the lumberjack closer to his goal.

It is the same with prayer. Every prayer lifted up in faith and in accordance with His will makes a difference. Every prayer reaches its destination. And every prayer is remembered. That is why the book of Revelation tells us that our prayers are like golden bowls full of incense that rise up before God (see Revelation 5:8; 8:3–4). Your prayers *do* ascend to heaven; they *are* heard at the throne of God. But good things often take time, and that is why, day by day, whether you see it or not, your prayers are making a difference.

Look at some of these lines from the apostle Paul where he describes how he prayed for different churches or individuals:

"I have not stopped giving thanks for you, remembering you in my prayers" (Ephesians 1:16).

"I thank my God every time I remember you. In all my prayers for all of you, I always pray with joy" (Philippians 1:3–4).

"We always thank God, the Father of our Lord Jesus Christ, when we pray for you, because we have heard of your faith in Christ Jesus and of the love you have for all God's people" (Colossians 1:3–4).

"We always thank God for all of you and continually mention you in our prayers" (1 Thessalonians 1:2).

"I thank God, whom I serve, as my ancestors did, with a clear conscience, as night and day I constantly remember you in my prayers" (2 Timothy 1:3).

The mighty apostle Paul, a true spiritual giant, prayed night and day for certain people. Over the course of years, he saw the fruit of his prayers. But it was anything but push a button and get a miracle. He persevered. He believed. And he gave thanks, even when he saw no evidence of change, and even when the people he prayed for resisted him. Not all prayers are answered instantly.

Consider the prayer that we call the Lord's Prayer. Jesus taught us to pray beginning with these words: "Our Father in heaven, hallowed be your name, your kingdom come, your will be done, on earth as it is in heaven" (Matthew 6:9–10). Hundreds of millions of people have prayed these words over the course of the last two thousand years, and we will continue to pray until Jesus returns. And yet every day, even though you may not see tangible answers to this prayer, it is being answered worldwide. People from every walk of life come to faith in Jesus, including atheists, agnostics, Muslims, Hindus, Buddhists and Jews. And the Gospel is having a powerful impact on whole regions in Africa and Asia.

Putting This All Together

There is no doubt that God sometimes answers our prayers instantly and dramatically, and we should be encouraged by that. When that happens to me, I write the answer down and share the news with others. At times like that, there is no denying God's reality. No one can tell you that He does not hear and answer prayer.

The problem is that over time we tend to forget those dramatic answers and live as if they never happened. This leads to discouragement, despair and even unbelief. May I encourage you to jog your memory and see if you can recall some undeniable answers to prayer? If so, let them be like footholds on the side of the mountain you are climbing, giving you confidence as you remember the faithfulness and the goodness of God. He has not changed.

Along with that exercise, understand the other aspects of prayer. You are building a relationship with God by sharing your heart with Him and telling Him your innermost thoughts. Be assured that He is listening carefully to every word. You are growing in character as He orchestrates things in your life to bring you into spiritual maturity, and you are growing in character as you determine to pray and not quit. Over the years you will look back with stunned amazement at the cumulative effect of your prayers. You will see the dramatic breakthroughs and the lasting transformation of lives.

Prayer does work when we understand its divine intent. And we will always be the better for it. No prayer that is offered up in harmony with God's will and in dependence on Him is ever prayed in vain. And when the veil is lifted one day, you will be stunned to see the effect of your prayers.

four

Permission to Doubt

n 2006, I was invited to participate in a panel discussion about Dan Brown's blockbuster novel *The Da Vinci Code*. In preparation for the discussion, I read the book carefully. Even though I was shocked by the book's claims (it was fiction but claimed to be based on facts), I was drawn in completely by Brown's writing skills. I could hardly put the book down.

In the years that have followed, I have read several of his other novels, the last one being *Origin*, which led me to ask myself, What is Dan Brown's problem? What happened in his upbringing that made him hostile to organized religion, in particular the Christian religion? The answer was not hard to find.

An article that the Associated Press published noted that Brown had shared this personal anecdote in a recent talk in New Hampshire. "'I owe everything to my parents,'" said Brown, whose father was a math teacher and whose mother was a church organist and piano teacher."[1] He said he was encouraged to ask questions at home as a child, and he believed in both his mother's religion and his father's science. But, he related, he became confused when the two conflicted.

One day at age thirteen he asked the priest at his mother's congregation how to reconcile what he perceived to be differences between the Bible and science. According to Brown the priest replied, "Nice boys don't ask that question."[2] And that, he explained in an interview on CBS, was the beginning of his search to find his truth.

How different things might have been if the priest had said, "What an excellent question! I'm so glad you asked. Let's explore it together." Perhaps if the priest had encouraged honest inquiry and had welcomed serious questions that explored apparent contractions between religion and science, Brown's life would have taken a very different direction.

Hard questions should not be discouraged. Doubts should not be squelched. True faith is not afraid of honest inquiry. Spiritual security breeds spiritual transparency.

Unfortunately, an opposite attitude often prevails in our churches and congregations. This attitude declares that to doubt is to commit the worst sin of all, and to have questions is to be disloyal. "How dare you question God and His Word!" This attitude only produces more doubt, which sometimes leads to complete unbelief, extreme skepticism, total apostasy and outright mockery.

A close friend of mine came to faith in 1971. He helped lead me to Jesus later that year. Both of us came out of a wild, drug-fueled lifestyle, and we both experienced radical conversions. Because of those radical conversions, we spent many hours in prayer and in the study of the Bible. There seemed to be a calling to preach on both of our lives, and two weeks apart we delivered our first sermons in August of 1973 at the age of eighteen.

But underneath the surface, my friend was wrestling with doubts and questions. He felt that he was not able to give voice to those doubts or raise those questions. This was not encouraged in our church, to say the least. He voiced very few of those doubts even to me.

Sometime later he was asked to preach again. Because he was struggling internally, preaching was an agonizing burden. Eventually this became one of the major factors that caused him to fall away from his faith. He remained away from the faith for more than forty years, after which time the Lord graciously brought him back.

Today, he is a committed believer who is strong in his faith. But this time around, he has a new feeling of freedom before the Lord. If he has questions about something in the Bible, such as a text that seems to present God in a negative light or that raises an ethical question, he feels little or no tension. He knows that Jesus is real, that his faith is real and that the Bible is God's Word. And he also knows that in this world we will have questions. If only he had felt this freedom decades ago, perhaps the last forty years would have looked totally different.

I am aware, of course, that there were many other factors that contributed to my friend falling away from the Lord. But feeling as if he could not express his doubts was certainly one of them, and it is one that could have been avoided easily. That is because almighty God, the Creator and Sustainer of all things, is not troubled by our questions or threatened by our doubts. As His children (especially those of us who are in leadership and ministry), we should not feel troubled or threatened. As Jude exhorts, we should "have mercy on those who doubt" or, as some translations say, "those who waver" (Jude 22).[3]

When was the last time you heard a sermon using Jude 22? We should show mercy—not condemnation, criticism, censure or condescending correction—to those who doubt.

And what, exactly, is doubt? Sometimes it is an inability to believe that God will do something for us personally. "I know the Bible says this, but I'm struggling to believe it will really happen for me." At other times, it is a struggle to believe that there really is a God. That includes trust that the God we believe in is the real God, that the Bible is truly His Word or that certain parts of the Bible are really inspired. Whatever the case, doubt eats away at our confidence and steals our peace.

If our whole life is based on faith, but we are not sure it is all real, how can we have peace, joy and confidence? How would you feel on your wedding day if you were riddled with doubts about the marriage? What if you found yourself questioning whether or not you really loved this person or if this person really loved you? Would you be joyful, or would you be anxious?

It is possible that this is how you have lived for years. You have wanted to believe, tried to believe and acted as if you believed, but in reality, you were in spiritual agony. What a difficult way to live! How God's heart must ache for you, and He would want you to know that this is not what He requires of you.

The Faith of a Father

We gain insight into this when we look at a dramatic encounter between the Lord Jesus and a distraught father. We'll look at the story as it is recorded in Mark 9, but you can also read about it in Matthew 17 and Luke 9.

Jesus had come down from a mountain with three of His closest disciples. He was confronted immediately with a crowd in turmoil. The religious leaders were arguing with His disciples. When He asked what was going on, the distraught father came forward. "Teacher, I brought my son to you, for he has a spirit that makes him mute. And whenever it seizes him, it throws him down, and he foams and grinds his teeth and becomes rigid. So I asked your disciples to cast it out, and they were not able" (Mark 9:17–18 ESV).

Jesus was stirred when He heard this. He replied, "O faithless generation, how long am I to be with you? How long am I to bear with you?" (Mark 9:19 ESV). He expressed an honest reaction to the great amount of unbelief that was in the air, even among His disciples. He then asked for the boy to be brought to Him, at which time the boy had a terrible seizure. "When the spirit saw him [the Lord], immediately it convulsed the boy, and he fell on the ground and rolled about, foaming at the mouth" (Mark 9:20 ESV).

What a dramatic, agonizing scene. It was a scene the father had observed too many times before. As he explained to the Lord, this had been the boy's lot since childhood. "And it [the demon] has often cast him into fire and into water, to destroy him. But if you can do anything, have compassion on us and help us" (Mark 9:22 ESV).

Jesus replied with these remarkable words, "'If you can'! All things are possible for one who believes" (Mark 9:23 ESV).

Yes, this was a strong rebuke to unbelief. Jesus was saying, "You are asking *if* I can? You are asking if I, the Son of God, the One who can calm a storm and raise the dead, can do anything in this situation? Did you actually say *if*? Everything is possible for the one who believes."

The boy's father responded immediately with these amazing words: "I do believe; help my unbelief!" (Mark 9:24 CSB).

And how did Jesus respond? Did He say to him, "Where is your faith, man?" Did He rebuke him and say, "You are no better than the religious hypocrites or My own disciples. You are so full of unbelief"?

Not at all. He commanded the spirit to leave the boy and never enter him again. He set the son free for life. He answered the father's cry despite his battle with faith.

You see, the father did believe, otherwise he would not have brought his boy to the Lord's disciples. And he wanted to believe, since he knew this was the only hope for his tormented son. Yet even as he professed his faith, he acknowledged his unbelief and asked for help. Jesus responded to the man's faith rather than choosing not to respond because of his unbelief.

My friend, God will help you believe. God will have mercy on your unbelief. God does understand, and He knows the condition of your heart. If He sees that you sincerely want to know the truth and that you are willing to give your all to Him if only you could be sure, He will not reject you.

The Faith That Doubts

What else could we expect? If the Father loved us enough to send His Son to die for us when we were sinful rebels, how much more will He help us—as His children—in our struggles to believe? After all, as much as simple, childlike faith is commendable, there is another kind of faith. It is a faith that struggles, a faith that wants to be sure but is not, a faith that battles with doubts, and a faith that is commendable in His sight. "Lord, I really want to believe, but I am struggling with unbelief." That is a prayer that is dear to His heart. You have permission to express your doubt.

What, then, do we make of the following strong word of rebuke?

> If any of you lacks wisdom, you should ask God, who gives generously to all without finding fault, and it will be given to you. But when you ask, you must believe and not doubt, because the one who doubts is like a wave of the sea, blown and tossed by the wind. That person should not expect to receive anything from the Lord. Such a person is double-minded and unstable in all they do.
>
> James 1:5–8

How do we reconcile these two concepts where one calls for mercy on those who doubt, and the other censors the doubter? And what about the very clear words that Jesus said to His disciples? "Truly I tell you, if you have faith and do not doubt, not only can you do what was done to the fig tree, but also you can say to this mountain, 'Go, throw yourself into the sea,' and it will be done" (Matthew 21:21).

Why did Jesus rebuke Peter for doubting? When the Lord was walking on the water in the midst of a storm and He beckoned Peter to walk on the water with Him, Peter began to do so. He walked on the water successfully until he took his eyes off of Jesus, because he became distracted by the wind and the waves. As he began to sink, he cried out to the Lord to save him, which Jesus did. But then the Lord said to Peter, "You of little faith. Why did you doubt?" (see Matthew 14:31).

Different Kinds of Doubt

How do we reconcile God's merciful heart toward doubters with His strong rebuke of doubters? I believe we are dealing with several different categories of doubt that are based on different heart conditions. Look with me at the following example of Zechariah who became the father of John the Immerser.

After the angel told him how he and his wife would have a child despite their advanced age, Zechariah asked, "How can I be sure of this? I am an old man and my wife is well along in years" (Luke 1:18). Gabriel responded, "I am Gabriel. I stand in the presence of God, and I have been sent to speak to you and to tell you this good news. And now you will be silent and not able to speak until the day this happens, because you did not believe my words, which will come true at their appointed time" (Luke 1:19-20). What a strong rebuke. It was as if Gabriel said, "How dare you doubt the very angel of the Lord!"

A few months later, Miriam (Mary) questioned this same angel. Gabriel came to tell her that she, a young virgin, would conceive and give birth to the Son of God. She asked, "How will this be, since I am a virgin?" (see Luke 1:34). This time, the angel's response to her question was totally different.

> "The Holy Spirit will come on you, and the power of the Most High will overshadow you. So the holy one to be born will be called the Son of God. Even Elizabeth your relative [this was Zechariah's wife] is going to have a child in her old age, and she who was said to be unable to conceive is in her sixth month. For no word from God will ever fail."
>
> Luke 1:35-37

That was it. No rebuke. No correction. No punishment. Only an explanation—a very glorious explanation at that.

What, then, was the difference? It was the same angel delivering two difficult to believe messages to two godly people whose responses were very similar. Zechariah asked how he could be sure of the promise since he and his wife were beyond child-bearing years, while Miriam asked how she could give birth to the Son of God since she was a virgin.

God saw a difference between the two. Zechariah, who should have known better and who should have believed, was rebuked. He seemed to be asking for a confirming sign, as if Gabriel's word was not enough. That is why God gave him a sign that was accompanied by rebuke. But to Miriam, who in apparent faith simply asked how the miracle would happen, He explained graciously through Gabriel how the Spirit would do His work. This helps us understand why in one verse doubt can be viewed one way, and in another verse it can be viewed very differently.

In the book of Jude, where we are called to have mercy on those who doubt, I believe Jude is speaking of someone who is weak and struggling but who wants to trust. We have focused on people such as this in this chapter (maybe this includes you?). But in the book of James, the focus is on someone who is double-minded or who wavers, not so much because of weakness, but because of lack of resolve. There is quite a difference between the two.

When it comes to commanding mountains to move—obviously a figure of speech for commanding massive spiritual obstacles to get out of our way—Jesus calls His followers to become strong in faith, to learn to trust Him, to recognize the power of the Spirit living within us and to understand the authority that we have in Jesus. In this context, He functions as a holy life coach who is challenging us to live up to our potential, so to speak. He is calling us to explore the power of faith.

As for Peter sinking in the water, there was no good reason for him to doubt. By this time, He had seen Jesus perform all kinds of extraordinary miracles. He had seen Him calm the wind and waves with a simple rebuke. Plus, at that very moment, he had seen Jesus walking on the water, and *he, himself,* was walking on the water. It is only when he took his eyes off of the Lord that he began to sink and cry out in terror. Peter should have known better. He was rebuked rightly for his doubt.

One size does not fit everyone. That means there are times when God will correct, chide or ask us lovingly, "Why did you doubt Me?" Rather than being put off by that, we should be encouraged by it. God is saying to us that we have more faith than we realize, that we are stronger than we know, and that He is confident we can do better. Be heartened by a word such as that.

If the rebuke is even stronger, as it is in the book of James, that means that we are living a double life willfully. We are of two minds, and we cannot decide who we will follow. When we are corrected with a strong word such as this, it means we need to take stock of our lives and make some serious, quality decisions. God will bless us as we do.

But then there are those of us who really want to believe, like the father of the tormented boy. We simply do not know how. We have learned the hard way that we cannot snap our fingers and manufacture faith. We cannot will ourselves to believe. That is where we cry out to the Lord with all sincerity and candor, saying, "God, I do believe—or, at least, I am trying to. Help my unbelief!" Or, "God, I want to believe in You, but I am not even sure You are real. If you are really there, please help me!"

Remember that Jude 22 said, "Be merciful to those who doubt." As we look at the context of this passage, it seems to refer to believers who have been led astray by false teachers and who are now wavering in their faith. But as noted by Professor Peter Davids, they are not to be condemned for their struggles. Rather, they should receive our compassion. Davids writes:

> Mercy is indeed a core Christian virtue; Jesus taught it (Matt 5:7; Luke 6:36; 10:37), and later writers emphasize it (Jas 2:13, which appears in a context of showing mercy instead of judgment). The church has often preferred judgment to mercy, but that is not what the Scriptures teach, for the followers of Jesus are told to show to others the mercy that God has already shown to them. So in Jude some are doubting, not sure who is right. Rather than condemning them for their uncertainty about the truth or their entertaining the possibility that the teachers whom Jude opposes could be right, Jude calls for mercy, being gracious toward them and showing the same type of acceptance and love that God shows.[4]

It is one thing to be a mocker, a hardened skeptic, a faultfinder or a complainer. It is another thing to be a struggler, someone who wants to believe but who wavers, or someone who would gladly take the plunge but is not sure which way is right. To a person such as that—perhaps, to you?—God says, "Come to Me with your baggage, your questions and your doubts, and make a commitment to keep coming, seeking and asking with a humble heart and an open mind. You will find the truth, and the truth will set you free."

Determined to Find the Truth

Shortly after I came to faith, my dad asked me to meet with the local rabbi. My father was thrilled that I was off of drugs, but as a Jew, he was concerned with my new Christian faith. I accepted his invitation gladly, as I was eager to share the Gospel with this rabbi. He befriended me quickly but then began to challenge what I believed. After all, I could barely read Hebrew whereas he had been studying it all his life. And he had learned it from his father, who had learned it from his father. Who was I to tell him what to believe? I was turning seventeen and relying on an old English translation, while he was reading straight from the Hebrew Bible and relying on brilliant rabbinic commentaries from previous generations. How could I teach him?

We continued to dialogue, and over time he introduced me to other rabbis. He was hoping something would spark within me that would call me back to our traditions. And some of the rabbis I met with were deeply sincere men, very learned and extremely kind. They seemed as passionate about God as I was. They also spent hours every day reading the Bible and praying. What made me right and them wrong?

I knew that Jesus had changed my life radically, and I knew that my ongoing experience with the Lord was real. At the same time, I was determined to love God with all my heart *and* all my mind, following the truth wherever it led. I continued with this attitude as I started college, all the way through earning my Ph.D. Year after year, my faith was challenged from a multitude of different angles, sometimes from a hostile (but brilliant) atheist professor and sometimes from a friendly (and also brilliant) traditional rabbi.

I did not stick my head in the sand, and I refused to accept cheap solutions to difficult problems. I continued in my determination to follow the truth wherever it led, and I sought God earnestly through the whole intellectual and spiritual process. Yet the more I did this, the stronger my faith became. I became more convinced about the things I believed, and my heart and my mind came into alignment.

So do not fear your questions or your doubts, whether they are experientially based or intellectually based. The One who is the Author of truth, the One whose knowledge surpasses our knowledge infinitely more than our knowledge surpasses that of an ant, is not troubled by your struggles. He will have mercy on you. He will make you strong. You must simply do your part, cry out to Him, seek Him, study and learn. He will not fail to do His part. One day you will realize that He has already done the heavy lifting.

Come to Him as you are today and say, "Lord, I do believe" or "I want to believe. Help my unbelief!"

five

Perhaps It Was Wrong Theology That Failed You?

See if you relate to the following scenario that depicts a devastating spiritual experience. You found yourself in a crisis. You or someone you loved needed a miracle, so you prayed. You believed. You stood firmly on God's promises. You felt sure that He would come through, but He did not. The answer never came. The breakthrough never materialized. The healing never happened. God failed you.

At least that is what you concluded. Either the God of the Bible was not true, or there was no God at all. And that was the end of your spiritual story. You could never believe the same way again.

But could there be another possibility? Could it be that God did not fail you at all? Could it be that it was faulty theology that failed you? Let's say you were taught that as a follower of

Jesus you had authority over demons and disease using passages such as these in support:

> When Jesus had called the Twelve together, he gave them power and authority to drive out all demons and to cure diseases (Luke 9:1).

> Jesus called his twelve disciples to him and gave them authority to drive out impure spirits and to heal every disease and sickness (Matthew 10:1).

> "Heal the sick, raise the dead, cleanse those who have leprosy, drive out demons. Freely you have received; freely give" (Matthew 10:8).

> "I have given you authority to trample on snakes and scorpions and to overcome all the power of the enemy; nothing will harm you" (Luke 10:19).

Let's say you were also taught that if someone did become sick, then the prayer of faith offered by the elders would make that sick person well (see James 5:14–16). That's because God promised to be our healer (see Exodus 15:26; 23:25–26; Deuteronomy 7:14–15), the one who forgives all our sins and heals all our diseases (see Psalm 103:1–5), and by whose stripes we are made whole (see Isaiah 53:4–5). And Jesus promised us that whoever believes in Him—that includes you and me—would not only perform the same miracles He performed, but they would perform even greater miracles (see John 14:12).

Maybe this was your biblically based theology. At times you even saw miracles that confirmed what you believed. Then you came down with a chronic, debilitating condition, and no matter what you did—praying, taking authority over the sickness, rebuking the devil or receiving anointed prayer—you were not healed. What happened to the promises? What happened to your God?

Or maybe you went through something even more extreme. Maybe you watched your child die of cancer. Or you lost a close loved one to a tragic, painful disease. What happened to mountain-moving faith? What happened to the power of the Spirit? What happened to the promises?

Some Christians go through horrific experiences such as these, but rather than lose their faith they simply adjust their theology. They realize that they had misconceptions about God or the Bible. They continue as strong believers, but they no longer hold to the same beliefs about healing and faith.

But with many others, their theology of healing and faith is so foundational to their entire relationship with God that when that theology fails, they assume God failed them. Either that, or the God they worshiped and followed does not really exist. This leads to a devastating emotional and spiritual collapse. Is this what happened to you?

If so, can we go back to those traumatic events? Your whole world has been destroyed, and your perception of reality is now uncertain. What is real and what is not? If you have lived through a crisis like this—or are living through one right now—you can explain the pain, trauma and upheaval far better than I can. Still, you are reading this book. Let's pursue some solid answers together.

The Easy Answer Versus the True Answer

It would be easy for me to say, "Actually, the days of healing and miracles are over. That was for New Testament times only. Jesus performed miracles to prove He was the Messiah, and the apostles performed miracles to vindicate their message. Now that we have that message—the New Testament—there is no more need for the miraculous."

In other words, I could tell you that you were taught incorrectly. You did not receive a healing miracle because the days of miracles are past. So, as agonizing as it was to watch your loved one die or to experience chronic pain and not be delivered, I could tell you this happened because God does not heal or deliver anymore. It was not God who failed you; it was your theology that failed you.

Yes, I could say those words to you, and there are certainly many Christians who would agree, but I do not hold to that theology. I believe that God still heals today. I believe that the days of miracles are not over. I believe that God responds to our faith. And when someone is sick, my first response is to pray for his or her healing. How, then, do we work this out? Does God heal or not? Should we expect miracles or should we not? Or is it hit or miss?

Let me say first that the Bible is very clear about God's healing power and His will to heal. He performed miracles in the past, and He performs miracles to this day. Even this passage in Jacob (James) tells us to expect healing in our local assemblies.

> Is anyone among you in trouble? Let them pray. Is anyone happy? Let them sing songs of praise. Is anyone among you sick? Let them call the elders of the church to pray over them and anoint them with oil in the name of the Lord. And the prayer offered in faith will make the sick person well; the Lord will raise them up. If they have sinned, they will be forgiven. Therefore confess your sins to each other and pray for each other so that you may be healed. The prayer of a righteous person is powerful and effective.
>
> James 5:13–16

It is not wrong, then, to pray for healing, and it is not wrong to expect healing. And there are millions of testimonies of miraculous healing even to this day. Back in 2017, I received this report from a colleague regarding a healing that took place through prayer in the late '90s in Pensacola, Florida. At the time, I knew nothing of it.

> The baby was four months old. Her eye was half shut, was lazy and was constantly leaking fluid. Doctors did not know why, and her medicine was not helping. You walked up during prayer time and laid hands on the baby's head without talking to the mother holding her. After you walked away, the mother looked down at the baby and watched the eye open, straighten, and the leaking stop. From that moment on [at this point, more than twenty years later] there was no problem, including no leaking.

That sounds like the Lord to me!

Randy Clark, a Christian leader who often teaches on the subject of divine healing, takes teams to pray for the sick. He teaches his teams what the Bible says about healing, and he gives them simple guidelines for prayer. These are ordinary Christians he takes along with him, not the cream of the crop or the elite. The following testimony is one of many amazing accounts he shared in his book *Eyewitness to Miracles*. This one involved a man who had been totally blind for fifty years.

> His eyes were white from about an eighth of an inch thickness of scar tissue that covered the entire pupil and cornea. Instead of Hispanic brown eyes, his were milky white. He was totally blind, having not seen a thing for fifty years, and he went blind as a five-year-old boy . . . [when a] man had accidently spilled muriatic acid in his eyes.[1]

The man came for prayer in one of Randy's meetings, and a woman prayed for his healing, but nothing happened. She prayed again and again and again—for four hours, even though the healing team members had been instructed not to stay too long with any one person since there were about 6,000 people in the meeting. But she felt a strong impression in her heart to keep praying for him, so she did.

Three days later Randy received a call from the man's pastor who said, "This man could not see anything when the night was over. Neither could he see anything the next day and night, but on the third morning, though he went to bed totally blind, he woke up with brand-new eyes and clear vision."[2] The doctors at the hospital where his records were kept and where his story was well known were absolutely astonished.

They kept asking him, "Tell us, again, how is it you can see?"

These are two examples of literally millions of miracles of healing and deliverance experienced by ordinary people after other ordinary followers of Jesus prayed for them in His name.

Yes, Jesus really rose from the dead, and He continues to perform miracles to this day. Book after book has been written on the subject that recount these extraordinary acts that are often with detailed documentation.[3] In fact, not only did Randy Clark document such miracles, but other scientific studies have provided similar documentation, including healing of the blind and deaf.[4]

Yet at the same time, millions of others are not healed. Most Christians who get terminal cancer are not miraculously healed. The vast majority of Christians who are blind, deaf or crippled do not receive miracles. That is why Randy Clark wrote a little book titled, *The Thrill of Victory—The Agony of Defeat*.[5] In the book, he not only recounts absolutely amazing testimonies of healing but also heartbreaking stories of those who were not healed.

What Is the Truth?

At this point, you're probably asking a few questions. How do we sort this out? Can we expect healing or not? And what is the "wrong theology" I am referring to when I say that perhaps it is wrong theology, not God, that failed you? Let me answer the second question first.

The wrong theology I am referring to is the theology that tells you that true believers never get sick. That if you have enough faith, you can just rebuke sickness and pain and, 100 times out of 100, the sickness and the pain will disappear. That people with the gift of healing will see perfect results. That a good God would never allow His children to suffer pain, let alone die of a debilitating sickness. That, in Jesus, you are even protected from car accidents and natural disasters. All if you have enough faith!

As we will see in chapter 9, the book of Job addresses this wrong theology head on. Sometimes tragic things happen to the godliest people in the world, the result of which is acute suffering. That's in the Bible, too. As with the subject of prayer, which we addressed in chapter 3, we have to look at healing the same way. We need to read all of the Bible and not just some of it.

Unfortunately, many Christians today have been taught a false message that leads to unrealistic expectations. And when those expectations are shattered, they lose faith entirely. They conclude that the Bible is not true and that the God of the Bible is not real. In reality, the problem was never the Bible or the God of the Bible. It was a false picture of the Bible and the God of the Bible.

To give you a vivid illustration, let's say you weighed 400 pounds, had arthritis in both knees, and suffered with severe insomnia. I came to you and said, "If you will change your diet and start to eat healthily, you will lose fifty pounds a month. Within two months, your arthritis and insomnia will disappear entirely." You try out the new, healthy diet for two months, after which you have lost a total of thirty pounds. But rather than being excited, you are discouraged.

"I thought I was going to lose fifty pounds a month! I should have lost one hundred pounds by now." And, of course, your arthritis and insomnia have not disappeared. With that, you conclude that the diet is a sham, and you go back to your unhealthy eating.

The problem was not the diet. The problem was wrong expectations. If you had stayed on the diet and made it into a lifestyle, you would have been able to reach and maintain your ideal weight within a few years. Those other conditions would probably have gone away as well.

It's the same with the Bible and healing. The promises are real, and there are countless testimonies of miraculous healing. They cannot be denied, and they point to the reality of God and the truthfulness of His Word.

But the Bible also speaks of people who were not healed. It even speaks of people close to the apostle Paul who were not healed. One was Timothy who was a spiritual son to Paul. Paul wrote to him urging, "Stop drinking only water, and use a little wine because of your stomach and your frequent illnesses" (1 Timothy 5:23). Wine was sometimes used medicinally in the ancient world, and Paul told Timothy to drink some because of his health issues.

Why didn't the mighty apostle drive the sickness out of Timothy, tell him to exercise his own faith for healing, or have others in the community pray for him? We simply do not know.

But we do know:

1. Paul was not afraid to speak openly about Timothy's frequent illnesses.
2. This did not mean that Timothy did not have faith.

3. He gave Timothy practical, medical advice rather than counsel him only to pray until a miracle happened.

In another letter, Paul says this in passing, "I left Trophimus sick in Miletus" (2 Timothy 4:20). We do not know why Trophimus was sick, but Paul was not afraid to say that he was sick. His sickness did not reflect badly on either of them. Some scholars believe that Paul, himself, battled with sickness, perhaps even chronically (see Galatians 4:13–14; 2 Corinthians 12:6–8; 1 Corinthians 2:3).[6] Yet without question, God performed many miracles through him. That means you can have the gift of healing without being healed yourself.

In this world people get sick, including followers of Jesus. There are men and women of God who are invalids. There are paraplegics and quadriplegics who are champions in the faith. That is a fact of life. One of the most joy-filled, confident men of God I have ever met was a brother from Africa who was living in Boston. When he was a boy, a serious disease ravaged his village and killed many. He went blind, but lived, and he considered himself blessed to be alive. After moving to the states and graduating from college, he attained a law degree and went into pastoral ministry.

Unfortunately, some Christians have been misled terribly by their teachers to the point that they will not even admit to being sick. "If I confess that I'm sick, then I'm agreeing with the devil. I will not acknowledge these lying symptoms!" Perhaps you once held to a theology like that.

A Holy Tension

What, then, is a right theology of healing? One extreme says that God no longer heals and that the promises of healing and miracles were for Bible days alone. The Bible clearly refutes that view, as does Church history. The other extreme says that God always heals and that if you have enough faith you will never get sick. Other verses in the Bible refute this, along with the experience of several billion believers over the last two thousand years.

The right theology leaves us with a holy tension. It promises healing and encourages us to ask God for healing, assuring us that miracles do happen. But it also reminds us that we are in a fallen, broken world, that we have not yet arrived in the perfect world to come, and that in this world there will be pain, sickness and premature death.

The good news is that God can be near to us right in the middle of our sickness. He can help us in the midst of our pain, and He can use us to touch others even while we are struggling. It is the same with our holiness and sanctification, which we'll cover in more depth in the next chapter. We are promised victory over sin and are told to consider ourselves dead to sin. And yet, we still battle with sin in this world. We will not attain perfect holiness until the world to come.

To repeat, we live with a holy tension. We are thrilled when we see miracles take place, and we pray for such miracles to happen. (We also thank God for medical science, and we recognize our responsibility to care for our body.) It is amazing to see sickness and pain leave instantly, and this points to the goodness and reality of God. When the Gospel is being preached in a new area, the miracles are often more pronounced as God makes Himself real to the people and confirms the message of Jesus. Jesus is alive, and miracles are for today.

Yet we also recognize that miracles are not the norm. Our bodies wear out, and there is a real devil who attacks and harasses. Calamities and tragedies befall us, and we sometimes get sick. That is in the Bible, too. It is not only for the wicked but for the righteous as well.[7]

So God did not fail you after all. A wrong theology may have let you down, and I am truly sorry you were taught poorly. That only poured salt into your wounds. But the solution is not to abandon the Lord. The solution is to abandon the wrong theology and to embrace the right theology of the Word. It may not always be simple, but it is true.

We live in the age of "already but not yet,"[8] meaning the age in which many of God's eternal promises have broken through in this world, but we have not yet seen the fullness of those promises. That means you can take every miraculous intervention as a token of the goodness of the world to come, a world in which there is no sickness, pain or suffering, while still living in this broken, imperfect world. And whether we are healthy or sick, or whether we live or die, we learn that Jesus is more than enough. Once you grab hold of that, you will never be shaken.

six

We Are Part Sinner and Part Saint

came to faith in Jesus in New York in the winter of 1971, which meant that everyone in the congregation was wearing long sleeves. The women wore long sleeved dresses and the men wore long sleeved shirts, normally with suit jackets. But beyond the outward appearance, I was amazed by the character of the people I got to know. What loving saints they were! They were joyful, kind and forgiving. I was especially impressed with the older believers, in particular some of the men in their sixties (which seemed ancient to me as a sixteen-year-old kid). I assumed they had always been saved.

As the temperature warmed up, the sleeve length changed as well. I was shocked by what I saw. Saintly old Brother Chris, who greeted us as we came through the doors and blessed us as we left, had a tattoo! (Remember, this was early 1972, and tattoos were far less common.) I learned that before Brother Chris came to the Lord he had been arrested and had served on a chain gang. At one point, he had been thrown into the trunk of a car to be killed, but God spared his life. Who knew?

Then there was his compatriot, Brother Chief. As a boy, he had caused much mischief. He would grab cats off the street, run over to a church building while a meeting was going on, open the front door, throw the cats in and run. The name stuck even though the mischief of his boyhood was far behind him. Many years later, I learned from his son that he had prayed for me daily for months before I came to faith, and he continued to do so for many years after.

But as time went on, I learned something else, and it was crushing. Some of the people in the church who I esteemed not only had checkered pasts, but some of them were *still* quite flawed. How could this be? I thought they were saintly. I thought that Jesus radically changed people. I thought our church was special. (For the record, Brother Chris and Brother Chief were always great examples.)

Looking back today, I recognize that many of these people were really devoted to the Lord and set fine examples in their personal lives. But they were hardly perfect. They did not shed their humanity once they were born again. They were saintly to some degree, but they were also sinful. And they probably had some ongoing strongholds in their lives. Does this deny the reality and power of the Gospel?

Maybe you had a similar experience, except that it was much more intense. Perhaps a spiritual leader hurt you deeply, maybe even to the point of abuse. Or perhaps it was not that extreme, but still very painful. Maybe the members of your church seemed to abandon you at your weakest moment or during your most difficult trial. And since God's people let you down, it caused you to question the reality of His existence. At the very least, it caused you to question your own congregation and its doctrines and beliefs.

Or maybe the failure was on your end. Maybe you disappointed yourself. Maybe there was a stronghold in your life or a sinful habit that you simply could not defeat. The Bible says that we have victory over sin, that Jesus broke the power of sin and that a true believer would not continue in sin (see John 8:32–36; Romans 6; 1 John 3:4–10). You wondered to yourself, *What is wrong with me? Why can't I change?*

In some cases, this leads to self-condemnation, hopelessness and backsliding. In other cases, this process leads to rejection of the Bible. Either way, the failure to overcome the power of sin can easily lead to a crisis of faith if you believe that God could never forgive you after did something ghastly. You think to yourself, *Surely, He has no interest in someone like me.*

Part Sinner, Part Saint

The fact is that even at our best when we are walking closely with the Lord, we are still part saint and part sinner, part transformed and part in the process of transformation, part spirit and part flesh. The New Testament is very clear that even leaders might fail and fall badly (see 1 Timothy 5:17–20).

This is not because God's grace is insufficient. It is because the Lord does not stop us from making sinful choices. He does not take away our freedom. The same way that Christians still need to sleep and eat as everyone else, our appetites and earthly desires do not disappear completely. That is why the Bible often urges us to be vigilant when it comes to battling fleshly lusts (see 1 Peter 2:11–12).

But the fact that people fail does not mean the Gospel is not true, and the fact that human beings make sinful choices does not mean that God is guilty. Would you prefer that He took away your free will to ensure that you never hurt anyone? If you don't want that to happen to you, then you cannot expect God to stop others from acting freely, even if that means their choices can hurt you. That is the price we all pay for our freedom.

We are in a broken world, and people do evil things. This is another reason why we need a Savior. He will never fail us or let us down. And when people hurt us and wound us, He will take us through. He will even make us better people if we cooperate with Him. You can be assured that our Savior fully understands what it means to be hurt, betrayed and abandoned even by His closest friends.

And yet, Paul does call the believers "saints" (1 Corinthians 1:2 ESV). Jesus said that we are to be the salt of the earth (see Matthew 5:13). The Church is supposed to shine (see Matthew 5:14–16; Philippians 2:14–15). And we are called to love one another as Jesus loved us (see John 13:34). But that doesn't mean that we always live up to the ideal. Why condemn the whole because of the sins and failings of some? This would be like a child concluding that parenting and families are bad because of an abusive father.

If you can step back from your personal hurt or disappointment, I bet you can find many wonderful qualities among your Christian friends. You probably witnessed genuine acts of sacrifice and compassion. You probably saw real kindness and compassion. Don't throw all of that away because some people really let you down.

You might say, "But you don't understand. It wasn't just that the pastor sinned against me. It was that the other leaders rallied around the pastor and then my friends rallied around the other leaders. Where was the love? Where was the justice? I found more loyalty in the bar than in the church."

I hate to hear that. Sometimes Christians do very ugly things. To make matters worse, they often cover their guilt with Scripture and prayer. What hypocrisy.

But remember that in the gospels, the ones Jesus denounced in the strongest terms were the religious hypocrites. The Lord hates this even more than you do. And you can be assured that if the people who sinned against you do not truly repent and make things right with you, they will have to deal with Jesus.

Read the following verse carefully and take it to heart. Although it refers first to little children, I believe it can be applied to God's children in general. Jesus said, "See that you do not despise one of these little ones. For I tell you that their angels in heaven always see the face of my Father in heaven" (Matthew 18:10). Our Father takes this very seriously indeed.

Reacting to Pain

Where does this leave you? When people hurt you, you have several choices. You can allow yourself to become bitter and angry, but this will bring you more turmoil and pain. You can develop a victim mentality and withdraw into your own shell, but this will sap you of life, vitality and vision. Or you can choose to forgive as God forgave you. You can determine to turn your stumbling blocks into steppingstones. Why let the devil win? Why let circumstances determine your destiny? Why let other people decide your future?

The Bible records disputes between leaders, including Paul and Barnabas, who had a falling out. And Paul had to rebuke Peter publicly (see Acts 15:36–41; Galatians 2:11–14). The Bible also records Peter's terrible denial of Jesus three times as Jesus was being beaten and interrogated (see Matthew 26:69–75). Yet God used Peter, Paul and Barnabas mightily in spite of their shortcomings.

Over the years, I have been hurt deeply and felt betrayed by people close to me. (And I imagine some have felt deeply hurt and betrayed by me, although I would never consciously do such a thing.) Yet overall, these were good people. They were not monsters. And some have become good friends again years after the painful disputes. There is a lot of good in God's Church, and we should not lose hope because of a bad experience (or even a series of bad experiences).

Something else you should consider is that what people intend for evil, God can use for good. The very thing meant to destroy us can end up saving many lives. Think of what happened to Joseph in the Bible. When he was seventeen, his older brothers, who were jealous of him, sold him into slavery and then faked his death so that their father would think he had been killed by a wild animal. What cruelty. He was purchased by the Ishmaelites, then was sold as a slave to an Egyptian master. Then, because he refused to have sex with his master's wife, she claimed that he had tried to rape her. The more innocent he was, the more he suffered.

He ended up as a prisoner in Egypt languishing in a dungeon where he would likely have died. But God had another plan. After suffering in prison from ages seventeen until thirty—for thirteen long years—he was supernaturally raised up by the Lord to become Pharaoh's right-hand man. In that position, he saved the nation of Egypt from famine and, more importantly, saved his own family, including all of his brothers. He said to the men who sold him into slavery, "You intended to harm me, but God intended it for good to accomplish what is now being done, the saving of many lives" (Genesis 50:20).

Perhaps the same could hold true for you. Perhaps people really did intend to hurt you—your own family or the larger family of the Church—but God is a redeemer who is at work turning tragedies into triumphs. And often, the worst things that happen to us become steppingstones for God's grace. This can be true for you. It's clear that Joseph became a better man as a result of his betrayal and pain. Without the terrible experience, he might not have developed the character qualities needed for him to fulfill his divine destiny.

It is true that there are some very wicked people who are living double lives, preying on the vulnerable one day and preaching from the pulpit the next. There are dangerous predators who are abusing the flock. But from my experience, having worked with leaders around the world for the better part of fifty years, these very bad apples are the extreme exceptions to the rule. Jesus warned us, saying,

> "Watch out for false prophets. They come to you in sheep's clothing, but inwardly they are ferocious wolves. By their fruit you will recognize them. Do people pick grapes from thornbushes, or figs from thistles? Likewise, every good tree bears good fruit, but a bad tree bears bad fruit. A good tree cannot bear bad fruit, and a bad tree cannot bear good fruit."
>
> Matthew 7:15–18

How, then, can we blame the Lord for the actions of corrupt people, especially when He warned us to be on our guard against them?

I don't mean that we should walk around full of suspicion, wondering if every pastor we meet is a sexual predator or money-hungry false prophet. Obviously, you want to be able to trust your leaders, which is how some of you got deeply hurt. Few things are more devastating than for your spiritual leader, the one who is supposed to represent Jesus, to sin against you.

But here is what you cannot forget: Jesus saw it, and it broke His heart. Your pain was His pain. Your wounds were His wounds. And until you are whole again, He will carry that pain. The worst thing that you could do is run *from* Him at a time such as this. Instead, run *to* Him. You will find that He will help restore your hope and renew your confidence. And you will find that over time He will send you some high-quality, faithful friends.

What if you disappointed yourself? What if you sinned to the point that you believe you have been disqualified from God's love? What if you looked at Scripture and then at your own life, and rather than saying, "The Bible isn't true," you concluded, "I'm obviously not a child of God. If I were, my life would be different."

It is certainly possible that you had a church experience rather than a Jesus experience, meaning, that you made a commitment to the Christian faith (or were raised in the Christian faith) rather than made a commitment to the Lord. In other words, it is possible that you were not truly saved or born again at all. But that is actually good news, since the door is wide open for you now to be truly born again, to become a genuine child of God, to receive forgiveness and new life and to be transformed by God's power. Maybe the reason you could never fly is because you had never received your wings.

If you realize that you may have had a form of religion without experiencing God's power, or if you now recognize that you were a false convert, cry out to God for mercy and forgiveness. Talk to Him right now as if He was in the room with you—in reality, He is! Tell Him honestly and candidly that you have sinned and have fallen short of His standards. Don't make excuses or blame others. Say that you believe that Jesus died for your sins and rose from the dead, confessing Him as Lord. God will hear your cry![1]

He will not refuse or cast you away. Not a chance! As Jesus said, "All those the Father gives me will come to me, and whoever comes to me I will never drive away" (John 6:37). Jesus also gives you this personal invitation: "Come to me, all you who are weary and burdened, and I will give you rest. Take my yoke upon you and learn from me, for I am gentle and humble in heart, and you will find rest for your souls. For my yoke is easy and my burden is light" (Matthew 11:28–30).

It may be, though, that the scenario I just described does not apply to you. To the best of your knowledge, you have asked the Lord to forgive you. You felt that most of your life was changed, but there were areas in your life that you could never conquer or that dragged you down continually. After a while, you gave up the fight, thinking, *What's the use? There's obviously something wrong with me, and God must hate me.*

Well, you are right, and you are wrong. There is something wrong with you, but God does not hate you. The fact is that there is something wrong with all of us. It is called the fallen human nature, the flesh, and sin. And as long as we live in this world we will be at war with the flesh.

That's why it is easier to be lazy than to be disciplined. That's why we have a sweet tooth and crave candy, chocolate and unhealthy sugars. That's why it's easier to oversleep than to get up early and why it's easier to overeat than to eat in moderation. That's why even a happily married man has to resist lustful thoughts toward other women. That's why we fall into so many sins: sins of the tongue, sins of the heart, sins of the body and sins of the mind. And, to say it again, that is why we need a Savior.

"But," you say, "I thought that Jesus actually changed us. I thought that the proof of the new birth was a new life. I thought that in Jesus we died to our sins and they no longer have mastery over us."

All that is totally true. Every word of it. At the same time, we often live through periods of life where we can relate to Paul's own experience.[2] He wrote:

> I do not understand what I do. For what I want to do I do not do, but what I hate I do. And if I do what I do not want to do, I

agree that the law is good. As it is, it is no longer I myself who do it, but it is sin living in me. For I know that good itself does not dwell in me, that is, in my sinful nature. For I have the desire to do what is good, but I cannot carry it out. For I do not do the good I want to do, but the evil I do not want to do—this I keep on doing. Now if I do what I do not want to do, it is no longer I who do it, but it is sin living in me that does it. So I find this law at work: Although I want to do good, evil is right there with me. For in my inner being I delight in God's law; but I see another law at work in me, waging war against the law of my mind and making me a prisoner of the law of sin at work within me. What a wretched man I am! Who will rescue me from this body that is subject to death? Thanks be to God, who delivers me through Jesus Christ our Lord! So then, I myself in my mind am a slave to God's law, but in my sinful nature a slave to the law of sin.

Romans 7:15–25

Can you relate to this? Have you felt like this in your own life? Be assured that the Lord understands. After all, He is the one who made you, He is the one who sees into your heart and life, and He is the one who inspired Paul to write these words. This is here for you.

Don't allow your sins and failures to separate you from God. Don't allow your personal disappointments—some of which may be terribly embarrassing and humiliating—to put a wall between you and the Father's mercy. Jesus shed His blood for your sins—every single one of them. In fact, before He died for you, He saw every sin you would ever commit, even the ugliest, the foulest and the most inexcusable. He saw those sins, and He died for those sins—and for you. And if you confess them afresh to God, He will wash you clean. That is what He does. That is who He is.

Overcoming

But the story does not end there. If you put your focus in the right place, you will learn to overcome. If you will not dwell on your failings, but rather on God's goodness and grace, you will see His Spirit working in your life. If you will keep looking to Jesus while looking away from your shortcomings and sins, you will find victory over your sins.

Look carefully at Paul's words. He explains to his readers that they have died to sin through Jesus, as symbolized by water baptism. Just as Jesus rose from the dead, so we also rise again in Him to live a new life.

> For we know that our old self was crucified with him so that the body ruled by sin might be done away with, that we should no longer be slaves to sin—because anyone who has died has been set free from sin. Now if we died with Christ, we believe that we will also live with him. For we know that since Christ was raised from the dead, he cannot die again; death no longer has mastery over him. The death he died, he died to sin once for all; but the life he lives, he lives to God.
>
> Romans 6:6–10

You say, "I put my faith in Jesus and was baptized, but I certainly didn't die to sin. In many ways, the battle is the same as ever."

I understand. But Paul didn't stop with verse 10. He also said, "In the same way, count yourselves dead to sin but alive to God in Christ Jesus" (Romans 6:11). Do you grasp what he is saying? Something real *has* taken place spiritually, but you must take hold of it. Something *has* changed, but you must make it your own.

Paul begins with the Greek word *logizesthe*, which means "consider yourselves" or "count yourselves." Specifically, it means that we are to count ourselves dead to sin but alive to God in Christ Jesus. Let me share with you the words of Professor Joseph Fitzmyer, a brilliant New Testament scholar, who writes in typical scholarly language. Read this through, and then I'll explain what he was saying in simple terms. Speaking of the word *consider*, he writes:

> It seeks to elicit the act of faith, which accepts the salvific event embodied in baptism. This is the conclusion of Paul's argument, as he expresses his view of the problem of the integration of Christian life. Ontologically united with Christ through faith and baptism, Christians must deepen their faith continually to become more and more psychologically aware of that union. Thus consciously oriented to Christ, Christians can never again consider sin without a rupture of that union. For they are "dead to sin." It is not just that they are to imitate Christ (because he has died to sin, so you too); Christians are also to arm themselves with the mentality that they are dead to sin; for that is what has happened to them in the baptismal experience.[3]

What Professor Fitzmyer is saying is that there was a real spiritual transaction that took place through our joining with Jesus. In a very real way we died to sin, and the power of sin was broken over our lives. But we must grow in our faith to take hold of that truth and to realize that we are not who we used to be. Sin is beneath us, and we have received power over it. As that truth becomes real to us, we will start to live differently.

Let's read Romans 6:11 once more, but this time we'll continue to verse 14:

> In the same way, count yourselves dead to sin but alive to God in Christ Jesus. Therefore do not let sin reign in your mortal body so that you obey its evil desires. Do not offer any part of yourself to sin as an instrument of wickedness, but rather offer

yourselves to God as those who have been brought from death to life; and offer every part of yourself to him as an instrument of righteousness. For sin shall no longer be your master, because you are not under the law, but under grace.

Romans 6:11–14

Paul is urging us to change our thinking. He is asking us to consider ourselves dead to the power of sin and to refuse to let sin reign in our bodies. We are to offer ourselves to God with every part of our body and mind. Because we are under grace rather than law, sin is no longer our master. When we were under law, we were slaves to sin. The law told us what to do and what not to do, but it did not give us the power to overcome. The law condemned us in our guilt.

In Jesus, we are under a new system—the system of grace. He took our condemnation so that we no longer stand condemned. When we were born again, we received a new nature by which we are empowered to say no to sin.

You do not have to be a slave to lust, hatred, greed, gossip, selfishness, bitterness, perversion or whatever sin enslaved you. You must renew your mind to the reality that the power of sin has been broken over your life. As you do that by meditating on God's Word, speaking out His promises (like the verses we read in Romans 6) and taking practical steps of wisdom to avoid temptation, you will see real change. You are an overcomer in Jesus. That, my friend, is spiritual reality.

It doesn't mean that you will never sin or fall short, but it does mean that the pattern of your life will be changed. And if you absolutely hit a brick wall that you cannot overcome, you can uproot that stronghold for good through prayer, counseling or deliverance. Countless millions attest to this reality.

Almost forty years ago, I had a friend who had been addicted to cigarettes for many years. He hated the habit and felt it was sinful in God's sight. Yet whatever method he tried, natural or spiritual, he could not get free. One day, I felt a tremendous prompting of the Spirit to pray for him, believing that the Lord was going to deliver him. He, too, felt the Spirit touch him as we prayed. The next day he smoked more cigarettes than any other day in his life, but saying with every cigarette, "Jesus has set me free! I am no longer addicted to smoking!"

And that was the last day he smoked a cigarette. As crazy as the story sounds, he was convinced that he whom the Son sets free is free indeed (see John 8:36). No matter what he was experiencing, he knew the Lord had worked in his life. Soon enough, it became a reality. He stopped smoking for good.

The same can happen with you. And it is not a matter of psyching yourself up or playing mental gymnastics, like trying to convince yourself that you are a bird, an airplane or an astronaut. It is, instead, a matter of getting your mind to grasp what is really true. It is similar to a coach telling a gifted athlete who has trained hard and is ready for victory, "You can do this!" For that athlete, it is simply a matter of taking hold of that reality. The British evangelical leader John Stott explains this in simple terms.

> This "reckoning" is not make-believe. It is not screwing up our faith to believe what we do not believe. We are not to pretend that our old nature has died, when we know perfectly well it has not. Instead we are to realize and remember that our former self did die with Christ, thus putting an end to its career. We are to consider what in fact we are, namely *dead to sin and alive to God* (11), like Christ (10). Once we grasp this, that our old life has ended, with the score settled, the debt paid and the law satisfied, we shall want to have nothing more to do with it.[4]

Think of it like this: You have been sick and in frail health for years, but through an amazing new treatment, you become healthy and well. But you still have the old mindset, so you continue to limit your physical activities. You think of yourself as sickly. One day your doctor sees you and says, "What are you doing? You are a healthy person! Start exercising and enjoying life. You are not sick anymore!"

Professor Leon Morris, a biblical commentator, says,

> Since Christ died to sin and since the believer is dead with Christ, the believer is dead to sin and is to recognize the fact of that death. This does not mean that he is immune to sinning. Paul does not say that sin is dead but that the believer is to count himself as dead to it. He feels temptation and sometimes he sins. But the sin of the unbeliever is the natural consequence of the fact that he is a slave to sin, whereas the sin of the believer is quite out of character. He has been set free. Paul tells him that he is to recognize that where sin is concerned he is among the dead. He has been delivered from its dominion. And death is permanent. Once united to Christ he must count himself as dead to the reign of sin forever. He is to reckon also that he is *alive to God*. His life now has a positive orientation; it is directed to the highest there is, the service of God.[5]

Did you grasp that? Before we knew the Lord, sin was the natural course of our lives. Now, in Jesus, it is "quite out of character." That's why we grieve and feel bad about sinning. Some of us used to boast about our sin. It was part of our identity, part of our lifestyle and something we indulged in gladly. Now it's the opposite. We do not want to live in it. We are ashamed of it. We know it is wrong. Why? Because we have a new nature. We are not who we used to be.

Again, what happens when you do sin and fall short? Jesus has it covered. He has already paid the price. Come to Him, acknowledge your guilt and receive forgiveness afresh, fully and completely. Be cleansed of every sin!

Of course, God's mercy is not an excuse to sin. It has negative consequences and is never our friend. Sin destroys. But knowing Jesus paid for our sins means that the Lord has everything covered. When we fall short, He is still our Savior. We can look to Him, and He will carry us higher until we are truly transformed. If you can understand this, the devil can never trip you up again, and your own mind cannot condemn you.

In fact, to be perfectly candid, we have no clue how ugly, foul and sinful we are outside of God's mercy. But He sees it all—perfectly, vividly, clearly. If we could see ourselves from His perspective, we would die of a heart attack instantly. Yet He not only sees our sin, but He calls us His beloved children. He calls us saints.

So I, too, will consider myself a saint even though I sometimes sin. In Jesus, I am an overcomer and a new creation who has a clean heart and an ever-renewing mind. In Jesus, so are you!

seven

Is the Bible an Outdated and Bigoted Book? (Part 1)

As I have read some of the stories of those who have walked away from the faith, especially in the younger generation, there is a theme that comes up over and over again. People declare, "I no longer believe the Bible is God's Word because it is filled with bigotry, violence and hatred. I once thought it was beautiful, but I can no longer accept what it says."

If that's your perspective, then this is hardly a debate about abstract philosophy or esoteric theology. This is about people, about your friends and family members. This is about your gay brother and his partner who are two of the nicest people you know. Is God sending them to hell because they're gay? They didn't ask to be gay. In fact, they prayed that God would take the feelings away. But He did not. Now He's going to damn them to eternal punishment because of the love they have for each other? You wouldn't be the first person to say, "If that's the God of the Bible, I don't want Him."

Others feel that the Bible is misogynistic in that it presents women as lower than men and affirms an oppressive patriarchal system. For others, the Bible's sanctioning of slavery is the deal breaker. The violence in the Bible, specifically the extermination of the Canaanites (including women and children) by Joshua and the armies of Israel, pushes others away. Is this any better than ISIS killing innocent victims in Allah's name?

It doesn't solve the problem when someone says, "Well, if God says it, I believe it and that settles it!" It's not enough when you're told, "You just have to trust God. He knows what He's doing." How does this help you if you're not even sure God exists? And if you do believe that He exists, do you really want to follow a God like that? How can you trust someone whose character you find repulsive?

Professor Richard Dawkins, one of the most famous contemporary atheists, wrote these stinging words:

> The God of the Old Testament is arguably the most unpleasant character in all fiction: jealous and proud of it; a petty, unjust, unforgiving control-freak; a vindictive, bloodthirsty ethnic cleanser; a misogynistic, homophobic, racist, infanticidal, genocidal, filicidal, pestilential, megalomaniacal, sadomasochistic, capriciously malevolent bully.[1]

Was he right?

Before we get into specifics, let me share with you some descriptions about the God of the Bible that were taken from the same Old Testament that Professor Dawkins referenced. Read these verses slowly and digest them. Let them paint a clear picture in your mind. This is a description of our heavenly Father.

> The LORD is compassionate and gracious, slow to anger, abounding in love. He will not always accuse, nor will he harbor his

anger forever; he does not treat us as our sins deserve or repay us according to our iniquities. For as high as the heavens are above the earth, so great is his love for those who fear him; as far as the east is from the west, so far has he removed our transgressions from us. As a father has compassion on his children, so the LORD has compassion on those who fear him; for he knows how we are formed, he remembers that we are dust.

Psalm 103:8–14

The LORD is gracious and compassionate, slow to anger and rich in love. The LORD is good to all; he has compassion on all he has made.

Psalm 145:8–9

He upholds the cause of the oppressed and gives food to the hungry. The LORD sets prisoners free, the LORD gives sight to the blind, the LORD lifts up those who are bowed down, the LORD loves the righteous. The LORD watches over the foreigner and sustains the fatherless and the widow, but he frustrates the ways of the wicked.

Psalm 146:7–9

For the LORD your God is God of gods and Lord of lords, the great God, mighty and awesome, who shows no partiality and accepts no bribes. He defends the cause of the fatherless and the widow, and loves the foreigner residing among you, giving them food and clothing. And you are to love those who are foreigners, for you yourselves were foreigners in Egypt.

Deuteronomy 10:17–19

But Zion said, "The LORD has forsaken me, the Lord has forgotten me." [God answers:] "Can a mother forget the baby at her breast and have no compassion on the child she has borne? Though she may forget, I will not forget you! See, I have engraved you on the palms of my hands; your walls are ever before me."

Isaiah 49:14–16

Who is a God like you, who pardons sin and forgives the transgression of the remnant of his inheritance? You do not stay angry forever but delight to show mercy. You will again have compassion on us; you will tread our sins underfoot and hurl all our iniquities into the depths of the sea.

Micah 7:18–19

The LORD appeared to us in the past, saying: "I have loved you with an everlasting love; I have drawn you with unfailing kindness."

Jeremiah 31:3

That is a picture of the God of the Old Testament. That is how His followers described Him based on their own experience and history with Him. And remember, all of this was written before Jesus came to earth and revealed the full extent of the Father's love. This was before the perfect Son of God died for all of our sins and before the Lord established a new and better covenant with Israel. Yet even here, in the pages of a book that some find troubling, we find the most beautiful, wonderful descriptions of God—a God full of wonder and goodness and compassion and love.

A God Who Takes Delight in His Creation

Generally speaking, those of you who are younger are more environmentally conscious than my generation, displaying much more care for creation. In that light, it's fascinating to see how the Bible describes God's intricate care in creating this world and filling it with all kinds of creatures. The Lord asked Job these questions after Job challenged God's justice.

"Do you know the time when the mountain goats give birth? Have you watched the calving of the deer? Have you counted the number of months they fulfill and do you know when it's time to give birth? They crouch, they bring forth their offspring, they send forth their young. Their little ones become healthy and grow strong in the open field. They leave, and don't return to them. Who set the wild donkey free and who loosed the cords of the onager, whose home I made the desert and his dwelling place the salt land? He scorns the din of the city; the shouting of the driver he doesn't hear. He ranges the mountains, his pastureland, searching after every green thing."

Job 39:1–8, my translation[2]

The God who cares about mountain goats and wild donkeys certainly cares about you and me. The Lord even asked Job, "Who provides sustenance for the raven when its little ones cry out to God, when they wander around without food?" (Job 38:41, my translation). Our heavenly Father set up an amazing ecosystem, and in the midst of it, He expresses His concern for baby birds. Does that sound like some kind of monster to you? You might be a tree-hugger, but God created that tree and designed the system that sustains it.

In another fascinating passage, the Lord asked Job, "Who carves out a channel for the torrents of rain and a path for the thunder bolts to rain upon a land without inhabitant, a desert devoid of man, to satiate the desolate wasteland and to cause the grass to sprout?" (Job 38:25–27, my translation).

You might ask, "What's the point of all this? What message am I supposed to get? What was God trying to tell Job?"

Remember that Job had questioned God's character when he felt that the Lord had treated him unfairly. (We'll discuss this more in chapter 10.) Yet in this passage, the Lord explains that some of His rain is poured out on uninhabited land. But why does this happen when no one sees what happens? No one is there (not animal, not human) to enjoy the fruit of the land. Yet even there, where no human eye can witness God's care and where no person can benefit from it, the dry land is satiated with life-giving showers. What does this say about the nature of the Lord? He is a God of life, not death, and He is a God of abundant flourishing, not deprivation. God is saying to Job, "Factor that into your equation when you try to figure out who I am."

Now, let's move from the realm of nature to the realm of human life. This same God who crafted the earth and the animal kingdom also carefully crafted us as human beings. He intricately designed our bodies in ways that the world's best scientists cannot match. As noted by author and biochemist, Isaac Asimov, the human brain is "the most complex and orderly arrangement of matter in the universe."[3]

But what, exactly, does this mean? Peter Line, who earned his Ph.D. in the area of neuroscience focusing on brain electrophysiology, wrote:

> The human central nervous system (CNS) consists of the brain and spinal cord, including roughly 100 billion nerve cells, and about 10 times more neuroglia, or supporting cells .... While the 1.4 kg mass (3 pounds) of tissue that makes up the brain might not look impressive, it is often described as the most complex arrangement of matter in the known universe. The 3-D world we experience, with sights, sounds, tastes, smells, and bodily sensations, is essentially constructed by our brains. Every second awake, signals from our environment of one kind

or another are converted into electrical currents (of ions—called action potentials) by sensory receptors in the skin or by special senses (like smell, vision, and hearing). These currents, bearing no obvious resemblance to the information they carry, travel into the brain via nerve fibres (cables, if you like), and there somehow the information is decoded. The original signal is interpreted so that a person sees the world in vivid colour, hears the sound of a waterfall, experiences the heat of a hot summer's day, feels a breeze on the skin, and smells the sausages on the barbeque. And this can happen all at the same time; i.e., really fast. How does the brain do this? No one knows, but it must involve signal processing way beyond our current understanding.[4]

How remarkable. We are living in the twenty-first century, and yet no one knows how the brain does much of what it does. It is "way beyond our current understanding." And these few paragraphs barely touch on the wonder of the human brain. It's the same with our heart, our circulatory system, our bones and our nerves. We are designed amazingly and intentionally, right down to the tiniest cells. In fact, the cell is a world unto itself, and evolutionary scientists cannot account for the development or the operation of the cell.[5]

And what about our DNA, in which God uniquely coded each of us as human beings? The Science Focus website gives us a perspective of the wonder of this divine code:

Try holding a piece of string at one end and twisting the other. As you add twist, the string creates coils of coils; and eventually, coils of coils of coils. Your DNA is arranged as a coil of coils of coils of coils of coils! This allows the 3 billion base pairs in each cell to fit into a space just 6 microns across.[6]

A human hair is fifty microns across, yet God squeezes three billion base pairs of DNA coding into a space that is eight times smaller than one human hair. Not only this, but, "If you stretched the DNA in one cell all the way out, it would be about 2m long and all the DNA in all your cells put together would be about twice the diameter of the Solar System."[7] What an amazing God! Who can even begin to fathom this?

Chaplain Roger Wilson paints a simple and clear picture of this truly miraculous design:

> I wonder if we really understand how we each one came to be. Let me share with you a stunning perspective. We all began in the same way, one cell from your mom found one cell from your dad. The cell from your mom carried half of your DNA and the cell from your dad carried the other half. They merged into one single cell. Out of this one cell the DNA began a brand new DNA code.
>
> This cell began to write out what we now know is the 3 billion character description of who you are, written in the language of God. This DNA, 3 billion characters, describes who God ordained you to be. In that one little simple cell. Scientists say that if you took the DNA out of that one little simple cell, and stretched it out, it would be 6 feet long, 3 billion characters. So amazing that if I would read your DNA, reading one character every second, night and day, it would take 96 years just to read the description of you.[8]

This is truly mind-boggling information, telling us more about our Creator than about ourselves. What kind of mind could design something such as this?

Male and Female

Yet there is something else that is revealed in this description of human origins, something that is also quite intentional. God made us male and female with the same purpose of excellence and exactitude. He uniquely designed our bodies right down to our DNA coding and made us for reproduction and intimacy. He specifically crafted our temperaments for complementarity—in other words, we supplement and complete each other. And He made us to thrive, multiply and fill the earth.

Just think about it. A husband and wife come together face-to-face in an act of sexual and romantic intimacy. In the midst of passionate love, a baby is conceived. At that very moment, that child has its own unique set of DNA coding. How is this even possible? Over the months, that baby is sustained within the mother's womb before it is delivered and nursed. The mother is made for this—literally. And for the mom and dad welcoming that child into the world, it really feels like a miracle.

Two men cannot produce this, no matter how much they love each other. Nor can two women. Their biology does not allow for it. They were not designed physically for each other regardless of the depth of their commitment. This is biology, not bigotry. And if you believe in a Creator, then this is all by design.

That's why, to this moment, every human being who has been born on this planet (aside from Jesus!) had a biological mother and father. And each human being is the unique by-product of his or her biological mother and father. To repeat, this is biology, not bigotry, and in saying this, I am not saying a single negative word about gays and lesbians. I am simply talking about how we were designed intricately and intentionally by God.

Think of it like this. In your kitchen drawer there are knives, spoons, and forks, each with a specific function. You eat soup with a spoon, not a knife or a fork. You cut meat with a knife, not a spoon or a fork. You pick up the pieces of meat with a fork, not a knife or a spoon. Each one has a specific function. That's why it was made the way it was made.

In the same way, you use a screwdriver for one thing, a hammer for another thing and a wrench for yet another thing. You also have one kind of saw for one kind of cutting and another kind of saw for another kind of cutting. There are specific functions for each tool. Using the right tool for the right job is the difference between success and failure.

I could go on with scores of different examples, but I'm sure by now you get the point. God fashioned males one way and females another way for very distinct purposes, both biologically and sociologically. The differences between us are intentional and essential.

If you were raised by your mother and father, you know that they had lots of different perspectives on parenting. When you were two years old, it wasn't your father shouting to your mother, "Be careful!" as she threw you into the air and caught you just before you hit the ground. No, it was your mom shouting, "Be careful!" as your dad hurled you high over his head.

It's also true that women have a tempering effect on men. They help domesticate them, and I mean that in the most positive sense of the word. (As a friend of mine asks, how many married men are in gangs?)

But when it comes to a man plus a man, you do not have the influence of a woman. That's why, on average, homosexual men have more sexual partners than do heterosexual men. (This holds true for homosexual couples as well. On average, they have more sexual partners over the years than do heterosexual couples.)[9] Something essential is missing in a male-male or female-female relationship, no matter how loving, committed or nice the couple may be. It's a matter of design.

Now, you might differ with some of what I have said, but I want to make sure one thing is clear: this is not a matter of bigotry or hatred. It is a matter of believing that our Designer knew what He was doing. If I tell you that a fish with gills was made for swimming and a bird with wings was made for flying, that would not be bigotry. That would be biology. It's the same when it comes to transgender issues. If we are convinced that God designed us with a beautiful biological purpose, why should we radically alter that purpose? Why should we remove a young woman's breasts or a young man's private parts and put them on hormones for life in an artificial attempt to turn them into the opposite sex? Doesn't it make much more sense to seek out the root cause of their dysphoria—their feeling of being trapped in the wrong body—and help them find wholeness from the inside out? How is that hate? How is that bigotry?

And in light of the marvel of the reproductive design of our bodies—it, too, is stunning, amazing and meticulously made—why on earth would we want to sterilize for life an eighteen-year-old who feels trapped in the wrong body? Wouldn't love call us to look for a better way, a way that does not mutilate perfectly healthy bodies and rob people of their ability to have biological children?

There are people who suffer from what is called body identity integrity disorder, where they feel they should not have a right leg or a left arm. Their mind map tells them something is wrong, and they have a desperate desire to remove a limb. (Some want to blind or maim themselves in other ways in order to feel whole.)[10] Why, then, do we criticize the doctor who saws off a perfectly healthy limb to give his patient peace of mind while commending the doctor who removes a woman's healthy breasts to give her peace of mind?[11]

And what do we say to the growing number of men and women, many of them in their twenties, who now deeply regret the decisions they made to amputate healthy body parts because of transgender identity?[12] If you have the courage, go to the SexChangeRegret.com website, and read some of the stories. Or read a book like *Trans Life Survivors*, compiled by

Walt Heyer, a man who lived as a woman for years and who also had radical sex-change surgery.[13] As Walt explains at the beginning of the book,

> *Trans Life Survivors* showcases emails from thirty or so people, selected from among hundreds who have written to me, concerning what many call "the biggest mistake" of their lives, or sex change. I present this representative group of gut-wrenching personal testimonies to put the transgender advocates on notice: we survivors know there is deep trouble in Trans La La Land. I wrote this book because I want others to catch a glimpse of the raw emotions and experiences of people who are harmed by the grand—and dangerous—experiment of cross-sex hormones and surgical affirming procedures.[14]

This is the voice of someone who lived the life, who understands the trauma of feeling as though he was trapped inside the wrong body, who took the hormones, who got the surgery, and who then realized that Jesus wanted to fix him from the inside out. Is this the voice of love or the voice of hate? And when we tell the parents of a ten-year-old that there is a better way than putting their child on puberty-blocking drugs, prescribing them a hormone regiment for life (to stop the body from functioning the way God intended it to function) and subjecting them to irreversible sex-change surgery while still in their teens, is this the voice of hatred or the voice of love?

Before you accuse me of exaggerating the issues, take the time to read Abigal Shrier's book, *Irreversible Damage: The Transgender Craze Seducing Our Daughters.*[15] And for solid arguments from a neuroscientist, see Dr. Debra Soh's *The End of Gender: Debunking the Myths about Sex and Identity in Our Society.*[16]

Those who identify as transgender are not physically sick people with diseased limbs that need to be amputated or with cancer-filled breasts that need to be removed. These are physically healthy people who need God's help from the inside out. Why mutilate the beautiful handiwork of the Lord? Why try to change them into something they were never meant to be? And again, even if you differ with some of this Scripture-based perspective, can you at least see that it makes sense and is motivated by genuine care?

Designed to Reproduce and Flourish

The first chapter of the Bible tells us that when God created the world of nature and the animal world, He designed everything to reproduce after its own kind. Trees, animals and people would not simply reproduce in a random way. Rather, each would reproduce after its own kind, with apple trees producing apples (and more apple trees), cats producing cats (rather than dogs), and humans producing humans. This is how they were designed.

With that in mind, ask yourself what would happen if a scientist put ten committed gay couples on an isolated island, five male couples and five female couples, all averaging twenty-five years old. The island is a true paradise, replete with farmlands and houses and everything needed for human thriving. And these couples, each madly in love, agreed to take part in a 100-year study. What would be their legacy after one century on this isolated island?

In keeping with the plan, 100 years after the experiment began, the grandson of the original scientist comes back to the island. What does he find? He finds a desolate, uninhabited island with some scattered graves and a couple of rotting skeletons. That's it. There were no future generations because there was no reproduction.

Now, ask yourself what would happen with the identical scenario, except the ten couples were all heterosexual. They, too, would all be gone in 100 years, but the grandson of the original scientist would meet a few of their older kids (quite aged by now), along with their kids and the kids of those kids. There would be multiple generations of children. There would be expanded farmlands and more houses. The original twenty might now be sixty or eighty or even one hundred. That's because God designed males to be with females and females to be with males, and He designed us for productivity.

That doesn't mean that every couple must have children or that some heterosexual couples will not be barren. And that certainly doesn't mean that gay couples threaten world population, as if the presence of gay couples on the earth stops heterosexual couples from having children. But it does mean that we were designed with a purpose, and to have a belief system that recognizes that this was the Designer's intent is not to be hateful or bigoted. That's why the Bible, following the Designer's guidelines, established marriage as the lifelong union of one man and one woman. Can you really call this homophobic?

Let's also think of this in terms of trajectory. Multiply truth endlessly and what do you have? Lots of truth. It is the same with love or goodness or any other truly virtuous trait. Multiply it over and over, and you end up with something wonderful.

But what if we do the same with hate, bitterness or anger? Keep multiplying that and soon enough you have murder, war and every kind of atrocity. What about sexual impurity? Multiply that over and over and soon enough you have every kind of imaginable (and even unimaginable) perversity. Would you agree?

Then let's apply this line of reasoning to issues of sexual orientation and gender identity. If you multiply "male and female He created them" from Genesis 1, you end up with generations of male-female relationships that are reproducing over and over. If you multiply different sexual orientations and variations in gender identity (represented in part by LGBTQ+), you end up with lists such as the following one. (These lists are real and are meant to be taken seriously; this one goes all the way back to 2013).

The following are the 56 gender options identified by ABC News:

- Agender
- Androgyne
- Androgynous
- Bigender
- Cis
- Cisgender
- Cis Female
- Cis Male
- Cis Man
- Cis Woman
- Cisgender Female
- Cisgender Male
- Cisgender Man
- Cisgender Woman
- Female to Male
- FTM
- Gender Fluid
- Gender Nonconforming
- Gender Questioning
- Gender Variant
- Genderqueer
- Intersex
- Male to Female
- MTF
- Neither
- Neutrois
- Non-binary
- Other
- Pangender
- Trans
- Trans*
- Trans Female
- Trans* Female
- Trans Male
- Trans* Male
- Trans Man
- Trans* Man
- Trans Person
- Trans* Person
- Trans Woman
- Trans* Woman
- Transfeminine
- Transgender
- Transgender Female
- Transgender Male
- Transgender Man

- Transgender Person
- Transgender Woman
- Transmasculine
- Transsexual
- Transsexual Female

- Transsexual Male
- Transsexual Man
- Transsexual Person
- Transsexual Woman
- Two-Spirit[17]

This list was compiled when Facebook yielded to pressure from LGBT activists who protested Facebook's limited choices when filling out personal bios for the social media giant. But it was not enough. Yes, 56 options were not enough (even though you could choose ten at once). Instead, Facebook added another option: fill in the blank![18] This is what happens when you deviate from the God-ordained pattern.

One person explained, "I'm not a girl or a boy, I'm a gender smoothie, I mix it all up together."[19] Another stated that he preferred not to be identified as male or female. Instead, he preferred to be called Tractor.[20] And we are supposed to embrace this as normal?

Today, on an increasing number of college campuses, professors are required to ask students how they want to be identified. Pronoun options include

- ve/vis/vir/verself
- jee/jem/jeir/jemself
- lee/lim/lis/limself
- kye/kyr/kyne/kyrself

- per/per/pers/perself
- hu/hum/hus/humself
- bun/bun/buns/bunself
- it/it/its/itself.[21]

There are even websites devoted to listing *multiple gender identities* (meaning, descriptions of people who claim multiple gender identities in their own lives). One site lists these: ambigender; bigender; blurgender; collgender; conflictgender; cosmicgender; crystagender; deliciagender; duragender; demiflux;

domgender; fissgender; gemelgender; gendercluster; gender-fluid; gendersea; genderfuzz; genderfractal; genderspiral; genderswirl; gendervex; gyaragender; libragender; ogligender; pangender; polygender; and trigender.[22] To repeat: this is what happens when you deviate from "male and female he created them" (Genesis 1:27).

To write these things does not mean that we are not compassionate toward those who struggle with their gender identity. Their pain is often intense, and I cannot imagine the internal anguish they have experienced. But it is love, not hatred, that causes us to shout out, "There is a better way than affirming someone as genderfractal or blurgender. Surely, this is not the intent of the Creator and the Designer."

Our Issue with an Aggressive and Destructive Agenda

Still, you might say, "But why do you conservative Christians make such a fuss about gays and transgenders as if they were the biggest problem in our country? Even if you disagree with them, why not leave them alone?"

The answer is that we did not start this war. We are simply responding to the encroachment of an aggressive LGBTQ agenda that has marched into our schools, our churches, our courts, our places of business, our social media networks and beyond. How can we not respond? As far back as 2014, I began to warn that those who came out of the closet wanted to put us—meaning conservative believers—into the closet. For sharing this warning, I was widely mocked and vilified. But a few years later, people began to say, "Bigots like you belong in the closet!"

Since then, we have seen people lose their jobs for holding to biblical values. We have seen students get kicked out of college programs for their Christian beliefs, and we have seen angry crowds calling for Christians to be thrown to the lions. We have seen godly conservatives compared to ISIS, the Taliban and the Nazis. And that is just the tip of the iceberg.[23]

We have also seen this aggressive agenda march right into our schools, to the point that nursery schools will not allow teachers to refer to their students as "boys and girls," since that would be making a gender distinction. We have also seen the latest fad that features drag queens reading to toddlers in libraries (supported by the American Library Association, no less). One of the drag queens stated plainly that the goal was to "groom" the children so they would be more accepting of homosexuality and the like.[24] Some of the drag queens have been previously arrested for sexual abuse of children.[25] Yet here they are reading to toddlers while being celebrated by the media.

It is not bigotry or hatred that causes us to stand. It is not hatred of gays, lesbians or transgenders as people. God forbid. It is love that is based on the Lord's design for humanity as found in the Bible that causes us to stand. We also believe the stories of the many ex-gays around the world (they are far more numerous than you would imagine).[26]

And we know that for some, radical change is possible. We also know that for everyone, a better life can be found in Jesus. What is so outdated, bigoted or hateful about this?

Seen, then, from a different perspective, the Bible, God's Word, is about beauty, about design, about flourishing and about liberation. It is anything but a dangerous book to be avoided. In its pages are found the ways of life.

Let's continue this discussion into the next chapter. There are solid answers for your deep questions and concerns.

eight

Is the Bible an Outdated and Bigoted Book? (Part 2)

As we continue looking at Scripture and asking who the God of the Bible really is, I'd like you to consider the following question. Do you think the human authors of the Bible would paint an amazingly beautiful picture of the Lord on one page, emphasizing His compassion and goodness and longsuffering, and then, on the very next page, depict Him as a cruel monster? Would that make sense? Would it be logical?

You might say, "That's the whole problem. I do see the passages about God being love, but what do I do with all the passages where God appears sadistic and cruel? Where He sanctions killing and destruction? Where His laws are outrageously harsh? It really sounds like two different gods are being described."

God Is Love

Let's take some time, then, to think this through together. Personally, I'm convinced that our God is always good and only good, meaning that nothing He ever does is bad. As Jacob (James) explained in the New Testament, "Every good and perfect gift is from above, coming down from the Father of the heavenly lights, who does not change like shifting shadows" (James 1:17). That is who He is. Or in the words of John, who knew Him very well, "This is the message we have heard from him and declare to you: God is light; in him there is no darkness at all" (1 John 1:5). John also wrote:

> Dear friends, let us love one another, for love comes from God. Everyone who loves has been born of God and knows God. Whoever does not love does not know God, because God is love. This is how God showed his love among us: He sent his one and only Son into the world that we might live through him. This is love: not that we loved God, but that he loved us and sent his Son as an atoning sacrifice for our sins.
>
> 1 John 4:7–10

Yes, God is love.

Even when the Bible speaks of God being holy, the authors are using that word as a positive term, an amazing term, a wondrous term. He is perfect love, perfect goodness, perfect justice, perfect compassion, perfect righteousness and perfect justice— all without stain, blemish or deviation. Perfect holiness is love perfected.

With this in mind, when we read other passages of Scripture that trouble us, we need to remind ourselves that the verses are all talking about the same God. There must be a good reason that He does what He does. Maybe there's an important perspective you are missing?

To give you an analogy, imagine that you walked into a room and saw an unconscious woman strapped to a table with her right leg cut off and lying on the floor, blood splattered everywhere. Next to her stands a man with a sharp saw, and both the man and the saw are covered with blood. What would you do? You would probably scream, run for your life—you might be next!—and then call 911.

But what if we change a few details? The woman on the table is your mother. She was rushed to the hospital after being found in a ditch by the side of the road where she was trapped in her car for three days in freezing weather. Her left leg has suffered severe frostbite, and the gangrene is about to spread to the rest of her body leading to her inevitable death. But the doctor, a skilled surgeon, has managed to amputate her leg. This surgery saved her life.

What would your reaction be now? You would be thankful your mother was alive, even while missing a limb, and you would be deeply grateful to the doctor who saved her life. The man with a saw goes from a monster to a lifesaver. A change in perspective changes everything.

It's the same with the God of the Bible. When we understand Him correctly, we understand that everything He does is good. We understand this not by sticking our heads in the sand and calling good evil and evil good, but rather by digging deeper and asking the question behind the question. Then we discover the truth.

Old Testament Laws

Let's consider some of the harsh penalties in the Old Testament for sexual sins. (I am *not* advocating these for today; I'm simply comparing the morality of ancient Israelite society with our society.) Adulterers would be put to death, as would Israelites who followed other gods. A man who raped an unmarried woman would be required to marry her—if that is what her father wanted—and he could never divorce her. Isn't this like punishing the woman twice? And what could be more draconian than executing adulterers?

What we don't understand is that the culture of the ancient Middle East was very different from the culture today, and harsh penalties such as these were fairly common in the surrounding nations.[1] In many ways, the biblical society was a far more moral society than ours today, one in which honor and shame played very important roles.

You might already be thinking, "The Bible can keep that world to itself. I wouldn't want to live in such a miserable society." Please allow me to challenge that thinking for a moment.

Consider a world in which virginity was prized and sexual intimacy was sacred, reserved for one's spouse. Imagine a world in which adultery was viewed as a horrific violation of trust and a shock to the community, and a woman's honor was valued highly as something to be cherished and protected. In a society such as that, the severe penalties for sexual sin were understandable. They were viewed as horrific violations of human dignity, as things that ought not to be done and as things that destroyed and degraded. Dare we, in 21st century America, judge the morality of such a society?

A recent study noted that in America:

> By the 2010s, only 5 percent of new brides were virgins. At the other end of the distribution, the number of future wives who had ten or more sex partners increased from 2 percent in the 1970s to 14 percent in the 2000s, and then to 18 percent in the 2010s. Overall, American women are far more likely to have had multiple premarital sex partners in recent years.[2]

And note that opening statement: "By the 2010s, only 5 percent of new brides were virgins." I wonder how ancient Israelites would view a society such as ours?

Who are we to look down our noses at biblical culture and question the morality of these ancient laws? Which culture is more moral, the culture of America today—with its rampant pornography, sexual perversion, sexually transmitted diseases (STDs) and broken homes—or the ancient biblical culture? Speaking of STDs,

- New estimates show that there are about 20 million new sexually transmitted infections in the United States each year.

- Young people, between the ages of 15 to 24, account for 50% of all new STDs, although they represent just 25% of the sexually experienced population.

- 46% of American high school students have had sexual intercourse and potentially are at risk for human immunodeficiency virus (HIV) infection and other STDs.[3]

An article published in 2018 in the *Los Angeles Times* stated that "among the 34 studies that included data on sending sext messages, the average prevalence was 14.8%. That means more than 1 in 7 teens admitted to—or boasted about—sending a sexually explicit message, photo or video of themselves."[4]

As for pornography, "64% of young people, ages 13–24, actively seek out pornography weekly or more often . . . . 35% of all internet downloads are estimated to be porn-related . . . . The 'teen' porn category has topped porn site searches for the last seven or more years." In addition, "Recorded child sexual exploitation (known as 'child porn') is one of the fastest-growing online businesses," and "624,000+ child porn traders have been discovered online in the U.S."[5]

Compare this to a society in which it was shocking for a woman to lose her virginity before marriage and where adultery carried the death penalty. Which society would you say was a more moral society? And do we as contemporary Americans have any right to make a moral judgment on these ancient Israelite laws?

As for the law that a man who raped a woman would be required to marry her and could never divorce her, that was meant for the protection of the woman. In fact, there are similar laws in some countries until this day.[6] You see, in some parts of the world, a woman who has been raped is considered unfit for marriage. Someone has defiled her, and, in that respect, she is damaged goods. To be consigned to singleness (and, therefore, barrenness) is considered a real curse. What, then, could benefit a woman who had been raped? Under Torah law, if a man raped a woman, he would have to care for her the rest of her life. She could not simply be used and discarded. The law was protecting her.

Again, that may seem offensive to us, but I can assure you that the current situation in America would seem more offensive to an ancient Israelite. I'm talking about our contemporary society in which nearly half a million women are raped every year. Reportedly, one out of every six women in America has been the victim of an attempted or realized rape in her lifetime. "Females ages 16–19 are 4 times more likely than the general population to be victims of rape, attempted rape, or sexual assault."[7]

Consider the lyrics of some chart-topping hits, including the 2020 song "WAP." It immediately jumped to number one on iTunes.[8] To call it vulgar, offensive and degrading to the women who performed it would be to understate its baseness. Yet it is one of an endless stream of sexually explicit and obscene songs that have flooded the airwaves for years now, with little children singing along without the slightest clue as to the meaning of the words. This provides a snapshot of our supposedly superior culture. Is it really to be preferred to the culture of the Bible?

As for the general harshness of Old Testament laws, consider that more than two million Americans are presently incarcerated, with over 150,000 serving life sentences.[9] More than 2,500 are on death row,[10] and, despite a steady decline in executions in our country, "1524 men and women have been executed in the United States since the 1970s."[11] So much for a merciful and compassionate society with high and lofty moral standards!

The point I'm making is simple. Just as we can question the morality of the ancient biblical society, even more can that ancient society question our morality. In fact, if you wanted to raise your children in a world where they would be less likely to sleep around as teens, less likely to get STDs, less likely to be treated as sexual objects, less likely to be raped and less likely to be addicted to drugs or alcohol, then you would choose the biblical world in a heartbeat. And this reflects the goodness of God: He truly wants what is best for us.

Again, there are biblical laws that seem very harsh from our perspective. "Anyone who curses their father or mother is to be put to death. Because they have cursed their father or mother, their blood will be on their own head" (Leviticus 20:9). We couldn't imagine a law like that today in a culture in which it's common for children to speak back and even curse their parents with minimal repercussions. But in the ancient world (and in much of the world today), parents were to be honored and revered, and it was unthinkable that a child would curse his own mother and father.

Not only so, but in ancient Israel, it was the norm for children to be raised by both their mother and father. The only reason for fatherless homes, generally speaking, would be the premature death of the father. Yet in America today, more than 25 percent of all children are raised in fatherless homes. And, according to the U.S. Department of Justice, children from fatherless homes account for:

- 63 percent of youth suicides
- 90 percent of all homeless and runaway youths
- 85 percent of all children that exhibit behavioral disorders
- 71 percent of all high school dropouts
- 70 percent of juveniles in state-operated institutions
- 75 percent of adolescent patients in substance abuse centers
- 75 percent of rapists motivated by displaced anger[12]

Which society would be the more moral, today's society or the ancient Israelite society? Which would be safer for your children? And, assuming that the law from Leviticus 20 was actually carried out from time to time, in which society would youth be more at risk?

Put another way, let's say that one teenager a year was put to death for cursing his parents in Old Testament times. (For the record, ancient Jewish rabbis questioned whether or not laws such as these were even enforced a single time in the history of Israel.)[13] Compare that to the thousands of teens who lose their lives every year to suicide or drug abuse, or who run away from home because of the breakdown in their families. Which society would be more compassionate to teenagers? Which society would provide a better moral framework for their upbringing and thriving? We have to compare apples to apples. When we do, we see that, in many important ways, the biblical world was much more moral than our world today.

Not only so, but we cannot focus primarily on Old Testament laws. We must continue reading into the New Testament where we learn that many of the Old Testament laws were given for specific purposes, including: keeping Israel separate from the nations so that it could survive as a people and bring the Messiah into the world (see Exodus 19:1–6; Leviticus 11:41–47); revealing the sinfulness of the entire world, proving that we are all guilty before God (see Romans 3:19–31); and demonstrating the destructiveness of sin (see 1 Corinthians 10:1–11). In other words, God visibly judged the people of Israel for their sins to show the rest of us how deadly sin was.

Once the Old Testament law had done its work, the New Testament took things to a higher ethical level, but without some of the strict legal penalties. Accordingly, some of the sins that carried the physical death penalty under the Old Testament (such as adultery, fornication and homosexual practice) carry a spiritual death penalty in the New Testament, meaning being excluded from God's eternal kingdom (see 1 Corinthians 5:1–13; 6:9–11).[14] And whereas the Israelites were commanded to drive out the Canaanites, we are not called to drive out people. Jesus calls us, instead, to drive out demonic spirits that destroy people's lives. There is quite a difference.

Israelites Versus Canaanites

You might say, "All that is fine and good, but what about the fact that God *did* call the Israelites to drive out the Canaanites? That is called genocide. How are you going to justify that?"

That is a very important question. The answer is that

(1) the Israelites did not commit genocide,

(2) the Canaanites were guilty of terrible wickedness, and

(3) God waited 400 years before enacting judgment on them, even though this delay caused the people of Israel real suffering while enslaved in Egypt.

This speaks of extreme patience on God's part, not extreme violence. Let's unpack these answers one at a time.

The reason I say that the Israelites did not commit genocide is because some of the inhabitants of the land of Canaan (which became the land of Israel) were driven out rather than killed, while others were neither driven out nor killed, but ended up living alongside the Israelites over the centuries (see Judges 1:21, 27–33). So, to set the record straight, this was not genocide.

That being said, the children of Israel did attack the Canaanites, marching into someone else's land and going to war over it. On top of that, they claimed to do this at God's behest. What kind of God is this?

Let me answer your question—which is a very good question—with several questions of my own. What if the rest of the biblical account is true, since it gives us further background? What if the native inhabitants had become so debased and wicked that they deserved judgment? What if they were like the Nazis or ISIS? Would we look at things differently?

According to Leviticus 18, the Canaanites were guilty of all kinds of gross sexual sins, including incest and bestiality. They also sacrificed their own children in the fire as an offering to the god Moloch. Should not people such as this pay a penalty? And yet, despite God promising the land of Canaan to Abraham and his descendants, the Lord explained to Abraham that his children would live in a foreign land and be oppressed for a period of 400 years (see Genesis 15:13–15), which is a longer time period than the entire history of the United States. Only after 400 years would the children of Israel return to Canaan, "for the sins of the Amorites do not yet warrant their destruction" (Genesis 15:16 NLT). In this passage, "the Amorites" is used with reference to the people living in Canaan.

Can you imagine waiting for 400 years before executing judgment, or waiting until the sin of the people was so heinous that it had to be dealt with? If anything, you could accuse God of being too lax, not too severe.

Let's hear what some biblical commentators have to say. First, we will listen to Professor Nahum Sarna, a Jewish scholar.

The fate and destiny of the future people of Israel is to be intertwined with that of other peoples. The history of all mankind is under the moral governance of God. The displacement of the native population of Canaan by Israel is not to be accounted for on grounds of divine favoritism or innate superiority (cf. Deut. 9:4–6). The local peoples, here generically called "Amorites" ... have violated God's charge. The universally binding moral law has been flouted and the inhabitants of Canaan have been doomed by their own corruption, as texts like Leviticus 18:24f. and 20:23f. explicitly aver. Yet God's justice is absolute. The limit of His tolerance of evil—four generations [meaning 400 years]—has not yet been reached, and Israel must wait until God's time is ripe. Divine justice is not to be strained—even for the elect of God, and even though its application relates to pagans.[15]

British Professor Derek Kidner, well-known for his practical insights into the Bible, said this:

This foretelling of bondage is doubly significant [meaning, Israel's bondage in Egypt], both in showing it to be a deliberate discipline with a planned outcome ... and in disclosing God's patience towards the inhabitants of Canaan. The clause *for the iniquity of the Amorite is not yet full* (16) throws significant light on Joshua's invasion (and, by inference, on other Old Testament wars), as an act of justice, not aggression. Until it was *right* to invade, God's people must wait, even if it cost them centuries of hardship. This is one of the pivotal sayings of the Old Testament.[16]

What an extraordinary statement. Abraham's descendants, the children of Israel, would languish in Egypt serving the Egyptians as slaves until it was right to invade the land of Canaan. And so, "God's people must wait, even if it cost them centuries of hardship." For good reason Kidner states that "this is one of the pivotal sayings of the Old Testament." God only acts with justice, and if we could have been there ourselves, we would have been amazed with His longsuffering.[17]

But there is still an unanswered, very important question: Why did God order the Israelites to exterminate the women and children as well? Or, even if we recognize that the women could be as wicked as the men, why kill the children? How is this possibly justified?

There are really only two answers that seem feasible when we remember how patient and longsuffering God was. One answer is that the wickedness of the parents was so deeply ingrained that the children themselves were corrupted. According to a 2020 article on Earth.com, a parent's moral compass can be passed on to his or her children.

> Eye and hair color, height, and even dimples are all physical traits we can inherit from our parents. But now, a new study has found that children can also inherit their parent's moral compass. The nature versus nurture debate shows that inherited traits and environmental influences each play a strong role in a person's upbringing, intelligence, personality, and worldview.[18]

If God knew this to be true about the children of the Canaanites, then the only way to end the spread of wickedness would be to deal with the children as well, as terribly harsh as that seems. It would be like amputating a gangrenous limb—to use my analogy from before, although, to be clear, a child is not a limb—in order to save the whole body. In this case, if the children of Israel did not survive, then the Messiah could not come into the world and we would not be saved. And had the Israelites intermarried with the Canaanites, they would have ended up following their gods and being wiped out as a distinct people. As for the eternal fate of those children, the Bible indicates that children are not fully responsible for their actions until they reach a certain stage of moral maturity. Because of this truth, a Canaanite child could be killed in this world and go straight to heaven (see Matthew 18:1–5; Deuteronomy 1:39).

The other possibility may sound extremely odd, but there are some top scholars who believe it to be true. The theory is based on an interesting text in Genesis 6 that seems to indicate that angelic beings took on human form, married women and produced children with them, giving birth to a mixed breed of giants. (I told you this sounded extremely odd, but it is a tenable theory.) This led to even more extreme depravity on the earth, and it was one of the reasons God sent the flood in Noah's day. The argument, then, was that the Canaanites were the descendants of this mixed breed of giants and had to be eliminated—men, women and children. They were corrupt to the core and they had to be removed for the good of the world.[19]

To be sure, the passages in the Bible calling for the killing of the Canaanites can be very troubling. But since we see how patiently God waited until executing judgment, and we see how patient He was throughout biblical history—giving people time to change their ways before taking action—we do best to reserve judgment, especially if the people were as wicked as the Bible describes.[20] And we must also remember that this was not the pattern through the ages. It was a one-time event with a one-time purpose.[21] (You can also ask yourself this question: If the God of the Bible is such a murderous tyrant, why does He allow millions of people every day to mock Him and reject Him without wiping them out? I know He has showed me infinite patience and mercy.)

What about Slavery?

What about the laws of slavery? How could the Bible sanction something so horrid? Actually, the Bible never sanctioned slavery as we know it in American and world history, in which people were brutally kidnapped, transported to a foreign land and sold as cattle. To the contrary, you can make the argument that the reason God put laws against slavery toward the top of the list was to say, "My children, you were slaves in Egypt and were terribly mistreated there, but that is not how you are to treat your own slaves." Israelite slaves would only serve for six years (in many cases an Israelite slave was like an indentured servant who sold his services out of financial need) unless they chose to work for their master for life. They were to rest on the Sabbath as everyone else did. And, for example, if their master knocked their tooth out, they would go free (see Exodus 20:8–11; 21:2–11, 27). What a contrast from slavery in Egypt.

Again, slavery was very common in the ancient world, as it has been common throughout much of human history. But Israelite law put significant safeguards in place to protect the well-being of slaves, also giving them viable paths to freedom. And in the New Testament world, where slavery was also the norm, Paul made the extraordinary statement that in Christ there was neither slave nor free (see Galatians 3:28; Colossians 3:11). In other words, while the social reality remained the same, there was now complete equality in Christ—a totally revolutionary concept—and that is why it was Christian leaders in history who helped lead the fight against slavery.

Paul said something else that was remarkable in the ancient world. He said that there was neither Jew nor Gentile in the

Messiah—again, meaning that there was complete spiritual equality, also a revolutionary concept—and that there was neither male nor female. In Jesus, men and women had equal footing. There was no caste system or class system. They were all one in Him.

Do you know how radical this sounded in the ancient world? But Paul knew that this was something Jesus had practiced. It is true, of course, that the twelve apostles were men, in keeping with the leadership role given to men in the Bible. But it is also true that women played an important part in the Lord's earthly ministry, sitting at His feet to hear Him teach, which was not a woman's place back then (see Luke 10:38–42), forming some of the core of His team (see Luke 8:1–3; Romans 16:1–16), playing honored roles in key narratives (see Mark 14:3–9; Luke 7:36–50; 8:42–48), and even being the first eyewitnesses of His resurrection, commissioned by the Lord to tell the apostles that He was risen (see Matthew 28:1–10). Yes, Jesus decided to appear to women first once He rose from the dead. Not only so, but the men—meaning the apostles—did not immediately believe the women when they came to tell their stories. The women appear to be more spiritual in these important accounts.

Women also played a key role in Paul's ministry (see his list of coworkers in Romans 16), and as the early Church grew and spread it had special appeal to women. It put women on an equal spiritual footing with the men, even if their respective leadership roles were different. It also required the same moral standards from men as it did from women, since in the Greco-Roman world, women were expected to be chaste while men could have their sexual fun. Not in the Church. Here, all were called to be chaste.

As for the larger charge that the Bible is a misogynist book, Bible teacher David Wilber reviewed all the relevant passages in his book, *Is God a Misogynist? Understanding the Bible's Difficult*

Passages Concerning Women. He also looked at the effects of modern feminism on women. What were his conclusions?

> The modern feminist movement cannot bring about true change in our society. It cannot deliver female dignity and equality. And in fact, some of the highest values of modern feminism (e.g., abortion) are directly contrary to women's rights, worth, and health. Secular feminism cannot solve the problem of female oppression and mistreatment in our society. So then what *does* work? The answer is biblical Christianity. We know Christianity changes the world and elevates the status of women because it already has. Christianity teaches us to value and protect women. Christianity teaches us that women are equal to men in worth and purpose.[22]

In short, while the Bible differentiates between some of the distinctive giftings of men and women (yes, men and women are different), the Bible does *not* teach that women are inferior to men. Absolutely not. In fact, while there is not one passage in the Bible that praises males as males, there is a lengthy passage in Proverbs giving praise to godly women. It reads:

> A wife of noble character who can find? She is worth far more than rubies. Her husband has full confidence in her and lacks nothing of value. She brings him good, not harm, all the days of her life. She selects wool and flax and works with eager hands. She is like the merchant ships, bringing her food from afar. She gets up while it is still night; she provides food for her family and portions for her female servants. She considers a field and buys it; out of her earnings she plants a vineyard. She sets about her work vigorously; her arms are strong for her tasks. She sees that her trading is profitable, and her lamp does not go out at night. In her hand she holds the distaff and grasps the spindle with her fingers. She opens her arms to the poor and extends

her hands to the needy. When it snows, she has no fear for her household; for all of them are clothed in scarlet. She makes coverings for her bed; she is clothed in fine linen and purple. Her husband is respected at the city gate, where he takes his seat among the elders of the land. She makes linen garments and sells them, and supplies the merchants with sashes. She is clothed with strength and dignity; she can laugh at the days to come. She speaks with wisdom, and faithful instruction is on her tongue. She watches over the affairs of her household and does not eat the bread of idleness. Her children arise and call her blessed; her husband also, and he praises her: "Many women do noble things, but you surpass them all." Charm is deceptive, and beauty is fleeting; but a woman who fears the LORD is to be praised. Honor her for all that her hands have done, and let her works bring her praise at the city gate.

Proverbs 31:10–31

Surely, if the Bible were misogynistic and demeaning to women, it would not include such a lengthy, beautiful passage that praises the woman's independence and strength. It is because of her that her husband and children thrive and look good. She is the key to their success, and she should get the praise she deserves.[23]

Contrast the passage we read above with today's society. Women are merchandised as sexual objects, magazine covers and websites are replete with scantily clad females, and teenage girls suffer from anorexia and bulimia in their quest for perfect bodies. This is also the society in which radical feminists despise men, reject marriage and shout in unison as they protest at pro-life rallies, "We will fight. We will win. Throw the fetus in a bin."[24]

May I encourage you to look again to the God of the Bible? May I encourage you to reconsider your position? In the last chapter, I quoted these verses: "The LORD is gracious and compassionate, slow to anger and rich in love. The LORD is good to all; he has compassion on all he has made" (Psalm 145:8–9). This is who He is to the very core of His being. The more you learn to trust Him, the more you see how good He is. And He is so committed to offering us mercy that He sent His Son to die in our place. As Paul wrote,

> You see, at just the right time, when we were still powerless, Christ died for the ungodly. Very rarely will anyone die for a righteous person, though for a good person someone might possibly dare to die. But God demonstrates his own love for us in this: While we were still sinners, Christ died for us. Since we have now been justified by his blood, how much more shall we be saved from God's wrath through him! For if, while we were God's enemies, we were reconciled to him through the death of his Son, how much more, having been reconciled, shall we be saved through his life!
>
> Romans 5:6–10

Open your heart to Him today and say, "Father, I really want to put my trust in You and believe that You are good. And I want to believe that Your Word is good as well. Open my heart and mind to see the truth—the real truth, the whole truth—and demonstrate Your goodness in my life." If you are sincere in praying those words, you will not be disappointed.

nine

The Problem of Evil

I f there is no God, then there is no problem of evil. There is simply suffering, pain, agony, calamity and death. In other words, if everything is natural, then human suffering does not present a moral or theological problem any more than a spider catching a fly presents a moral or theological problem. That is what nature does. Things happen.

God and Human Suffering

But if there is an all-loving, all-knowing, all-powerful God, then the suffering of this world presents a moral and theological problem. Why would such a God create a world where there is so much pain? And how can He sit by idly while babies starve to death and natural disasters wipe out whole communities?

In the words of Jon Steingard, a young man raised in the faith who became the lead singer of a Christian rock band before renouncing his faith,

If God is all-loving and all-powerful, why is there evil in the world? Can he not do anything about it? Does he choose not to? Is the evil in the world a result of his desire to give us free will? OK then, what about famine and disease and floods and all the suffering that isn't caused by humans and our free will?[1]

Those are piercing and painful questions. Yet they are questions that must be asked, since more people lose their faith in God because of suffering than because of theology.[2] This is where the rubber meets the road. This is where we live.

But what if I told you that God is also troubled by human suffering? I know that sounds confusing and even contradictory—after all, if the Lord does not like the state of things, He has the power to fix it. But once we understand God's heart in the midst of our pain, we will understand His goodness and love even more deeply.

Kazoh Kitamori, who lived from 1916–1998, was a Japanese theologian who wrote a provocatively titled book shortly after World War II. The name of the book was *Theology of the Pain of God*, and it was based on this very profound concept.

> The heart of the gospel was revealed to me as the "pain of God." This revelation led me to the path which the prophet Jeremiah had trodden (Jeremiah 31:20). Jeremiah was a "man who saw the heart of God most deeply" (Kittel). I was allowed to experience the depths of God's heart with Jeremiah. . . . We dare to speak about this "pain of God." . . . We must pronounce the words "pain of God" as if we are allowed to speak them only once in our lifetime. Those who have beheld the pain of God cease to be loquacious, and open their mouths only by the passion to bear witness to it.[3]

What did he mean by the "pain of God"? Why would an almighty God experience pain, or more acutely, why would

He choose to experience pain? According to Basilea Schlink (1904–2001), founder of the Evangelical Sisterhood of Mary in Germany and a courageous opponent of the Nazis, "Anyone who loves as much as God does, cannot help suffering. And anyone who really loves God will sense that He is suffering."[4]

What an incredible idea. The love He has for us, a love far greater than anything we can imagine, means that He must suffer intensely because of our suffering. Can you imagine how intense God's pain must be if this is really true?

When you read about a stranger dying in a car accident, you might feel a little sad. But if it is someone close to you—a family member or a dear friend—you experience shock and agony. The pain is palpable and the grief is overwhelming. Can you imagine, then, how God must feel because of His passionate love for His creation?

Old Testament scholar Terence Fretheim wrote a book titled *The Suffering of God* that focused "on the theme of divine suffering, an aspect of our understanding which both the church and scholarship have neglected."[5] But what does this all mean? How can God suffer? And why would He choose to create a world that would bring Him so much suffering? More importantly, how does any of this help us deal with our own suffering?

In the first chapter of Mark's gospel, Jesus encountered a man with leprosy, which was an untouchable, unclean, even disfiguring condition (see Mark 1:40–45).

The man appealed to Jesus, saying, "If You are willing, You can make me clean" (Mark 1:40 NASB). How did the Lord respond? Most of our translations read: "*Moved with compassion*, Jesus stretched out His hand and touched him, and said to him, 'I am willing; be cleansed'" (Mark 1:41 NASB, emphasis added). This would be consistent with other healing miracles recorded in the gospels where Jesus was moved to heal out of compassion (see Matthew 14:14; Luke 7:11–15). His heart went out to the sufferer. Being moved by compassion, He removed their sickness.

But that may not have been the case in this situation, as there are other ancient manuscripts of Mark that read, *"Moved with indignation,* Jesus stretched out his hand and touched him, saying, 'I am willing. Be clean!'"* (Mark 1:41 NET, emphasis added). Based on this reading, Jesus was angry when He saw this man's suffering and pain. But why, exactly, was the Son of God angry?

According to New Testament scholar Robert Guelich, the anger "must stem from the setting of the illness and what it represented as a distortion of God's creature by the forces of evil . . . . Jesus' anger is a 'righteous anger' that recognizes the work of the Evil One in the sick as well as the possessed."[6]

When Jesus saw this man in his suffering and disfigurement, He saw it as a terrible distortion of God's intent for the human race. He saw it as a satanic distortion, and it moved Him to anger and then to an act of healing. That's one reason why Jesus spent so much time healing the sick. He was pointing toward God's ideal for humanity, showing us what His Father intended, reversing what was wrong, undoing the work of Satan and of sin and pointing toward a better world yet to come.

You don't like the way this world is? God doesn't either. In fact, He hates certain things that take place. Yet in the midst of it, He is at work for good purposes. In the end, He will bring something beautiful out of it. As expressed by quadriplegic Joni Eareckson Tada, "God permits what He hates to accomplish what He loves."[7] Put another way, the only way we can arrive at our ultimate destination and live out the fullness of our divine destiny is to pass through this fallen and broken world.

But, to repeat, God Himself is hurt by tragedy and suffering, and Jesus was even angered by it. In the words of Isaiah, "In all their [Israel's] distress he too was distressed" (Isaiah 63:9). Even when He brings correction and judgment, the Bible tells us that, "He does not enjoy hurting people or causing them sorrow" (Lamentations 3:33 NLT). He may not explain to us all of the reasons for our suffering, and He may not tell us why He apparently does not intervene more (although, to be sure, He definitely does intervene, as many believers could attest), but this much is sure: He cares deeply, and He is suffering with us.

Let me paint a picture for you to help underscore this point. Imagine that you're a Christian living in Haiti when a terrible earthquake decimates your city. Thousands have been killed and thousands more are missing, many of them buried in the rubble. All electricity is out, the water system is polluted and the city is plunged into chaos. But you have survived. So you immediately join a rescue team that is trying to dig people out of the debris. Yet your heart is bursting as you dig, forcing you to cry out, "Jesus, where are You? How could You let this happen? Don't You care?"

To your shock, you look to your right, and there He is. It is Jesus. He is on His knees digging through the rubble, His hands torn and bleeding as tears pour down His cheeks. At that moment, you say to yourself, "I don't know why He didn't stop this, and I have no idea who or what caused this earthquake. But I can't blame Jesus. It's obvious that He cares, too!"

It was in that spirit that Pastor Tim Keller wrote,

> If we again ask the question: "Why does God allow evil and suffering to continue?" and we look at the cross of Jesus, we still do not know what the answer is. However, we know what the answer isn't. It can't be that he doesn't love us. It can't be that he is indifferent or detached from our condition. God takes our misery and suffering *so* seriously that he was willing to take it on himself.[8]

That is why Anglican leader John Stott stated, "I could never myself believe in God, if it were not for the cross."[9] It is through

Jesus that God enters into our suffering, bears our pain, carries our disease, demonstrates His love and dies for our sins. You may want to blame God for your suffering, yet here He is, coming into our world, standing right next to us, paying for our sins and pouring out Himself to death so that you and I can be freed from bondage and live forever. Obviously, He is not the one at fault.

At this point, though, we are back to where we started. The question remains: Why would God create a world like ours if it hurts Him, too, to the point that He sent His Son to die for us? Why do it at all?

Free to Choose

The answer is simple. God was moved by love. He wanted to have an extended family, a people who could enjoy His goodness forever, a people He could love and who would love Him, a people who would experience abundant life forever. But our love for God must be freely chosen, not coerced or forced. Love requires freedom of choice.

But freedom has consequences, and the choices every generation has made—including ours—have had disastrous effects. They have brought destruction on our race and a curse on our planet. (By the way, from a biblical perspective, we are related intimately to our planet, and our sin against God affects the earth as well.)

We are living in a fallen, broken world that is both cursed and blessed. It experiences both cruelty and love, tsunamis and sunshine, a world of contradictions, a world that reflects the contradiction of our own nature as people who are created in the image of God and yet fallen. "God made men and women true and upright; we're the ones who've made a mess of things" (Ecclesiastes 7:29 MSG). This describes the schizophrenia of the human race. We are capable of incredible good and extraordinary wickedness, and sometimes we find both extremes inside our own hearts.

But if there is to be real life, there must be freedom of choice.[10] In the words of C. S. Lewis, "Try to exclude the possibility of suffering which the order of nature and the existence of free wills involve, and you find that you have excluded life itself."[11] He also said, "Free will, though it makes evil possible, is also the only thing that makes possible any love or goodness or joy worth having. A world of automata—of creatures that work like machines—would hardly be worth creating."[12]

You might say, "Look. I didn't ask for this. I didn't ask to be put in this world." That is true. But what is it that you cherish most as an individual? Isn't it your very existence and your ability to make choices for your life? Yet those are the very things you fault God for giving you. That's why so few take their own lives, and that's why all of us fight intensely to keep our freedom.

But our existence and our freedom are gifts that come with consequences. When we realize how much evil there is in the world, it's amazing that we can enjoy a beautiful sunset, experience years of good health or have fun with our friends. If anything, God is being amazingly merciful, not judgmental, toward us.

So which would you prefer? Would you prefer that you, your family and your friends had the opportunity to exist rather than never having existed at all? And would you prefer freedom of choice over being a robot? If you answered yes to both questions, then the result is earth as we know it.

Still, you could rightly say, "But if God foresaw that there would be so much pain, why did He decide to create the world?" The answer is that He sees all of eternity, and He sees that it will be worth it all in the end. He is making something beautiful out of us.

According to Scripture, we are in a transition age, a war zone of sorts, and that's another reason why so many things seem to be out of order and wrong. In fact, that's why Jesus taught His followers to pray, "Your kingdom come, your will be done on earth as it is heaven" (Matthew 6:10). God's perfect Kingdom is not yet here, and His perfect will is not yet being carried out in full. What we pray for, long for, and work for is the perfect age to come—God's Kingdom—on a renewed earth where there will be no sickness, pain, injustice, evil or death. We will experience life to the full.

In fact, someone has suggested that rather than thinking of the world to come as the afterlife, we should think of this present world as the before-life—or, as some call it, the Shadowlands—and the world to come as the time when we really experience the fullness of life. In the words of the ancient rabbis, this world is the vestibule to the world to come, and the world to come lasts forever.

Most of us are probably working to make this world a better place. But trying to improve the world is not enough. (In fact, it seems that the more "civilized" we become, the more people we kill, with the 20th century being the bloodiest by far.)[13] God's plan is to usher in a massively better world, a world of wonders beyond our wildest dreams, a world filled with the beauty and the knowledge of God.

But in this transition age there is much evil and suffering. The Bible likens it to giving birth: The whole world is in the pains of childbirth with all creation groaning for the end of suffering and death. A better world is at hand, but it will be birthed out of this present, decaying world as we work together with God (see Romans 8).

That's why what happens in this world matters deeply, after all, this is where we live and where we experience the ups and downs of life. But this is only the beginning and not the end of the story. During our journey through these Shadowlands, God is at work in the midst of our suffering. Even when people do evil things against His will—things that He hates—He can take those things and use them for greater good. All the while, He is shaping and developing us. You can almost think of this present life as our time inside the womb. The world to come is life outside of the womb. From inside the womb it is hard to fathom life on the other side, just like it's hard to fathom that we ever lived inside our mother's womb.

Of course, if you take away the reality of the world to come, suffering becomes all the more meaningless and life all the more purposeless. If there is no world to come, some will never be rewarded for their sacrifices and others will never be punished for their wickedness. The scales of justice will never be set right, and our dreams will remain simply dreams. But if there is a world to come, then our lives are only chapters in a great big book. It is a book with an ending that is almost too good to be true. But it *is* true, because God *is* good, and God *is* love. Ultimate meaning will emerge from the seeming chaos and uncertainty of life. Good will drive out evil, and love will drive out hate.

There Can Be a Redemptive Side to Suffering

It is true that this world is filled with death and evil, but God can bring life out of death and good out of evil. Sometimes what appears to be the worst thing that happened to you can end up being the best thing that happened to you.

God is the great redeemer, and what society, circumstances or Satan mean for evil God can cause to turn out for greater good. Alexander Solzhenitsyn was a Nobel Prize–winning Russian author who was imprisoned for speaking out; yet he said this about his imprisonment: "I nourished my soul there, and

I say without hesitation, 'Bless you, prison, for having been in my life!'"[14]

Does this happen in the case of every tragedy? Certainly not. But Scripture is clear on this: If we give our lives to God and ride out the storm with Him, He will cause everything to work for ultimate good, either in this world or in the world to come (see Romans 8:28).

The Bible also teaches that we grow as human beings through suffering and adversity. In fact, it is often difficult to grow *without* some level of adversity. How many elite athletes never experienced defeat? How many people of strong character never had to overcome failure, disappointment and sometimes even tragedy? A world without adversity, obstacles or setbacks would lack many of the most important dynamics of life.

God's Word explains that suffering can produce compassion and build character (see Romans 5:1–5). Suffering can also remind us of the shortness of life and help us to focus on what really matters. It has the potential to jar us out of the spell of narcissistic materialism. There is more to life than eating, drinking and having fun, and what we sometimes call the good life is often the shallow life.

My wife, Nancy, expressed it like this in an email she sent to me in February, 2011:

The way things are now has been in God's plan all along. Not that God likes an evil world, but this is *not* His plan B. God wanted to create a man to His desired specifications. A glorious man. One that would move in unison with Him, one that would have His mind and heart. One that would work alongside and in union with Him. But in order for this man to have all the elements that God desired, the Fall was a necessary part of the plan. It was not a failure, but a feature of the design.

God does not relish sin, but there was no way that free man could have God's nature inside, with all the important and indispensable elements, and be righteous and holy, unless he fell, and then was redeemed by God Himself. God could not just put His Spirit inside and then we go on from there. The things that man has gone through were necessary to complete the man.

God wanted us to be free to "choose life." Man had to make an independent decision to choose life over death and good over evil. Choice (with the knowledge of evil) and the acceptance of redemption changed something in the essence of man. It changed his nature and character. He became a creature that is different from the one that was created at the beginning, and this is exactly what God was after. Man, being granted the privilege to live eternally *after* the fall and *after* his redemption, was a different man entirely, compared to the same man being given life eternal *before* the fall and *before* the redemption.

This is a powerful insight that can change our perspective deeply. I encourage you to give it some prayerful thought. In short, God did not cause us to sin, and He did not orchestrate the Fall. He created us with freedom of choice, knowing the wrong choices we would make and the suffering those choices would bring. But He also knew that through the cross, our redeemed state in the end would be far greater than our perfect state at creation.

Our Own Sin Is the Cause of Much Suffering

Right now, however, we are in this fallen, unredeemed world, and we often make sinful choices that hurt ourselves and others. But even when our suffering is the consequence of our sin, that suffering can serve as a warning or deterrent or wake-up call that helps us get back on the right path. As the psalmist said, "Before I was afflicted I went astray, but now I obey your word" (Psalm 119:67).

And notice carefully that the psalmist does not blame others, and he certainly does not blame God. In the same way, we have no right to blame God for the messes we sometimes get ourselves in, yet we often do that very thing (see Proverbs 19:3). Some of us leave God out of our lives for years at a time, then we find ourselves in a mess that is due to our sinful choices, and we suddenly become religious and wonder where God is.

But where it is written that the Lord is obligated to bail us out of the pit that we dug for ourselves? Where did we get that notion? Since when does He exist simply for the purpose of delivering us from the consequences of our wrong choices?

We should not minimize the extreme damage our sin can produce in our lives and in the lives of others. Yet, to say it again, God is a redeemer, and some would not be enjoying God's blessing and favor had they not hit bottom and learned from their mistakes. Perhaps your own life can rise higher after reaching such terrible lows.

Ultimately, there *is* purpose and meaning to life, and one day, it will all make sense and be worth it. But I repeat: If you take God and His purposes out of the picture, what do you have? The answer is absolute random suffering with no silver lining and no future hope. And that leads me to these thoughts about what God might say to an atheist after death.

An Atheist Calls Out the Lord

In 2015, Stephen Fry, an outspoken gay British actor and atheist, was asked what he would say to God if such a being really existed and he encountered him/her/it after death. His reply was passionate, eloquent, defiant and irreverent.[15] According to Fry, God is "utterly evil, capricious and monstrous" along with "mean-minded, stupid." How might the Creator respond to being described in such a way?

The first error made by Fry was assuming he would be able to speak at all in God's presence, having no idea that he would suddenly encounter perfect purity, unimaginable love, absolute goodness, untainted justice, blazing truth and unadulterated light. In a moment, he would be overwhelmed by his own sinfulness—not so much as an atheist but as a human being—his selfishness, his arrogance, his carnality and his hypocrisy.

Rather than rebuking God he would be reproaching himself and wailing aloud, "I am so very sorry for who I am and what I have done. Could you possibly have mercy on a wretch such as me?"

But what of the substance of his remarks? What if he could have his say with God? How would the Lord respond? Fry was outraged that a God who was allegedly loving and compassionate could allow such terrible suffering among His creation, stating that he would say to the deity, "Bone cancer in children? What's that about?" He also declared that he would say, "How dare you create a world in which there is such misery that is not our fault? It's not right. It's utterly, utterly evil."[16]

God might say to him, "I applaud you for your moral indignation. In fact, you got it straight from Me. If you were simply the result of a freak, unguided evolutionary accident and your brain waves were the result of neurons firing, you would have no more moral indignation than a zebra being eaten alive by lions or a mouse being swallowed by a rattlesnake.

"The very fact that you care and that you know that such suffering is not right is a reflection of My image in you. But in reality, you don't know the half of it. I am in constant pain because of the suffering of My creation. The cries and agony are in My ears day and night" (see Exodus 2:23–25).

The Lord might also say, "There is something else you are missing. Your own race commits the most horrific, barbaric atrocities day and night—willfully and with premeditation—from burning people alive to raping little children, from kidnapping and torturing innocent victims to blowing up hundreds of people at a time. Yet I don't step in and wipe them all out. Why? Because I am more longsuffering than you could ever imagine, and I have created you with a free will so that you could choose to love Me or hate Me. Would you prefer that I take your freedom from you? Or would you prefer that you never existed?"

In the interview, Fry had his guns fully loaded, stating that he would say to God, "Why should I respect a capricious, meanminded, stupid god who creates a world which is so full of injustice and pain?"[17]

The Creator might reply, "What you fail to understand is that for Me to create a world inhabited by free moral agents involves the possibility of evil and great suffering, and it is the freedom of the human race that has produced the agony of the human race."

"But," Fry would surely protest, "bone cancer in children is surely not their fault. Natural disasters that wipe out thousands in a moment of time are surely not our fault."

To quote his exact words, "Yes the world is very splendid, but it also has in it insects whose whole life cycle is to burrow into the eyes of children and make them blind."[18]

In response, the Lord might say, "Doesn't it seem contradictory to you that I could make such an incredible universe and world that is filled with such beauty, splendor and majesty, one in which human beings stand as the pinnacle of My creation and one in which all things were crafted with precision and skill beyond all mortal calculation, and yet also include those deadly insects you mentioned? Did you ever wonder about that?

"If only you had seen the world before the Fall, you would have been stunned by its beauty and perfection. And if you could see the world to come—a world devoid of pain and heartache, a world devoid of plague and pestilence, a world devoid of murder and rape and a world of indescribable wonder and beauty—you would be astonished beyond words.

"It is human sin that has polluted this world, and I am in the process of turning this terrible evil into something incredibly good. And although this completely transcends your understanding—remember that what you don't know is infinitely greater than what you do know—it will be worth it all in the end."

According to Fry, "The god who created this universe, if he created this universe, is quite clearly a maniac, an utter maniac, totally selfish. We have to spend our lives on our knees thanking him. What kind of god would do that?"[19]

To this God might say, "Does anyone force you to look at beauty? Does anyone require you to appreciate good? I call on My creation to worship Me to remind them of who I am and who they are. It is My prerogative as Creator to do so. And as they gaze on Me and recognize My holy qualities, they are raised up in character, attitude and faith. They become more like Me and come into the fullness of My image in them. Whatever I do for My glory I also do for your good, if you only recognize who I am and humble yourself before Me."

Fry claimed that, "Atheism is not just about not believing that there is a God . . . . It's perfectly apparent that he is monstrous. Utterly monstrous and deserves no respect whatsoever. The moment you banish him, life becomes simpler, purer, cleaner, more worth living in my opinion."[20]

To the contrary, as countless millions will attest, it is the moment you truly come to know Him and experience Him that life takes on real meaning. And we come to know Him most fully through Jesus.

Perhaps God would have ended things on that note, saying, "What you have overlooked is that I am not some indifferent bystander. I get involved in the pain of My creation. In fact, through Jesus I entered into this world and took the place of sinners, rebels, tyrants, scoundrels, mass murderers and every other foul expression of humanity, giving My Son as a payment for your transgressions. I did this so that you, along with every other person who has ever lived, might go free and enjoy My blessing forever. Are you really going to reproach me, Stephen?"

A caller to my radio show suggested that at the root of atheism was a sense of divine betrayal, as if God had somehow let the person down in his moment of greatest need. After this happened, he concluded that He must not be there at all.[21] One of my friends often says that what many atheists really feel is, "There is no God, and I hate Him."

Perhaps this is what happened to Fry as well. Or perhaps, as a gay man, he felt excluded by the Church and rejected by God. Either way, I imagine the moment that Fry meets the Lord after death, the Lord will pinpoint the root of Fry's atheism. I can imagine that at this moment, he might dissolve in tears having seen the love of the Father for the first time.

The good news is that, as of this writing, Stephen Fry is still alive and breathing. Where there is life, there is hope. And you are alive and breathing as well. So, turn the page, and let's see what Job has to say to us about the problem of suffering. There is one more perspective we need to consider.

For the moment, take hold of this reality: Jesus has been anointed by God to

Comfort all who mourn; to grant to those who mourn in Zion— to give them a beautiful headdress instead of ashes, the oil of gladness instead of mourning, the garment of praise instead of a faint spirit; that they may be called oaks of righteousness, the planting of the LORD, that he may be glorified.

Isaiah 61:2–3 ESV

Right now, He wants to replace the ashes of mourning in your life with a crown of beauty. It is a small foretaste of the endless beauty that is to come.

ten

What Would Job Say?

A re you familiar with the story of Job? We don't know all the details of his life, but he may have lived about 4,000 years ago, and God Himself said that there was no one on earth like him (see Job 2:3). He feared God, he shunned evil and he and his family were incredibly blessed. Then, suddenly and without notice, calamity struck. In one day, he lost all of his possessions and, far more tragically, all ten of his children. And yet he refused to curse God, choosing instead to worship Him. Even when he was subsequently afflicted with a terrible disease, he still thanked God. In the end, he was restored to divine favor, and his possessions were doubled. God gave him ten more children, and he lived happily ever after.

But that is only part of Job's amazing story. There's much more to be told, and the missing parts of the story are the ones you'll find especially relevant if you're struggling with your faith.

Let's begin by taking a deeper look at why Job suffered in the first place. After all, if he was so righteous and blessed, how could such calamities strike him? Doesn't God protect His beloved children?

According to the first two chapters of the book, Satan challenged God by claiming that no one served Him out of love. The enemy alleged that people worshiped Him with ulterior motives, doing it for outward blessings rather than for intimate relationship. According to Satan, people (including Job) loved God because of what He did for them, not because of who He was. Consequently, Satan alleged, if God were to take everything from Job, he, too, would curse the Lord.

God took up the challenge and allowed Satan to destroy all that Job had, including his own children and his health. But Job would not yield. He continued to worship God no matter what was taken from him, and Satan lost the challenge.

That's the story that unfolds in the first two chapters of the book. But the book of Job is 42 chapters long. What happened the rest of the way? And why did the Lord allow Satan to raise his hand against a righteous man like Job? We'll answer the question of why later in this chapter. For now, let's answer the question of what happened in the next forty chapters of the book.

Job had three friends who learned of his terrible turn of fortune, and they traveled together to console him. When they saw how great his grief was, they said nothing. All of them sat together in silence for seven days. Then Job spoke up, cursing the day of his birth and wishing that he had never come into the world.

These words surprised his friends—they had never heard him speak this way—and so Eliphaz, apparently the eldest of the friends, gently corrected Job, chiding him for his outburst and stating that all human beings were sinful and unclean in

God's sight. The way he understood it, the Lord evidently saw something wrong in Job, which is why He disciplined him. He wanted Job to be more righteous.

But Job knew this was not the case. He knew he was not being disciplined by the Lord. And the kind of torture that Job was experiencing was hardly the way God disciplined His children. It seemed to Job as if God was acting out of character and that He had become a tyrant and a bully. In response, Job spoke out what he was feeling.

This shocked the friends, who were forced to come to an unpleasant conclusion: Job was not a righteous man after all. They had misjudged him in the past, thinking he was someone he was not. Now they saw the real Job. He was positively wicked! That must be why God judged him. He was getting what he deserved, and that was why his children were killed, too. And they told him these very things to his face! You can be assured that Job had something to say back to his friends.

On and on the dialogue goes, with Job speaking, then one of his friends, then Job, repeating the cycle several times through. And while Job makes some incredible statements of faith along the way, he also levels some heavy accusations against the Lord. (Remember, this is all recorded in the Bible, meaning that God wanted it there and that the biblical authors were not scandalized by it.) Job spoke the following words that are anything but meek and reverent.

- Why won't You take your eyes off me? You won't let up on me long enough for me to swallow my spittle. Even if I have sinned, what have I done to You, You Watcher of mankind? Why have You made me Your target so that I'm now a burden to myself? (7:19–20, my translation).
- It is one and the same, therefore I will say it: both those full of integrity and the wicked He destroys. When a

scourge brings sudden death, He mocks the plight of the innocent. The earth is given over to the power of the wicked; He covers the face of its judges; if not Him, then who? (9:22–24, my translation).

- Is it a good thing for You that You oppress and spurn the labor of Your hands but appear gloriously on behalf of the counsel of the wicked? Do You have eyes of flesh? Do You see as a mortal sees? Are Your days like the days of a mortal and Your years like those of a man that You seek out my iniquity and search for my sin, although You know that I am not guilty and that no one can deliver from Your hand? (10:3–7, my translation).

- But now He has worn me out. You have made desolate my whole community! You have shriveled me up: my gauntness serves as a witness that rises up and testifies against me. He has torn [me] apart in his anger and treated me with hostility. He has gnashed his teeth at me; my adversary sharpens his eyes against me. They have opened their mouths wide against me; scornfully, they smite me on the cheek; they mass themselves together against me. God has handed me over to the ungodly and cast me into the hands of the wicked (16:7–11, my translation).

- I was at ease and He shattered me; He grabbed me by the scruff of the neck and pulverized me; He set me up as His target. His archers surrounded me; He pierced my kidneys, showing no mercy, spilling my gall on the ground. He breached me with breach upon breach; He ran at me like a mighty warrior. I have sowed sackcloth on my skin and buried my honor in the dust. My face is red from weeping and on my eyelids is deep darkness— Although I have committed no violence and my prayer is pure (16:12–17, my translation).

Did you know that these words were recorded in the Bible? Earlier, after losing his possessions and his ten precious children, he said, "Naked I came out of my mother's womb and naked will I return there. YHWH gave and YHWH took away. May YHWH's name be praised!" (Job 1:21, my translation). Then, after losing his health and having his wife encourage him to curse God and die, he said, "You speak like one of the foolish women speaks. Shall we receive only the good from YHWH and not receive the bad?" (Job 2:10, my translation). This was the same Job! In fact, if you can grasp it, *the Job who challenged God was as much a man of faith as the Job who worshiped God.* He pleaded his case *against* God *to* God.

We said earlier that our Father is not troubled by our doubts, nor is He bothered by our probing questions. In the same way, He is not troubled by harsh accusations spoken out of broken hearts. He understands our weaknesses. He knows that from our perspective things on earth are not fair. He is aware that from our vantage point God sometimes seems distant (if He exists at all) or, worse still, downright cruel. And when His children who are in the midst of deep grief and agony speak harsh words about Him, He is not offended, nor does He feel the need to defend Himself. That's why Job's words are recorded in the Bible. It is the Lord's way of saying, "I understand that sometimes you may feel exactly the same way Job felt in the midst of your own severe trial, and I am not going to strike you down for your insolence."

Of course, it's is wonderful if we can continue to praise God in the midst of our trials as Job did in the first two chapters of the book. But we are not always able to, and Job's speeches are recorded in the Bible to remind us that sometimes, through loss and pain, we might speak rashly.

How, then, did the Lord respond? If He did not kill Job, which Job thought might happen for his insolence, what did He do?

He revealed Himself. He made Himself known. He spoke to
him out of a whirlwind and described the beauty and majesty
of His creation and His mastery over all other powers. He ex-
posed Job's (and our) incredible ignorance with questions such
as these (that were meant as a loving but strong rebuke to Job's
accusations):

> "Where were you when I laid the foundations of the earth? Tell
> me, if you have understanding. Who established its dimen-
> sions, if you know, or who stretched out a (measuring) line over
> it? On what were its bases sunk and who laid its cornerstone,
> when the morning stars sang together and all the divine be-
> ings shouted for joy? [Who] shut up the sea with doors when
> it burst out from the womb and came forth, when I clothed
> it with a cloud and made thick darkness its swaddling cloth,
> when I established a limit for it and set up bars and doors, and
> I said, 'Up to here you may come and not beyond; here your
> proud waves stop'?
>
> Have you in your lifetime commanded the morning or
> caused the dawn to know its place so that it takes hold of the
> corners of the earth and shakes the wicked from it? [The earth]
> is changed like clay under a seal, [its features] stand out like a
> garment. And the light of the wicked is withheld from them and
> the upraised arm is broken."
>
> 38:4–15, my translation

The Lord even asked him, "Do you know the time when
the mountain goats give birth? Have you watched the calving
of the deer? Have you counted the number of months they
fulfill and do you know when it's time to give birth?" (39:1–2,
my translation).

Put another way, the Lord was saying, "Job, who are you
to tell Me how to run My world when you can't even tell Me
when the mountain goats birth, let alone tell Me where you

were when I was creating the universe? There is a whole lot you do not know. In fact, what you do not know is infinitely more than what you do know. There is so much more to the story (including your story) than you could ever imagine, and if you could see the whole picture, it would make perfect sense. But you cannot, because you are a human being and I am God. So, rather than answer all your questions—even if I did, you don't have the capacity to understand all the answers—I will reveal Myself to you. And when you see Me, you will not have any more questions."[1]

And how did Job respond to God's words, which took up chapters 38–41 in the book? He began by saying, "I know You can do everything and that no plan of Yours can be thwarted." In other words, "I recognize that you are almighty God!" Then, he quoted God's earlier challenge to him, when the Lord had asked him, "Who is this who obscures counsel without knowledge?" Job answered, "Surely I declared [things] that I did not understand, things too wonderful for me that I did not know."

Next, Job quoted another, earlier challenge that the Lord had presented when He said to Job, "Listen, now, and I myself will speak. I will ask you, and you will inform me." Job responded to this challenge with these important words: "I had heard about You by the hearing of the ear but now my eye has seen You. Therefore I repudiate [everything] and repent on dust and ashes" (42:2–6, my translation).[2]

To paraphrase, "Now that I have seen Your majesty, wisdom, power, and beauty, I realize how foolish I was to speak so harshly about You. What did I know? The fact is that I did have a relationship with You in the past, but it was from a distance. Now I have seen You with my own eyes; therefore, I repudiate everything I said, and I repent deeply. You are the majestic, wise and good Creator, and You are the ruler of the universe. That is enough for me!"

Yet as he said these words, he was still suffering physically and nothing around him had changed. He had still lost everything, and he was still a rejected, lonely, materially bankrupt man. But everything changed inside of him, and that was more than enough. It was only after that the outward restoration began to come.

How Does This Apply to You?

What can we take away from this in our own lives? First, it is okay to be angry. It is okay to feel as if God let you down or betrayed you. It is okay to give vent to your grief.

But you cannot stop there. Through prayer (even desperate, gut-wrenching prayer), through worship, through the Word (even through reading Job), you must have your own encounter with God. When He reveals Himself to you, not only will the questions disappear—especially the agonizing questions of why—but the pain will begin to heal. God's presence is the ultimate restorative agent.

Yet there's still more to the story of Job, and what you are about to read will shock you. You see, after the Lord spoke to Job and put him in his place, the Lord turned and rebuked Job's friends. Yes, He rebuked the ones who seemed orthodox and pious, the ones who said, "God blesses the righteous and curses the wicked, so Job must be wicked." And what did God say to the friends? Speaking to Eliphaz He said,

> "My anger is kindled against you and your two friends because you did not speak what was right concerning Me as did my servant Job. Now, take for yourselves seven bulls and seven rams and go to My servant Job and offer them up as a burnt offering on your behalf. Job My servant will pray for you for I will show him favor so as not to deal with you according to your folly, for

you have not spoken what is right concerning Me as did my servant Job."

42:7–8, my translation

What? "Eliphaz, you and your friends did not speak what was right concerning me *as did my servant Job.*" Job spoke rightly about God? Did he not attack Him and accuse Him of being a cosmic tyrant and a moral monster? But that is some of the incredible message of the book. Yes, God is very proud of His faithful servant Job. He called him "My servant" three times in these two verses, as well as in chapters one and two. And it was Job, not the friends, who spoke rightly about God. Talk about an unexpected turn of events!

You see, it is only because Job was such an extraordinary man that Yahweh saw fit to speak to him from the whirlwind at such length and with such self-disclosure. To Job's friends, He said a few words, and they were words of a very different character. As Jesus said to His disciples centuries later, "No longer do I call you servants, for the servant does not know what his master is doing; but I have called you friends, for all that I have heard from my Father I have made known to you" (John 15:15 ESV).

This rebuke must have come as quite a shock to Job's three friends, who presumably felt vindicated deeply after the Lord rebuked Job at such length.

"Surely," they thought to themselves, "we were in the right, and Job was in the wrong. I'm glad poor Job finally recognizes it."

Rather, God expressed His extreme anger toward them, saying, "You did not speak what was right (Hebrew, *nekhonah*) concerning Me as did My servant Job."

But what, exactly, does *nekhonah* mean? Old Testament scholar Tryggve Mettinger states that "the Job speeches depict a God who is not merely amoral but actively immoral, the omnipotent tyrant, the cosmic thug."[3]

How, then, could God possibly say that Job had spoken rightly of Him? And in what sense did the friends fail to speak what was right concerning the Lord?

Let's start with Job's friends. By spouting rigid theology about the Lord and by misapplying conventional (and often true) wisdom, they misrepresented Him to Job. They spoke from an intellectual and religious point of view rather than from a relationship point of view. As they tried to be God's spokesmen, they grossly misrepresented Him.

Job, on the other hand, spoke from the heart and was convinced that what he was experiencing did not reflect who God really was. Because of his devotion to the Lord, he felt that he had to challenge Him. This, too, was an act of faith!

It had appeared to Job that God was a monster, and he foolishly accused God of monstrous acts. What he didn't know was that the Lord didn't do these things to Job, nor did He instigate them. He had his reasons for allowing Job to suffer such an attack, but the one who instigated and carried out the attacks was Satan. This is a very important point. Our heavenly Father does not indiscriminately slaughter or afflict His children. That is not who He is, and we make a serious mistake when we blame Him or judge Him based on what the devil does.

In that sense, too, Job spoke what was right about the Lord. What he experienced reflected more of the character of Satan than the character of the Father. Put another way, Job knew that the character of God was one of absolute justice, but he also knew that his treatment was terribly unjust. This discrepancy caused him to say that there must be something wrong with the deity rather than with himself. So on the one hand, to say that God was smiting Job for his sins was to speak wrongly of the Lord. On the other hand, to accuse Him of acting wrongly, even though not accurate, was to speak rightly of Him.

In summary, as explained by Job commentator Norman Habel, "The blunt and forthright accusations of Job from the depths of his agony are closer to the truth than the conventional unquestioning pronouncements of the friends."[4]

Or, in the striking formulation of Donald Kraus, "Therefore Job is better off than his friends, and Job's seeming blasphemy is more pleasing to God than the friends' conventional piety."[5]

In the words of the Israeli scholar Yechekzel Kaufman, "The friends are guilty of clichés and empty phrases, while Job's challenge to God reflects a moral duty to speak only the truth before him."[6]

And William Reyburn notes:

> Job's friends have insisted that Job's calamities were God's punishment for his sins. Job maintained that he had not brought this punishment on himself through sin. So the friends are saying things about God that are not true. Job is correct in what he is saying about God, but he draws conclusions from it that make God out to be unjust. It is for these wrong conclusions that Job has just repented.[7]

This is in keeping with Job's extraordinary integrity, as he could not compromise his character and deny what he knew to be true (namely, his own spiritual history of loyalty to God), and he would have been lying if he had simply stated, "Obviously, I deserve to suffer like this because I have been such a wretch." His error, again, was to come to a very wrong conclusion— namely, that God must be cruel and cavalier. There was obviously a whole dimension to the story that Job had missed entirely. In a real sense, then, while it is dreadfully wrong for a human being to accuse God of misconduct (see Isaiah 10:5–15;

45:9–10; Romans 9:19–24), it is quite right to expect Him to act in keeping with His character. Job was rebuked for the former expression and commended for the latter.

As expressed by Job scholar Robert Gordis:

> Far from denying Job's insistence that justice must somehow inhere in the universe, the Lord vigorously confirms it. Job has spoken the truth not only about his unmerited suffering but "about Me," the nature of God. Thus the Book of Job demonstrates what could have been inferred *a priori* [meaning, by the very nature of things]—a God without justice is no God to an ancient Hebrew.[8]

This is the God of the Hebrew Bible. This is the God of Job. This is our God.

You still might ask, "But if this God is good and just, why did He allow Job to be targeted by Satan? What did He have to gain from this, and how was this fair to Job?" In reality, Job serves as a microcosm of the human race in that God allowed him to go through something truly horrific to emerge far better in the end. In the case of Job, his suffering was undeserved. In the case of our race, much of our suffering is very much deserved. But in both cases, God has our long-term, best interests in mind. And along the way, He will vindicate His name.

What Satan meant for evil, God used for good. He did this first by demonstrating to the watching angelic world, along with billions of readers through the ages, that people do serve Him because of who He is and not only because of what He does. Second, while Satan wanted to destroy Job, God used the unmerited attacks to reveal things in Job that he didn't know were there. This made him a far better man and brought him into a more intimate relationship with God. Third, in the end, Job was doubly blessed. The fact that he had ten more children (rather than twenty) points to his reunion with them in the world to come. Satan took everything away. God gave it back double.

But there is still more to the story. Job was special enough that, in a sense, he took a hit for all of us, teaching us that sometimes inexplicable things happen to godly people. When these tragedies and losses occur, we can learn what *not* to do from the book of Job.

On the one hand, we should not do what the friends did, accusing Job of sin. "Job, you must be a really bad person, otherwise, this would not have happened to you!"

On the other hand, we should not do what Job did, accusing God of sin. "God, you're obviously not who I thought You were, otherwise You wouldn't have treated me so badly."

Instead, recognizing that there are things happening behind the scenes that we do not see or understand, we should resolve to worship God no matter what—and I mean worshiping Him as a good, loving, faithful God—believing that He will bring light out of darkness, healing out of pain and redemption out of calamity. In the end, we will know God better and have more to offer to others who are in pain. As the old poem by Ugo Bassi says:

> Measure thy life by loss instead of gain;
> Not by the wine drunk, but the wine poured forth
> For love's strength standeth in love's sacrifice;
> And whoso suffers most hath most to give.[9]

The apostle Paul learned a similar lesson while enduring a terrible Satanic attack that drove him to prayer. He had received such incredible revelations that the Lord allowed Satan to attack him in order to keep him humble. He wrote:

> Therefore, in order to keep me from becoming conceited, I was given a thorn in my flesh, a messenger of Satan, to torment me.

Three times I pleaded with the Lord to take it away from me.
But he said to me, "My grace is sufficient for you, for my power
is made perfect in weakness." Therefore I will boast all the more
gladly about my weaknesses, so that Christ's power may rest on
me. That is why, for Christ's sake, I delight in weaknesses, in
insults, in hardships, in persecutions, in difficulties. For when
I am weak, then I am strong.

2 Corinthians 12:7-10

What an incredible statement, and what an incredible
insight: when I am weak, then I am strong. We don't know
exactly what Paul's thorn was—there is much speculation
among scholars, ranging from a physical illness to extreme
persecution—but whatever it was, Paul said it was sent to
torment (or harass) him.[10] The Greek verb literally means "to
strike or beat with the fist, either once or repeatedly," and it
was used to describe the way Jesus was beaten (see Matthew
26:67; Mark 14:65). Paul said that this was his own experience
at Satan's hand, and yet somehow it was allowed by the Lord,
and in the end, it served for Paul's good and for the good of
those to whom he ministered.

Earlier in this same book, Paul described a harrowing experience that he and his team lived through—just barely. He wrote:

We do not want you to be uninformed, brothers and sisters,
about the troubles we experienced in the province of Asia. We
were under great pressure, far beyond our ability to endure, so
that we despaired of life itself. Indeed, we felt we had received
the sentence of death. But this happened that we might not rely
on ourselves but on God, who raises the dead. He has delivered
us from such a deadly peril, and he will deliver us again. On him
we have set our hope that he will continue to deliver us.

2 Corinthians 1:8-10

The experience was hellish and far beyond their ability to endure, to the point that they were convinced they were going to die. But God brought them out of it—if you are reading this book, then you are not dead either, despite what you have endured—and, once again, they came out the better for it. They grew in character and endurance and they had more to give to others. As Paul said, God "comforts us in all our troubles, so that we can comfort those in any trouble with the comfort we ourselves receive from God" (2 Corinthians 1:4). In the end, they came to know God more deeply.

Like Job, they experienced hell on earth, but the things that were intended to destroy them were used for greater good. Rather than wipe them out, these painful trials made them better people, more godly people, more faith-filled people, more confident people and, most of all, people who really knew the Lord.

May He reveal Himself to you as well, even in the midst of your severe trial. The God of Paul, who is the God of Job, is also your God! You can trust Him with your life, in this world and in the world to come. In the end, you will see that He never did you wrong and that He only had your best interests in mind—for now and forever.

eleven

Seek Him Until

I truly hope that you have been greatly encouraged by reading this book. I hope that your questions have been answered, that a burden has been lifted and that you are starting to regain confidence in your relationship with God. Hope lives again! The words that follow will encourage you even more, and they will invite you to come into an even deeper fellowship with the Lord.

On the other hand, you might feel anything but encouraged. You came across this book, or a friend strongly recommended it to you, and you have read it through. Even though you have arrived at the very last chapter, your heart still aches. You have found no cure. You want to believe but cannot find faith. And you still do not know if God is there.

My friend, do not lose hope. The words that follow are your lifeline. This chapter was written for you. The God who put this book in your hands is the God who will see you through—if only you will do one essential thing. Allow me to explain.

Journal Reflections

A friend of our family who is involved in ministry, we will call him J. T., shared some journal entries with me. These are entries that reflect many years of spiritual agony. Despite having had a real born-again experience, he was riddled with doubts, and he asked many questions: Does God really exist? If so, is He genuinely good? Why are so many Christians able to connect deeply with Him, but I feel as if I am outside the camp? And what do I do with the endless questions that arise in my heart regarding unanswered prayer, the terrible suffering of humanity and the behavior of the God of the Old Testament?

Try as he might to find faith by reading the Word, quoting Scripture. and making an effort to fend off doubt, unbelief was always at the door hounding him. Although he didn't want to try to manufacture faith, and in doing so deceive himself, when he tried the "Christian" methods to build faith, nothing had any long-term effect. That root of unbelief was always there, lurking under the surface.

As for being honest with God, sometimes J. T. was so grieved that he would rail at God. At other times, he recognized this behavior as ugly sin, and he repented and asked for forgiveness and mercy. Who can live with this kind of spiritual schizophrenia, especially when you are supposed to be ministering to others?

After struggling like this for *decades*, he came to a breaking point. He was determined to seek God or die trying. I can honestly say that I have never seen a man seek God the way that he did. He pursued Him every way he knew how, day and night, month in, month out.

The Lord honored J. T.'s determination and no quit mentality—there was an uncompromising, holy stubbornness and tenacity—that refused to let go or accept that God would not honor His Word and keep His promises when He said, "You

will find Me when you seek Me with all our heart and soul."[1]
Although J. T. wrestled with the question of God's reality—*Am I
seeking someone who is not really there?*—he knew that if God
was real, He would have to keep His promise.

During this time of intensive, prolonged seeking, the Lord
met him powerfully, revealing deep parts of Himself—His goodness, character, love and beauty. But even after these encounters, the root of doubt would sometimes surface again, making
J. T. feel like a miserable failure. *Why*, he wondered, *do I keep
falling back into unbelief when God has so powerfully met me and
so graciously revealed Himself?*

I want to share some of J. T.'s journal entries with you. Please
remember that this journal expresses the raw emotions of a
man who is in deep spiritual pain. It is not intended to be a
fine literary work—or even grammatically correct. Instead, it
reflects a man crying out to God. He wrote:

> The problem keeps arising—unbelief. No matter what I do, no
> matter how I determine to believe at all costs, the doubt always
> arises, even after I have determined to "believe and not doubt."
> Then, because You don't come, I become unsure if You really
> exist. If You do exist, then I question Your compassion. Would
> a father treat his child like this?—keep himself at a distance and
> make them beg for his presence, make them pine after him—it
> seems so cruel. So I get condemned for these thoughts and I
> fear that You can never come because I am accusing You and
> I have not fulfilled Your requirements. I don't understand the
> benefit of Your refusal to help me now. I am so hungry for Your
> presence. Why do You stay away from me?
>
> I have left everything. I have done all that I know to do. I have
> poured over Your Word. I have sought You with all my heart—for
> hours upon hours day after day. I have looked for You as for hid-
> den treasure. I have asked for "the richest of fare" as You promised
> in Your Word I would receive if I would seek You. Whatever I am

missing, I am unable to perceive it, and I have asked You to show me what it is that I lack. You do not show me. All I want is You. It seems that if You would come to me and bless me with Your abiding presence, then that would encourage me and demonstrate that You genuinely care and are not some legalistic tyrant.

I don't know what is required—what I am doing wrong. If it is because faith is required, then I am in trouble, because the very thing I need to bring Your presence is missing from my soul. I don't know if I can legitimately ask You to help me with my faith (although I do). I just long to be delivered from this torture, this torment! I cannot change myself, but think that somehow I am supposed to because "without faith, it is impossible to please God," and "When he asks, he must believe and not doubt, because he who doubts is like a wave of the sea, blown and tossed by the wind. That man should not think he will receive anything from the Lord" so, the responsibility seems to be mine. The fact that I continually seek You has to show that I have SOME kind of faith—why would I do it unless I thought there was the possibility You were really there and would actually answer. I don't seem to have any capacity to change this. I cannot deliver myself. There is no manufacturing faith. It must be real. This is beyond my ability. I WANT to believe.

I hate that I always point a finger back at You. I do not know what else I can do to make myself believe You with all my heart and fully trust that You will show up and enable me to experience what others have experienced. Every day I fail at this and fear that I will never get out of this vicious cycle. Please, please help me. I cannot do this without Your intervention.

Can you relate to these agonizing words? Sometimes J. T. would even experience dramatic ups and downs in the very same day:

Morning: Somehow, I just have to find faith. Even when I read the Word, I question its validity. Sometimes God's way seems barbaric, or unsophisticated—it just seems like stories. I have to swallow the entire thing—like a child. But it is such a FIGHT. It seems my mind just won't let me go where my heart wants to. Even after reading the Word to build faith, reason challenges me. How can I get my mind to believe what I want to believe?? Because there are so many promises in the Word that the Church never experiences—not even close—it appears that the entire thing is not real—no visible answers to prayer. How do I take hold of faith? How do I become like a little child? How can I change my mind, when it seems that even the Word can't change me?

Evening: All I have to do is believe. That's it. I don't have to fast, or pray for hours, or beg, or work, or strive, or moan, or groan, or plead. Just believe and it is a sure thing. It is done. It is a fact. There is nothing I have to do for it. God is the one who does the work—I just believe Him. This is the way He set things up, the way He ordained we would receive answers to prayer. There is no possibility that it can't be so because of what Jesus said: "Nothing will be impossible for you if you believe." "I will do whatever you ask for in My name." "I tell you, whatever you ask for in prayer, believe that you have received it, and it will be yours." "If you do not doubt in your heart, but believe that what you say will happen, it will be done."

. . . I have prayed that He would strengthen me—my mind, my spirit. I have asked Him to take me all the way through—over and over again. I do believe that this is His process and that He has TOTAL victory for me. I do believe it's mine.

All of these journal entries were made during J. T.'s season of intense prayer and seeking. He would encounter the Lord and be overwhelmed with His love, only to plunge back into times of spiritual darkness. This process is reflected in this journal entry one year later:

What can I say? I am still in the same wretched condition I have always been in. I cannot find God. I look and look, but I cannot find Him. I still am not sure He even exists. How can I deny the fact that all of His claims about Himself—His loving kindness, His promises, His faithfulness, His compassion like a father— that all of that seems absent in this world. It's as if we have to believe that black is white, that goodness and compassion and love as we understand it is somehow different from God's apparent love and compassion. We are left to suffer in this world with no help or even comfort.

The innocent, the righteous, they suffer just as much as anyone. Where is the compassion of our heavenly Father???? How long can I go on making excuses for God? If I don't understand and my eyes are blind, then why oh why doesn't He give me understanding? I have asked, I have begged, I have pleaded for understanding . . . so that I might love Him and agree with Him and His ways.

What did Jesus accomplish on the cross? It seems that one impossibility (the requirement of being good and righteous and fulfilling God's laws) has just been replaced with another impossibility (perfect faith). How are we to believe when there is seemingly so little evidence of His love (according to what is written in the Word and based on what God says about Himself)? When so little if any of His promises have come through, how can we possibly have faith to really believe? There is nothing tangible. Nothing to hang on to. The apostles looked right in the face of Jesus, and still it was hard for them to believe. What hope is there for us who have not seen Him?

My own experience . . . I cry out and cry out . . . and nothing. There is no evidence of His presence—no evidence of His caring. How much can flesh and blood take? Like Job, are we made of bronze? No, we are not perfect like Job, but isn't that what Jesus came for? To forgive our sins and imperfections and bring us to the Father. What else can we do but cry out to God? If we are blind or wrong, then GOD, help us to see it and we will repent!!!!!!!!!!!!!!!

A few months later, he wrote the following entry in which he spoke about a prayer that he had prayed *after* encountering God during those months of intensive seeking. He thought that he had broken through for good, and he wanted the Lord to prove the reality of his faith. He wrote:

> What did I know way back when I started seeking God? I asked Him to test me, test my faith. I wanted Him to prove me so that I would know what I was made of. Boy, did I fail!!!! My heart was to be unswervingly loyal to Him, even in the little things . . . no matter what. But I failed because I couldn't feel Him or see Him or see any evidence of His hand . . . so I gave up hope.

But God did not quit. He did not give up on J. T., and He has not given up on you. You can see how the Lord was drawing J. T. to Himself in the following entry, written about the same time as the previous entry:

> Father, I love You with all my heart. You are everything to me. I want You, only You. Nothing holds any meaning to me without You. I am so hungry for You—for Your presence, Your ABIDING presence. I long to see You, touch You, feel You. I am desperate for You. Sometimes I just ache. There is something, something of what and who You are that I must have. Visit me Father. Fill my deepest longing. You are the creator of the universe, the creator of ALL things. You have everything in Your essence that can satisfy me fully, that can bring me to that place of being so one with You that I am utterly filled with Your Glory. One look from You, one touch, one glance—I want to be with You all the time. I want to walk with You. Bring me to the ultimate of what I, as a human, walking on this earth, can be in You.

J. T. also realized that once God had given him a promise, he had to take hold of it, refusing to let go whether he felt anything or not. And since he had experienced the reality and presence of God, he knew beyond question that His Word could be trusted. J. T. wrote:

> Even when I am not conscious of the presence of God, I must walk in what I've found to be true. God made a promise to Abraham, and that was it. It didn't matter that God wasn't mentioning the promise every second of the day, Abraham took God at His word . . . period.

And yet still, almost two years after months of intensive seeking, the deep doubts rose again. Can you feel the torture J. T. lived with? He was someone who wanted to love and believe God with all his heart, and yet he could not retain the breakthrough.

> My sin of unbelief. I am just like the wandering Jews in the desert. God touches and delivers me, I then get a surge of faith and consecration, the next trial or delay comes, and poof, I doubt and end up back in the pit of unbelief—EVERY TIME! God has delivered me every time, but I soon forget. When I was in trouble a couple of years ago, I absolutely believed that if I sought Him, He would show up and deliver me . . . and He did. I had faith in Him. Not only did He show up to deliver me from my trouble, but He changed my insides and gave me precious treasures from Himself . . . rubies and diamonds. He gave me HIS heart, bits of Himself, and I trampled on it with my unbelief and ungratefulness. I neglected to recognize the treasure I had been given. I have gone back on EVERY promise I made to Him and discarded everything I knew to be right and true because I was unable to walk with Him in faith and wait patiently for Him. I let fear and unbelief dominate me. He had proven Himself to be trustworthy when I had reached out in faith, but somehow I could not see that.

Unexpectedly, almost one year later, J. T. felt supernaturally drawn to the Lord, burdened to seek Him afresh:

Where do I start? There is grace on me to start seeking again. I don't know why. I haven't done anything different, it's just on me. I am still in such pain over the suffering of humanity and how it all fits with God in this world. I just can't wrap my brain around it, and I just can't let it go either and live a normal life seeing the vast difference between the reality of what I see, and the promises of God . . . they are on opposite ends. I can't just ignore the reality of what is happening in the world/church and the promises in the word of God . . . . They don't meet. Something is wrong. Oh, how I long to see the promises of God be a reality. How, how, how??

And then this entry a few months later:

The shield of faith can extinguish ALL the flaming arrows of the devil. Not just a few, but all. We have complete victory over the devil by our faith. Our pure faith will extinguish every damnable flaming dart . . . every one of them. Our faith is the only sure way to victory. We must do EVERYTHING to guard our faith in God. If it is not strong, our victory is not assured. Whatever does harm to our faith must be dealt a death blow.

It was sometime after this, as J. T.'s trials at last seemed to be a thing of the past, that he railed against God during a moment of testing, as if the Lord had not met him in that secret place during those months of seeking. He was deeply rebuked by the Lord in his heart—and *from that moment on*, the test of his faith ended, for good. He repented of scorning God's incredible grace, and he never looked back. God literally changed him on the inside. The doubts were removed, and the questions were resolved. The pain, agony, unbelief and torment truly vanished and have never returned.

God heard his cry. He paid attention to his pain. He did not turn a deaf ear, even though, for years on end, it seemed as if He did not hear or even care. But when J. T. finally made the determination to seek God as if his very life depended on it, the lasting breakthrough came. And even though it was challenged on and off for the next few years, the fruit of his prayers followed him. This resulted in permanent transformation. No more doubts and no more unbelief! God was faithful to His promise.

One year later, J. T. received an alarming medical report from the doctor concerning his health. But when he heard the news, a momentary, intense wave of fear was replaced with a deep sense of joy to the point of giddiness. Supernatural faith was at work in his life! He did not even have to try. God had changed him. J. T. wrote:

> God did a miraculous thing when He changed me . . . absolutely miraculous!! I was one who was at the end of everything with no hope of change. He totally, supernaturally shot faith into me. It was nothing I could work up. I couldn't try to believe, I couldn't try to be at peace.
>
> When the doctor's office called with the negative report, initially, there was a rush of fear, an overwhelming sensation that felt like the bottom had fallen out. But it was only for a second, and then that was immediately ripped out by God Himself, and faith was shot into me instead . . . it was instant, and it shot right in! And then there was TOTAL peace and rest. God was the one who did the work of faith . . . not me. All I did was cooperate and bring every stray thought captive. I was giddy with faith and expectation. Giddy with confidence and rest.
>
> REMEMBER, REMEMBER, REMEMBER what God has done! He will do it ALL . . . ignore anything else . . . only believe. God imparted faith, not so I would fail, but so that I would succeed. "Now it is God who has made us for this very purpose

and has given us the Spirit as a deposit, guaranteeing what is to come." 2 Cor 5:5 We live by faith, not by sight. "Now to Him who is able to do immeasurably more than all we ask or imagine, according to his power that is at work within us, to Him be glory in the church and in Christ Jesus throughout all generations, for ever and ever! Amen."

What, then, can you learn from these incredibly moving entries, some of which may have brought you to tears? First, you are not alone. Other people have gone through what you are going through. You can cling to Him and throw yourself on Him, and He will not let you go. He is real, and He will not forsake you.

Second, if you are determined to seek Him, you will find Him. His promises are sure. As He said to the children of Israel who were scattered around the world, "But if from there you seek the LORD your God, you will find him if you seek him *with all your heart and with all your soul*" (Deuteronomy 4:29, emphasis added). And this: "You will seek me and find me when you seek me *with all your heart*" (Jeremiah 29:13, emphasis added). There is something about seeking Him with all our heart, all our soul, all our desires and all that is within us. And when we do, we will find Him. Guaranteed. "He rewards those who earnestly seek Him" (Hebrews 11:6).

As J. T. journaled,

> The wonderful things of God do not come cheaply—that would diminish who He truly is. Of course, the knowledge of God is free and He longs to give Himself to us. He has made it very simple—just believe Him. But oh, to believe, to truly believe, takes knowing Him intimately, and that doesn't come cheaply. To know Him, really know Him, takes all that we have, all that we are. To give ourselves to Him—totally. That is the only thing

that can bring us to true faith, immovable faith. Father, bring me there—to You.

You might say, "I would love to seek the Lord for hours every day, but it's not possible. I have a job. I have a family. I have responsibilities. I barely have one hour free a day, let alone ten or twelve hours." The good news is that God looks at the heart, not the clock. He looks at the longing of your soul, at the deepest yearnings of your being. He can see when you are truly hungry. He can hear the silent cry. When you set your heart to seek Him, your prayer can ascend to heaven even while working a job or changing diapers. And when you are in pain—especially emotional pain—you will feel that pain no matter what you are doing. Let that pain, the pain of spiritual frustration and doubt and alienation, become a prayer.

You can cry out from your heart while working behind a desk, studying for an exam, or homeschooling your children. The hunger is always there. The desire never ceases. It is something that cannot be quenched. If you are determined to see a breakthrough no matter what, that breakthrough will come. He promised.

The problem with many of us, if we were to be totally honest, is that all too often we are not that determined to seek God. We do not want the breakthrough badly enough. We choose to put other things first, from mindless social media to sports, entertainment, and hobbies. We expect God to interrupt our activities and manifest His presence.

But if we will put aside those distractions and continue to cry out to Him, He *will* hear our cry. Our God will answer! As He promised through the prophet Isaiah, our high and lofty God is drawn to the lowly and the hurting. He will revive you! (See Isaiah 57:15).

When it comes to seeking His face, it's not that we are trying to earn something from Him or win some kind of brownie points. Instead, it is our declaration that nothing matters to us more than truly knowing Him, that being in an intimate relationship with Him is the most important thing in our lives, and that we are making room for Him to come and fill us. He will not go where He is not desired.

What would happen, then, if you shut out every distraction and sought the Lord with all your heart and all your soul? What would happen if you said no to everything unnecessary and unessential, spending every free hour on your face before God crying out for breakthroughs, for visitation, for transformation or for empowerment? What would happen if you took a break from social media and entertainment? What would happen if you did this for one week, let alone for weeks or months on end? Soon enough, you would not even recognize yourself. The transformation would be that dramatic.

Finding God is like finding wisdom. Your search will be rewarded:

> My son [or daughter], if you accept my words and store up my commands within you, turning your ear to wisdom and applying your heart to understanding— indeed, if you call out for insight and cry aloud for understanding, and *if you look for it as for silver and search for it as for hidden treasure*, then you will understand the fear of the LORD and find the knowledge of God.
>
> Proverbs 2:1–5, emphasis added

> I love those who love me, and *those who seek me diligently find me*.
>
> Proverbs 8:17 ESV, emphasis added

Nothing of real, lasting value in life comes cheaply. And so, it should not surprise us that the thing that matters most, the thing that is of inestimable, indescribable value—namely, a deep, intimate, personal relationship with our Creator—does not simply drop down from heaven. It must be pursued with diligence. And those who make that pursuit will not be disappointed. "Those who look to him are radiant, and their faces shall never be ashamed" (Psalm 34:5 ESV).

What Is Stopping You?

In the end, there is nothing more important than knowing the truth about God and having a personal relationship with Him. If He's not real, or if we cannot really know Him, then we should move on to other things. But if He is real, if He put us here for a purpose, and if He, the Almighty, offers to be our heavenly Father, then nothing can be more important than taking Him at His Word, taking hold of His promises and seeking Him with everything inside of us until He fills every fiber of our being with His goodness and His love.

This is more important than the career choices we make. It is more important than our education, more important than our social status and more important than the friends we have or the person we marry. Knowing Him, understanding His will and entering into a real and vibrant relationship with Him must be our priority. When we make that determination, not simply for a minute or a day but in a lasting way, we will not be disappointed. We will find the one for whom our hearts long.

You might say, "But that's exactly what I tried to do! I was determined to seek the Lord until I found Him. I was determined to break through and take hold of His promises. But I failed miserably. I kept falling short. I simply didn't have it in me. What am I supposed to do?"

You can turn your weakness into strength. In other words, you can go to Him as a failure, as someone who is weak. You can tell Him, "I really want to know You intimately and to walk closely with You, but I keep falling short. I can't do this without You! I am too weak." All through the day, let that be your cry.

When the thought comes to mind, open your heart and plead Your case: "Father, if you don't do something dramatic in my life, I'm not going to make it!"

Do it when you wake up in the morning. Do it while you drive to work. Do it when your mind takes a break from work. Do it when you are about to fall asleep at night.

"God, I need You! I need Your help! I don't have the strength to seek You with all my heart."

And then, something will happen. You'll realize that, little by little, you *are* seeking Him more deeply. That cry *is* becoming more consistent. He *is* helping you. Soon enough, as surely as the sun rises, you will encounter the Creator of the universe. He will bless your life. Your job is to keep pursuing Him until the answer comes, no matter how many times you fall short. The answer will certainly come. No one is as faithful as He.

In fact, in the midst of your seeking, there is a word of encouragement for you from the brilliant French mathematician, Blaise Pascal (1623–1662). He wrote, "Jesus says: Console yourself, you would not seek me, if you had not found me."[2]

The very fact that you hunger and thirst for God is a sign that, on some level, you already know Him. The fact that you seek Him means that, on some level, you have already found Him. Now, you must press in until the breakthrough comes.

John G. Lake, a pioneer missionary to South Africa early in the twentieth century, and a man who endured much suffering and loss, once said:

> No matter what your soul may be coveting, if it becomes the
> supreme cry of your life, not the secondary matter, or the third
> or fourth, the fifth, or tenth, but the supreme desire of your
> soul, the paramount issue—all the powers and energies of your

spirit, soul and body are reaching out and crying to God for the answer—it is going to come![3]

You can rest your life on that promise. It is going to come!

So do what you can do, taking your little, human steps toward Him. And the Lord will do what only He can do, which is taking His massive, divine steps toward you, until He takes you into His arms and assures you of His infinite and undying love. And if you fall flat on your face, even plunging into sin and disobedience, return to Him with humility and confession, and He will wash you clean. Then, begin to seek Him anew.

And should you wonder if He is really good, look again to the cross where Jesus died in your place and showed you how deeply our heavenly Father loves you. He showed us how committed He is to make you His own, both in this world and forever. God's love shouts to you and me from the cross. He is pursuing us.

So take that step today, and do not stop seeking the Lord until He satisfies the longing of your soul. He will! As Hosea declared,

"After two days he will revive us; on the third day he will restore us, that we may live in his presence. Let us acknowledge the LORD; let us press on to acknowledge him. As surely as the sun rises, he will appear; he will come to us like the winter rains, like the spring rains that water the earth."

Hosea 6:2-3

Your heavenly Father, who loves you more deeply than you could ever imagine, will touch you, change you and fill you. He will hear the cry of your heart. He will restore, even redeeming your past mistakes and failures. What Satan, sin or society meant for evil in your life, He will turn to good. And as you lean hard on Him for the rest of your days, He will never, ever fail.

And you will learn that His ways are always for the best. In the ever-true expression of Paul, "The one who calls you is faithful, and he will do it" (1 Thessalonians 5:24).

I leave you with J. T.'s words:

> It is true that God is the one that has changed me. It has been His work all along, and not the power of positive thinking or my working it up, or my own strength. He did it all by His power and Spirit. I see that over these years, going through the severe trial of my faith, and feeling empty and abandoned, I see that there has been absolutely nothing I could do to change the situation. I could not change my mind and have lovely loving thoughts towards Him. I could not muster faith. I could not love God deeply the way I wanted to. I could not thrill myself with thoughts of His awesomeness. No amount of reading the Word, or praying, or fasting brought me any relief or comfort or excitement in God. Nothing seemed to be able to bring me into His presence the way I so deeply desired.
>
> Certainly, if I had lifted myself up by my own bootstraps during those initial months of seeking when I had received a great breakthrough, I would have been able to do the same thing again—but I could not. GOD WAS THE ONE WHO INFUSED FAITH INTO MY SOUL.
>
> I had always known that the Word taught that God gives each of us a measure of faith, but I felt like I had been shortchanged somehow, unable to truly believe in Him. Yet when I sought Him earnestly, He changed it all. The Lord fixed my deepest problem!
>
> God wants me to always recognize His working in and for me. Never to forget His reality. I must guard my heart and mind with all diligence. It means my life. I must cling to Him every second.

He will prove Himself faithful.

Notes

Preface

1. "In U.S., Decline of Christianity Continues at Rapid Pace," *Pew Forum*, October 17, 2019, https://www.pewforum.org/2019/10/17/in-u-s-decline-of -christianity-continues-at-rapid-pace/.

2. These closing words are based on a famous quote from missionary pioneer Adoniram Judson (1788–1850): "The future is as bright as the promises of God." Given the amount of personal suffering experienced by Judson, these words take on greater significance. Don Dozier, "'The Future is as Bright as the Promises of God'-Adoniram Judson," *Don's Desk*, July 12, 2010, http://dozier don.blogspot.com/2010/06/future-is-as-bright-as-promises-of-god.html. For a powerful, full-scale biography of Judson, see Courtney Anderson, *To the Golden Shore: The Life of Adoniram Judson* (King of Prussia, Pa.: Judson Press, 1987).

Chapter 2: What If There Is No God?

1. Ira Stanphill, "God Can Do Anything but Fail," 1946.

2. See Stephen C. Meyer, *Signature in the Cell: DNA and the Evidence for Intelligent Design* (New York: HarperOne, 2010). See also Wayne Jackson, "Five Questions About Evolution that Charles Darwin Can't Answer," *Christian Courier*, 2020, https://www.christiancourier.com/articles/1579-five-questions -about-evolution-that-charles-darwin-cant-answer. See also Don Batten, "15 Questions for Evolutionists," *Creation Ministries International*, 2020, https:// creation.com/15-questions-for-evolutionists.

3. Stephen Cave, "There's No Such Thing As Free Will," *Richard Dawkins Foundation for Reason & Science*, May 17, 2016, https://www.richarddawkins .net/2016/05/theres-no-such-thing-as-free-will/.

4. Tamler Sommers, "Can an Atheist Believe in Free Will?," *Psychology Today*, January 22, 2009, https://www.psychologytoday.com/us/blog/experiments-in-philosophy/200901/can-atheist-believe-in-free-will.

5. J. D. Greear, "If There Is No God, There Is No Free Will," *J. D. Greear Ministries*, September 26, 2017, https://jdgreear.com/blog/no-god-no-free-will/.

6. J. D. Greear, "If There Is No God, There Is No Free Will."

7. Denyse O'Leary, "Has Science Shown That Consciousness Is Only an Illusion?," *Mind Matters News*, January 21, 2019, https://mindmatters.ai/2019/01/has-science-shown-that-consciousness-is-only-an-illusion/.

8. As quoted in Denyse O'Leary, "Has Science Shown That Consciousness Is Only an Illusion?," *Mind Matters News*, January 21, 2019, https://mindmatters.ai/2019/01/has-science-shown-that-consciousness-is-only-an-illusion/.

9. Steven Pinker, *How the Mind Works* (New York: W.W. Norton and Company, 2009), 78.

10. Dinesh D'Souza, *What's So Great About Christianity?* (Carol Stream, Ill.: Tyndale Publishers, 2008), 15–16.

11. D'Souza, *What's So Great About Christianity?*, 15–16.

12. D'Souza, *What's So Great About Christianity?*, 15–16.

13. *Conservapaedia*, s.v. "Atheism and fertility rates," December 13, 2019, https://www.conservapedia.com/Atheism_and_fertility_rates.

Chapter 3: Does Prayer Really Work?

1. "Not to faint (μη ἐνκακειν [*mē enkakein*]). Literally, not to give in to evil (ἐν, κακεω [*en, kakeō*], from κακος [*kakos*], bad or evil), to turn coward, lose heart, behave badly." A. T. Robertson, *Word Pictures in the New Testament* (Nashville: Broadman Press, 1933), Lk 18:1.

Chapter 4: Permission to Doubt

1. The Associated Press, "'Da Vinci Code' author Dan Brown speaks in NH," *The San Diego Union Tribune*, May 18, 2012, https://www.sandiegouniontribune.com/sdut-da-vinci-code-author-dan-brown-speaks-in-nh-2012may18-story.html.

2. Tony Dokoupil, "The Evolution of Dan Brown," *CBS This Morning*, October 1, 2017, https://youtube.com/watch?v=4TEfnncv-nU.

3. For *doubt*, see ESV, NIV or NASB; for *waver*, see CSB, NET, TLV, NLT.

4. Peter H. Davids, *The Letters of 2 Peter and Jude*, The Pillar New Testament Commentary (Grand Rapids, Mich.: Eerdmans, 2006), 100–101.

Chapter 5: Perhaps It Was Wrong Theology That Failed You?

1. Randy Clark, *Eyewitness to Miracles: Watching the Gospel Come to Life* (Nashville: Thomas Nelson, 2018), 7.

2. Clark, *Eyewitness to Miracles*, 8.

3. For a nuanced anthropological study by a professor of religious studies with a Ph.D. from Harvard, see Candy Gunther Brown, *Global Pentecostal and Charismatic Healing* (New York: Oxford University Press, 2011).

4. See Randy Clark, *Eyewitness to Miracles*; see also Candy Gunther Brown, *Testing Prayer: Science and Healing* (Cambridge, Mass.: Harvard University Press, 2012).

5. Randy Clark, *The Thrill of Victory—The Agony of Defeat* (Mechanicsburg, Pa.: Global Awakening, 2011).

6. While many interpret Paul's reference to a thorn in the flesh as a physical sickness, I do not share that interpretation.

7. As you study the Bible, you see that books like Proverbs present perennial and general truths, similar to "Heavy cigarette smoking will shorten your life." The statements are generally true, but not without exceptions. Some people smoke cigarettes for years and yet live to advanced ages, while others who live cleanly die prematurely. That is why other books of the Bible, like Ecclesiastes, address the exceptions to the rule. In the end, the wisdom of Proverbs holds true, since the exceptions prove the rule.

8. Dr. Michael A. Milton, "How Is the Kingdom of God 'Already but Not Yet'? What Else Does the Bible Say?," *Christianity.com,* May 30, 2019, https://www.christianity.com/wiki/god/how-is-the-kingdom-of-god-already-but-not-yet-what-else-does-the-bible-say.html.

Chapter 6: We Are Part Sinner and Part Saint

1. For more information on this process, please visit www.billygraham.org/story/how-to-be-born-again/.

2. For an in-depth discussion of the interpretation of Romans 7, see my book *Go and Sin No More: A Call to Holiness* (Ventura, Calif.: Regal Books, 1998), 265–284.

3. Joseph A. Fitzmyer S.J., *Romans: A New Translation with Introduction and Commentary, Anchor Yale Bible* (New Haven: Yale University Press, 2008), 438.

4. John R.W. Stott, *The Message of Romans: God's Good News for the World, The Bible Speaks Today* (Downers Grove, Ill.: InterVarsity Press, 2001), 179.

5. Leon Morris, *The Epistle to the Romans, The Pillar New Testament Commentary* (Grand Rapids, Mich.: InterVarsity Press, 1988), 256.

Chapter 7: Is the Bible an Outdated and Bigoted Book? (Part 1)

1. Richard Dawkins, *The God Delusion* (New York: Houghton Mifflin, 2006), 51.

2. Michael L. Brown, *Job: The Faith to Challenge God: A New Translation and Commentary* (Peabody, Mass.: Hendrickson, 2019).

3. Isaac Asimov, "In the Game of Energy and Thermodynamics You Can't Break Even," *Smithsonian Institute Journal,* June, 1970.

4. Peter Line, "The Incredible Human Brain," *Creation Ministries International*, July 2018, https://creation.com/the-incredible-human-brain.

5. Stephen C. Myer, *Signature in the Cell: DNA and the Evidence for Intelligent Design* (New York: HarperOne, 2010).

6. Hannah Ashworth, "How long is your DNA?," *Science Focus,* 2020, https://www.sciencefocus.com/the-human-body/how-long-is-your-dna/.

7. Ashworth, "How long is your DNA?"

8. Roger Wilson, "God's Miracles Start in the Miracle of Creating Your DNA," *Statesman News Network*, September 25, 2018, https://www.statesman.com/news/20160904/gods-miracles-start-in-the-miracle-of-creating-your-dna.

9. Sara Nelson Glick, Martina Morris, et al., "A Comparison of Sexual Behavior Patterns Among Men Who Have Sex with Men and Heterosexual Men and Women," *Journal of Acquired Immune Deficiency Syndromes*, May, 2013, 60(1): 83–90, https://www.ncbi.nlm.nih.gov/pmc/articles/PMC3334840/.

10. Naveed Saleh, "Body Integrity Identity Disorder," *Very Well Mind*, February 20, 2020, https://www.verywellmind.com/amputating-a-healthy-limb-1123848.

11. "Surgeon defends amputations," *BBC News*, January 31, 2000, http://news.bbc.co.uk/2/hi/uk_news/scotland/625680.stm#:~:text=The%20surgeon%20who%20amputated%20healthy,Falkirk%20and%20District%20Royal%20Infirmary.

12. See the painful stories compiled at https://www.parentsofrogdkids.com/.

13. Walt Heyer, *Trans Life Survivors* (self-published, 2018).

14. Heyer, *Trans Life Survivors*, 1.

15. Abigal Shrier, *Irreversible Damage: The Transgender Craze Seducing Our Daughters* (Washington, DC: Regnery Books, 2020). See also the important new movie *In His Image*, available for free viewing at InHisImage.movie.

16. Dr. Debra Soh, *The End of Gender: Debunking the Myths about Sex and Identity in Our Society* (New York: Threshold Editions, 2020).

17. Russell Goldman, "Here's a List of 58 Gender Options for Facebook Users," *ABC News*, February 13, 2014, https://abcnews.go.com/blogs/headlines/2014/02/heres-a-list-of-58-gender-options-for-facebook-users.

18. Michael Brown, "My Gender Is: 'Fill In the Blank'," *Christian Post*, February 27, 2015, https://dev.christianpost.com/news/my-gender-is-fill-in-the-blank.html.

19. "Do We Need More Than Two Genders?" *BBC News,* January 13, 2016, https://www.bbc.com/news/health-35242180.

20. Michael Brown, "Call Me Tractor," February 18, 2014, *Townhall*, https://townhall.com/columnists/michaelbrown/2014/02/18/call-me-tractor-n1796635.

21. Michael Brown, "Compassion for Transgender People Shouldn't Change Our Language," *Christian Post*, August 8, 2016, http://dev.christianpost.com/news/compassion-for-transgender-people-shouldnt-change-our-language.html.

22. "Multigender," *Nonbinary Wiki*, July 18, 2020, https://nonbinary.wiki/wiki/Multigender.

23. Michael L. Brown, *Outlasting the Gay Revolution: Where Homosexual Activism Is Really Going and How to Turn the Tide* (Washington, DC: WND Books, 2015).

24. James Risdon, "Drag Queen Admits He's 'Grooming' Children at Story Hour Events," *LifeSite*, November 27, 2018, https://www.lifesitenews

.com/news/watch-drag-queen-admits-hes-grooming-children-at-story-hour
-events.

25. Elizabeth Johnston, "Mass Resistance Uncovers a Third 'Story Time' Drag Queen with a Criminal Record," *ActivistMommy.com*, August 31, 2019, https://activistmommy.com/mass-resistance-uncovers-a-third-story-time -drag-queen-with-a-criminal-record/#.

26. Read the stories at www.changedmovement.com.

Chapter 8: Is the Bible an Outdated and Bigoted Book? (Part 2)

1. Dennis Bratcher, "Israel's Codes of Conduct Compared to Surrounding Nations," *The Voice*, 2018, http://www.crivoice.org/lawcodes.html. More broadly, see John Oswalt, *The Bible Among the Myths: Unique Revelation or Just Ancient Literature?* (Grand Rapids, Mich.: Zondervan, 2009).

2. Nicholas H. Wollfinger, "Counterintuitive Trends in the Link Between Premarital Sex and Marital Stability," *Institute for Family Studies*, June 6, 2016, https://ifstudies.org/blog/counterintuitive-trends-in-the-link-between -premarital-sex-and-marital-stability.

3. DoSomething.org, "11 Facts About Teens and STDs," *Do Something*, https://www.dosomething.org/us/facts/11-facts-about-teens-and-stds.

4. Karen Kaplan, "Ten Things You Should Know About Teen Sexting," *Los Angeles Times*, February 2018, https://www.latimes.com/science/sciencenow /la-sci-sn-teens-sexting-20180226-htmlstory.html.

5. "20 Mind-Blowing Stats about the Porn Industry and Its Underage Consumers," *Fight the New Drug*, May 19, 2020, https://fightthenewdrug.org/10 -porn-stats-that-will-blow-your-mind/.

6. Wikipedia, "Marry Your Rapist Law," *Wikipedia.com*, September 6, 2020, https://en.wikipedia.org/wiki/Marry-your-rapist_law.

7. "Victims of Sexual Violence: Statistics," *RAINN*, 2020, https://www.rainn .org/statistics/victims-sexual-violence.

8. Brian Cantor, "Cardi B & Megan Thee Stallion's 'WAP' Reaches #1 On US iTunes Sales Chart, Scores Big Spotify and Apple Playlist Looks," *Headline Planet*, August 7, 2020, https://headlineplanet.com/home/2020/08/07/cardi -b-megan-thee-stallions-wap-blasts-into-top-5-on-us-itunes-sales-chart -scores-big-spotify-apple-playlist-looks/.

9. Niall McCarthy, "Report: The Number of People Serving Life Sentences in the U.S. Is Surging," *Forbes*, May 5, 2017, https://www.forbes.com/sites /niallmccarthy/2017/05/05/report-the-number-of-people-serving-life-sen tences-in-the-u-s-is-surging-infographic/#cd36a25691d9.

10. "The Death Penalty in 2019: Year End Report," *Death Penalty Information Center*, December 17, 2019, https://deathpenaltyinfo.org/facts-and-research /dpic-reports/dpic-year-end-reports/the-death-penalty-in-2019-year-end -report.

11. "Executions Overview," *Death Penalty Information Center*, https://death penaltyinfo.org/executions/executions-overview.

12. Wayne Parker, "Statistics on Fatherless Children in America," *Live About*, May 24, 2019, https://www.liveabout.com/fatherless-children-in-america-statistics-1270392.

13. See "Rebellious Son," Jewish Virtual Library, https://www.jewishvirtual library.org/rebellious-son.

14. Note that the end of verse 13, "Purge the evil person from among you," is taken from Deuteronomy where it refers to a literal, physical punishment that potentially included the death penalty. Here it refers to disfellowshipping.

15. Nahum M. Sarna, *Genesis, The JPS Torah Commentary* (Philadelphia: Jewish Publication Society, 1989), 117.

16. Derek Kidner, *Genesis: An Introduction and Commentary, Tyndale Old Testament Commentaries* (Downers Grove, Ill.: InterVarsity Press, 1967), 136.

17. For other perspectives, some of which minimize the degree to which innocent men, women and children were killed by the Israelites, see John H. Walton and J. Harvey Walton, *The Lost World of the Israelite Conquest: Covenant, Retribution, and the Fate of the Canaanites* (Downers Grove, Ill.: IVP Academic, 2017); Paul Copan, *Did God Really Command Genocide?: Coming To Terms With The Justice Of God* (Grand Rapids, Mich.: Baker Books, 2014); Stanley Gundry, ed., *Show Them No Mercy: 4 Views on God and Canaanite Genocide* (Grand Rapids, Mich.: Zondervan, 2003).

18. Kay Vandette, "Children Inherit Conscientiousness from Their Parents," *Earth*, April 4, 2020, https://www.earth.com/news/children-inherit-conscientiousness-parents/.

19. Obviously, there are strong objections to this point of view, including: 1) the Bible nowhere states this explicitly; 2) only some of those wiped out by the Israelites were associated with races of giants. For the larger issue, see Bodie Hodge, "Nephilim: Who Were They?," *Answers in Genesis*, July 9, 2008, https://answersingenesis.org/bible-characters/who-were-the-nephilim/.

20. For a very different and highly controversial reading of these texts, see Gregory A. Boyd, *The Crucifixion of the Warrior God: Volumes 1 & 2* (Minneapolis: Fortress Press, 2017) and *Cross Vision: How the Crucifixion of Jesus Makes Sense of Old Testament Violence* (Minneapolis: Fortress Press, 2017).

21. This would also extend to the destruction of Amalek (see Exodus 17:8–16; Deuteronomy 25:17–19; 1 Samuel 15).

22. David Wilber, *Is God a Misogynist? Understanding the Bible's Difficult Passages Concerning Women* (n.p: n.p., 2020), 144.

23. For a very fair treatment of the relevant texts (and the broader subjects covered in this chapter), see David T. Lamb, *God Behaving Badly: Is the God of the Old Testament Angry, Sexist and Racist?* (Downers Grove, Ill.: IVP Books, 2011).

24. David Larson, "Annual March for Life Rallies in Raleigh Against Abortion," *North State Journal*, January 22, 2020, https://nsjonline.com/article/2020/01/annual-march-for-life-rallies-in-raleigh-against-abortion/.

Chapter 9: The Problem of Evil

1. Eric Manning, "Without Training, the Church Will Create More Jon Steingards," *The Stream*, June 6, 2020, https://stream.org/without-training-the-church-will-create-more-jon-steingards/.

2. According to Steingard's Instagram post in which he announced his loss of faith, every close friend he has who is his age and who was raised in the church struggles with these same questions. Jon Steingard, *Instagram*, May 20, 2020, https://www.instagram.com/p/CAbHm1olt7w/.

3. Kazoh Kitamori, *Theology of the Pain of God* (Richmond, Va.: John Knox Press, 1965), as cited in *Sown in Weakness, Raised in Glory: From the Spiritual Legacy of Mother Basilea Schlink*, compiled, edited, and published by the Evangelical Sisterhood of Mary (Darmstadt, Germany: 2004), 82–83, 19–20.

4. Kitamori, *Theology of the Pain of God*, 167.

5. Terence E. Fretheim, *The Suffering of God: An Old Testament Perspective* (Philadelphia: Fortress Press, 1984), back cover.

6. Robert Guelich, *Word Biblical Commentary Mark 1–8:26, 34A* (Grand Rapids, Mich.: Zondervan, 1989), 74.

7. Joni Eareckson Tada, "The Hope of Glory," *Joni and Friends*, January 14, 2019, https://www.joniandfriends.org/the-hope-of-glory/.

8. Tim Keller, Twitter post, https://twitter.com/timkellernyc/status/1249095725469876224?lang=en.

9. John R.W. Stott, *The Cross of Christ* (Downers Grove, Ill.: InterVarsity Press, 2006), 326.

10. Thankfully, in the world to come, there will be no possibility for us to sin. We have already called on the Lord to save us and given our lives to Him, so we have made our choice, and in the eternal age, there will be no flesh, no sinful world, no devil, and no temptation, so we will never be bothered by sin again.

11. C. S. Lewis, *The Problem of Pain* (San Francisco: HarperOne, 2015), 25.

12. C. S. Lewis, *Mere Christianity* (New York: HarperCollins, 1980), 48.

13. Francis P. Sempa, "The Bloodiest Century," *American Diplomacy*, January 2007, http://americandiplomacy.web.unc.edu/2007/01/the-bloodiest-century/.

14. Alexander Solzhenitsyn, *The Gulag Archipelago: An Experiment in Literary Investigation*, Scribd.com (New York: Harper and Row, 2007), 617, https://www.scribd.com/document/130747181/Gulag-Archipelago-II.

15. Henry McDonald, "Stephen Fry Calls God an 'Evil, Capricious, Monstrous Maniac,'" *The Guardian*, February 1, 2015, http://www.theguardian.com/culture/2015/feb/01/stephen-fry-god-evil-maniac-irish-tv.

16. McDonald, "Stephen Fry Calls God an 'Evil, Capricious, Monstrous Maniac.'"

17. McDonald, "Stephen Fry Calls God an 'Evil, Capricious, Monstrous Maniac.'"

18. McDonald, "Stephen Fry Calls God an 'Evil, Capricious, Monstrous Maniac.'"

19. McDonald, "Stephen Fry Calls God an 'Evil, Capricious, Monstrous Maniac.'"

20. McDonald, "Stephen Fry Calls God an 'Evil, Capricious, Monstrous Maniac.'"

21. Michael L. Brown, "What Would God Say to an Atheist? and Thoughts on 'Redemption and Revenge,'" *The Line of Fire*, February 4, 2015, http://www.lineoffireradio.com/2015/02/04/what-would-god-say-to-an-atheist-and-thoughts-on-redemption-or-revenge/.

Chapter 10: What Would Job Say?

1. In these divine speeches, the Lord also spoke of His complete mastery over the fearsome creatures Behemoth and Leviathan, who represented the forces of chaos and darkness. They were no match for Him, meaning that there was no evil or wicked device that could thwart His plan.

2. For the meaning of repenting on dust and ashes, see Brown, *Job: The Faith to Challenge God*, 293, 438–444.

3. Michael L. Brown, *Job: The Faith to Challenge God: A New Translation and Commentary* (Peabody, Mass.: Hendrickson, 2019), 295.

4. Brown, *Job*, 295.

5. Brown, *Job*, 295.

6. Brown, *Job*, 295.

7. Brown, *Job*, 295.

8. Brown, *Job*, 296.

9. Alfred Henry Miles, ed., *Women Poets of the Nineteenth Century* (New York: E.P. Dutton and Co., 1907, Bartleby.com, 2011), poem number 293.

10. I agree with those biblical scholars who understand Paul's thorn to be the extreme nature of the persecution he experienced for preaching the Gospel, as summarized in 2 Corinthians 11:23–33.

Chapter 11: Seek Him Until

1. This is a paraphrase of several verses that we will quote later in the chapter.

2. Ryan M. Thurman, "Blaise Pascal Quotes," Apprenticeship to Jesus, September 19, 2007, https://apprenticeshiptojesus.wordpress.com/2007/09/19/blaise-pascal-quotes/.

3. John G. Lake, *Spiritual Hunger and Other Sermons*, edited by Gordon Lindsay (Dallas: Christ for the Nations, 1987), 7.

Michael L. Brown, (Ph.D. from New York University), is the founder and president of AskDrBrown Ministries and of FIRE School of Ministry in Concord, North Carolina. He has served as a visiting or adjunct professor at seven leading seminaries. He is host of the nationally syndicated daily talk radio show, *The Line of Fire*, and he hosts TV shows on METV (Middle East TV), GOD TV, NRB TV and other networks. He has written more than 40 books and 2,000 opinion pieces, has taken the Gospel message around the world and has debated some of the toughest questions of our day on university campuses. Learn more at www.askdrbrown.org.

More from Michael L. Brown

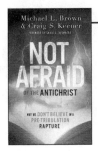

Despite the popular theology of our day, Christians should *not* expect to get out of tribulation or the end times. In this fascinating, accessible book, two respected, award-winning Bible scholars walk you through what the Bible *really* says about the rapture, the tribulation and the end times. And what they show you will leave you full of hope.

Not Afraid of the Antichrist with Craig S. Keener